Unreal Engine Game Development Cookbook

Over 40 recipes to accelerate the process of learning game design and solving development problems using Unreal Engine

John P. Doran

[PACKT]

PUBLISHING

BIRMINGHAM - MUMBAI

Unreal Engine Game Development Cookbook

First published: November 2015

Production reference: 1271015

Published by Packt Publishing Ltd.
Livery Place
35 Livery Street
Birmingham B3 2PB, UK.

ISBN 978-1-78439-816-3

www.packtpub.com

Cover image by John P. Doran

Credits

Author
John P. Doran

Reviewers
Katax Emperore
Dennis Glowacki
Devin Sherry

Commissioning Editor
Edward Bowkett

Acquisition Editors
Reshma Raman
Owen Roberts

Content Development Editor
Rohit Kumar Singh

Technical Editor
Chinmay S. Puranik

Copy Editor
Swati Priya

Project Coordinator
Mary Alex

Proofreader
Safis Editing

Indexer
Hemangini Bari

Production Coordinator
Nitesh Thakur

Cover Work
Nitesh Thakur

About the Author

John P. Doran is a technical game designer who has been creating games for over 10 years. He has worked on an assortment of games in teams comprising of just himself to over 70 students, mod, and professional projects.

He previously worked at LucasArts on *Star Wars 1313* as a game design intern. He later graduated from DigiPen Institute of Technology in Redmond, WA, with a BSc in game design.

He is currently working as a designer in DigiPen's research and development branch in Singapore. He is also the lead instructor of DigiPen-Ubisoft Campus Game Programming Program, instructing graduate level students in an intensive, advanced- level game programming curriculum. In addition to that, he also teaches and assists students on various subjects and gives lectures on C#, C++, Unreal, Unity, game design, and more.

He is also the author of *Building an FPS Game with Unity*, *Unity Game Development Blueprints*, *Getting Started with UDK*, *UDK Game Development*, and *Mastering UDK Game Development*, and has co-authored *UDK iOS Game Development Beginner's Guide*, all by Packt Publishing. You can find more about him on his website, http://johnpdoran.com.

A big thank you goes to my brother Chris and my wife Hien for being supportive and patient with me as I spent my free time and weekends away from them to finish the book.

On that same note, I also want to thank Samir Abou Samra and Elie Hosry for their support and encouragement while working on this book, as well as the rest of the DigiPen Singapore staff.

Thanks so much to Owen Roberts who approached me to write again, Rohit Kumar Singh for keeping me on track, as well as everyone else at Packt, who were helpful, as always!

Last, but not least, I'd like to thank my family as well as my parents Joseph and Sandra Doran, who took me seriously when I told them that I wanted to make games for a living.

About the Reviewers

Katax Emperore was born in January 1974. Since his childhood days, he loves board games, science magazines, comic books, and graffiti painting. Katax was introduced to the IT world when he got his first game platform, *Fire Attack* from the *Game & Watch* series by Nintendo, back in the '80s. While spending hours on it, he became curious about the process of creating games.

As a teenager, Katax owned *Amiga 500* by Commodore on which he played hundreds of games. However, one of the games stuck with him, *Shadow of the Beast* by Psygnosis. He was enamored by the quality of graphics, music, and FX sounds involved in the game. Katax realized that he would like to learn to create such games, and this was the first step. Today, he can design and develop any game on various web pages and platforms.

The Amiga platform created a high-quality gaming experience supported by an advanced hardware architecture that was way ahead of its time. It was a high-profile computer with real stereo sound supported by the advanced Direct Memory Access technology for multiprocessing. On this platform, Katax learned many aspects of programming, multitasking, DMA, interactive applications, I/O port mappings, graphic design, and 3D. When Microsoft introduced Windows 98, he got serious about programming, 3D, and graphic design, which led him to base his education, and later his career, in the IT industry.

Around this time, Katax experienced live performance of digital visual art improvisation, over music known as VJ performance. He was influenced by Jimi Hendrix's style of improvising each track on a live stage. His style visualize forms, colors, and brightness of images and videos, by playing live visual transitions over each pixel on the screen. Katax believes that it's necessary for each game designer/developer to be a part of some art movement or activity because it helps you in your career, both technically and spiritually.

Katax's favorite bands/artists include Klaus Schulze, Tangerine Dream, Hawkwind, and Jimi Hendrix.

I am grateful to John Carmack from id Software for his efforts and great work on 3D graphics programming. What he invented and developed back in the '90s was the beginning of the wonderful genre of first-person shooter games, which is my personal favorite. Also, I would like to thank Westwood Studios for introducing the Command and Conquer (C&C) series to the gaming world. This game pioneered many aspects of the modern real-time strategy games, which later powered many subgenres in this area as well. Great job, thank you!

Dennis Glowacki, with over a decade of experience rising from the modding and indie community he released several Source and Unreal Engine projects before breaking into the AAA industry where he contributed as an environment artist on *Mortal Kombat X* and *Battlefield: Hardline Premium*. He has been awarded the titles of Unreal MVP and Unreal 4 Founder's Club member by Epic Games.

He has also worked on *Source SDK Game Development Essentials* by Packt Publishing and *How to Become a Video Game Artist* by Watson-Guptill Publications, New York.

I would like to thank Trey McNair for all the pro tips he traded with me at Electronic Arts and Rohail Leghari for making me a better teacher.

Devin Sherry is originally from Levittown on Long Island, New York. After graduating from Island Trees High School in 2010, he studied game development and game design at the University of Advancing Technology, where he earned his BA in game design in 2012.

During his time in college, he worked as a game and level designer with a group of students, called Autonomous Games, on a real-time strategy-styled, third-person shooter called *The Afflicted* using Unreal Engine 3/UDK. It was presented at GDC in 2013 at the *GDC Play Showcase*. It is with this group of developers that he learned the valuable skillsets in the field of game development using the Unreal technology.

Today, he works as an independent game developer, located in Tempe, Arizona. He works on both personal and contracted projects. His achievements include the title *Radial Impact*, which can be found in the Community Contributions section of the Learn Tab of Unreal Engine 4's Launcher and can be purchased on Steam. You can find his work on his YouTube channel, Devin Level Design, where he educates viewers on game development within Unreal Engine 3, UDK, and Unreal Engine 4. He also works with the indie game development community on various projects using the Unreal technology.

Whenever he can, he works in the field of technical support as well. In the realm of game development, he has worked with groups such as Autonomous Games, Virtus Studios, and Nordic Games to develop titles in both the independent and AAA sectors.

He has also co-authored *Unreal Engine 4 Physics Essentials* by Packt Publishing.

I would like to thank my parents, my brother, and my friends for supporting my work and passions. I dedicate my work for this book to my nana. Thank you, everyone, for the love and support.

www.PacktPub.com

Support files, eBooks, discount offers, and more

For support files and downloads related to your book, please visit www.PacktPub.com.

Did you know that Packt offers eBook versions of every book published, with PDF and ePub files available? You can upgrade to the eBook version at www.PacktPub.com and as a print book customer, you are entitled to a discount on the eBook copy. Get in touch with us at service@packtpub.com for more details.

At www.PacktPub.com, you can also read a collection of free technical articles, sign up for a range of free newsletters and receive exclusive discounts and offers on Packt books and eBooks.

https://www2.packtpub.com/books/subscription/packtlib

Do you need instant solutions to your IT questions? PacktLib is Packt's online digital book library. Here, you can search, access, and read Packt's entire library of books.

Why subscribe?

- Fully searchable across every book published by Packt
- Copy and paste, print, and bookmark content
- On demand and accessible via a web browser

Free access for Packt account holders

If you have an account with Packt at www.PacktPub.com, you can use this to access PacktLib today and view 9 entirely free books. Simply use your login credentials for immediate access.

Table of Contents

Preface

Unreal Engine 4 (UE4) is a complete suite of game development tools made for game developers by game developers. A truly powerful tool for game development, there's never been a better time to use it for both commercial as well as independent projects.

Unreal Engine Game Development Cookbook explores the creation of real-time interactive simulations or games. Key aspects of UE4 will be explored to make UE4 more accessible to readers and gear them with the knowledge so that they can focus on creation, knowing where they need to go if they run into issues.

What this book covers

Chapter 1, Getting Acquainted with the UE4 Interface, starts you off with learning Unreal Engine 4's interface and explores the most commonly used aspects in development.

Chapter 2, Level Design – Building Out Levels or Greyboxing, puts readers in the shoes of a level designer, building rooms and using materials to make them look nicer.

Chapter 3, Creating Quality Interior Environments, shows how you can polish your levels using meshes and particle systems and teaches you how to mesh a map properly and work with groups.

Chapter 4, Building the Great Outdoors – Exterior Environments, teaches readers about how to work with terrain, add trees and rocks, build rivers, and stream multiple levels in the game at once.

Chapter 5, Lights, Camera, Action – Cinematics, shows readers how to create an opening cutscene, play matinees, and deal with player movements in videos.

Chapter 6, Lighting and Shadows, introduces different types of lights in Unreal Engine 4 and teaches you how to make them mobile like a flashlight the player can carry. It also explains how to create dynamic lighting with a day/night cycle.

Chapter 7, Art Pipeline – Working with Materials, explores Unreal's art pipeline, teaching you how to create a number of materials from a simple image and glowing mirrors, and makes you see through walls.

Chapter 8, Blueprint Scripting – Level Effects, shows you various ways to use blueprints, the visual scripting language of Unreal Engine 4. It teaches you how to build a number of things from flickering lights to doors and flashlights.

Chapter 9, C++ Programming – Gameplay, introduces C++ programming in Unreal Engine 4. It lets you create your own development environment and a basic gametype. It also explains you how to work with networking, save and load games with keyboard commands, and create custom blueprint nodes.

Chapter 10, User Interface, brings you some insight on Slate and the UMG Editor to create a number of UI elements, including health bars and an animated main menu to tie your whole game together.

Chapter 11, Publishing and Deployment, teaches you how to package your project and create an installer for it to get it out into the world for others to play.

What you need for this book

For developing projects with Unreal Engine 4, it is recommended that your computer has the following specifications:

- ▸ A desktop PC or Mac
- ▸ Windows 7 64-bit or Mac OS X 10.9.2 or later
- ▸ Quad-core Intel or AMD processor, 2.5 GHz or faster
- ▸ NVIDIA GeForce 470 GTX or AMD Radeon 6870 HD series card or higher
- ▸ 8 GB RAM

UE4 will run on desktops and laptops below these recommendations, but performance may be limited. While most of the recipes can be completed on Mac or Windows, the writer has created them using a Windows machine.

Who this book is for

Unreal Engine Game Development Cookbook is intended for readers who are getting used to Unreal Engine 4 and would like to have guidance when it comes to particular parts of the engine. It also targets those who want a handy reference for brave beginners to learn at an accelerated pace. Level designers can use this book to gauge their understanding of the editor, check for specific problems, and discover gems they may not have come across before.

Sections

In this book, you will find several headings that appear frequently (Getting ready, How to do it..., How it works..., There's more..., and See also).

To give clear instructions on how to complete a recipe, we use these sections as follows:

Getting ready

This section tells you what to expect in the recipe, and describes how to set up any software or any preliminary settings required for the recipe.

How to do it...

This section contains the steps required to follow the recipe.

How it works...

This section usually consists of a detailed explanation of what happened in the previous section.

There's more...

This section consists of additional information about the recipe in order to make the reader more knowledgeable about the recipe.

See also

This section provides helpful links to other useful information for the recipe.

Conventions

In this book, you will find a number of text styles that distinguish between different kinds of information. Here are some examples of these styles and an explanation of their meaning.

Code words in text, database table names, folder names, filenames, file extensions, pathnames, dummy URLs, user input, and Twitter handles are shown as follows: "In this recipe we will extend and customize the built in GameMode class to do just that!"

A block of code is set as follows:

```cpp
void ACookbook_Chapter9GameMode::StartMatch()
{
  Super::StartMatch();

  if (GEngine)
  {
    GEngine->AddOnScreenDebugMessage(-1, 10.0f,
                                     FColor::Yellow,
                                     "Hello World!");
  }
}
```

When we wish to draw your attention to a particular part of a code block, the relevant lines or items are set in bold:

```cpp
/** Base look up/down rate, in deg/sec. Other scaling may
    affect final rate. */
UPROPERTY(VisibleAnywhere, BlueprintReadOnly, Category=Camera)
float BaseLookUpRate;

// Saves the game
void SaveMyGameFile();

// Loads the game
void LoadMyGameFile();

// Called every frame
void Tick(float DeltaTime);

protected:

/** Called for forwards/backward input */
void MoveForward(float Value);
```

New terms and **important words** are shown in bold. Words that you see on the screen, for example, in menus or dialog boxes, appear in the text like this: "Switch to the **New Project** tab and you'll be given a selection of various templates to use for projects."

Warnings or important notes appear in a box like this.

Tips and tricks appear like this.

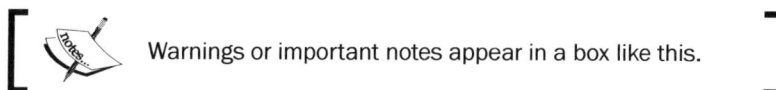

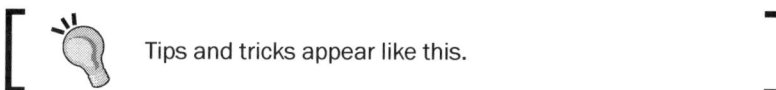

Reader feedback

Feedback from our readers is always welcome. Let us know what you think about this book—what you liked or disliked. Reader feedback is important for us as it helps us develop titles that you will really get the most out of.

To send us general feedback, simply e-mail feedback@packtpub.com, and mention the book's title in the subject of your message.

If there is a topic that you have expertise in and you are interested in either writing or contributing to a book, see our author guide at www.packtpub.com/authors.

Customer support

Now that you are the proud owner of a Packt book, we have a number of things to help you to get the most from your purchase.

Downloading the example code

You can download the example code files from your account at http://www.packtpub.com for all the Packt Publishing books you have purchased. If you purchased this book elsewhere, you can visit http://www.packtpub.com/support and register to have the files e-mailed directly to you.

Downloading the color images of this book

We also provide you with a PDF file that has color images of the screenshots/diagrams used in this book. The color images will help you better understand the changes in the output. You can download this file from https://www.packtpub.com/sites/default/files/downloads/8163OT_ColorImage.pdf.

Errata

Although we have taken every care to ensure the accuracy of our content, mistakes do happen. If you find a mistake in one of our books—maybe a mistake in the text or the code—we would be grateful if you could report this to us. By doing so, you can save other readers from frustration and help us improve subsequent versions of this book. If you find any errata, please report them by visiting http://www.packtpub.com/submit-errata, selecting your book, clicking on the **Errata Submission Form** link, and entering the details of your errata. Once your errata are verified, your submission will be accepted and the errata will be uploaded to our website or added to any list of existing errata under the Errata section of that title.

To view the previously submitted errata, go to https://www.packtpub.com/books/content/support and enter the name of the book in the search field. The required information will appear under the **Errata** section.

Piracy

Piracy of copyrighted material on the Internet is an ongoing problem across all media. At Packt, we take the protection of our copyright and licenses very seriously. If you come across any illegal copies of our works in any form on the Internet, please provide us with the location address or website name immediately so that we can pursue a remedy.

Please contact us at copyright@packtpub.com with a link to the suspected pirated material.

We appreciate your help in protecting our authors and our ability to bring you valuable content.

Questions

If you have a problem with any aspect of this book, you can contact us at questions@packtpub.com, and we will do our best to address the problem.

1
Getting Acquainted with the UE4 Interface

In this chapter, we'll cover the following recipes:

- ▶ Installing UE4 and folder structure
- ▶ UI overview
- ▶ Navigating the viewport
- ▶ The Content Browser overview
- ▶ Importing your own content

Introduction

UE4, created by Epic Games, is a robust game engine that contains several different game development tools, which can create any kind of game imaginable, with many areas for specialization. It would be good for newcomers to the Engine to first have a basic understanding of what the entire Unreal Engine consists of and then dive into the different areas that they are interested in.

These first recipes may seem a bit difficult for those who are unfamiliar with game development, but after a short period of time, it will become second nature to them. In this chapter, readers will gain some fundamental knowledge and have some awareness that will help and prepare them for the upcoming chapters.

Installing UE4 and folder structure

Now, in order to use UE4 at all, we have to have it installed on our computer. Even after we install it, we may also want an overview of what it is. In case you haven't installed it yet, here is how you can do this.

How to do it...

Now that we have our project set up, let's get started with creating our player:

1. In the web browser of your choice, go to `http://unrealengine.com`.

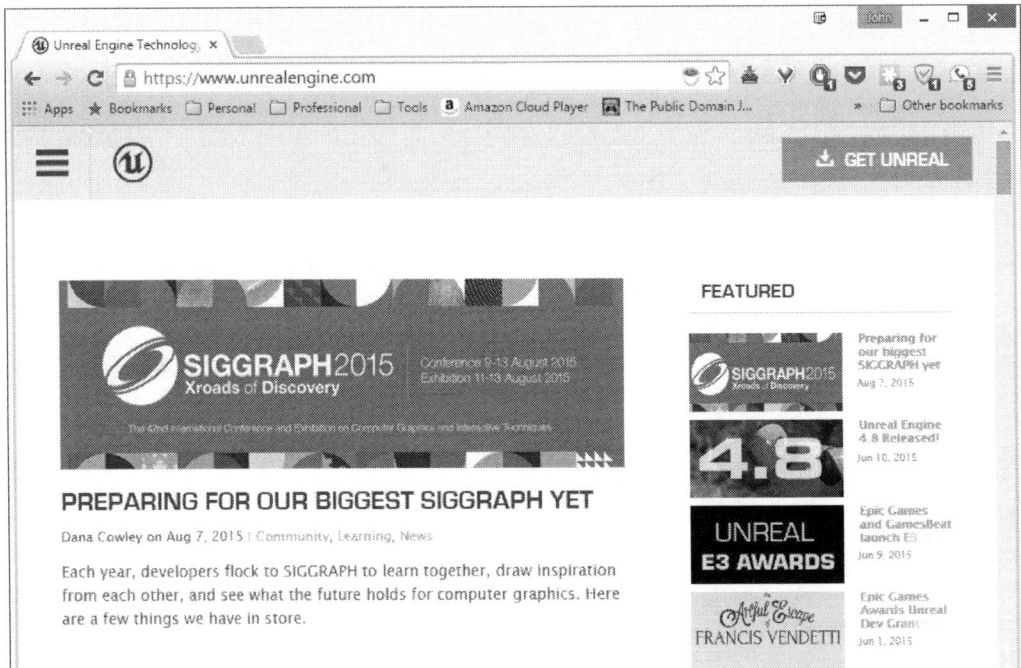

2. Once on this page, click on the light blue **GET UNREAL** button.

3. Once on the **Join the Community** page, fill out the information and create your account!

   It's important at this point to note the subscription plan that Unreal has for its user. You need to pay a 5 percent royalty to Unreal for any games that you publish. Of course, if the title is released for free, you don't need to pay anything.

If you happen to be a student who is 13 or above and are enrolled in a degree or diploma granting course of study, GitHub has a pack of resources for student developers that currently includes free subscription to Unreal Engine 4 for a year. If you have a school-issued e-mail address, valid student identification card, or other official proof of enrollment, check it out at `https://education.github.com/pack`.

If you happen to be a teacher or school administrator, it may also be possible to get access to UE4 for your school. Find out more at `https://www.unrealengine.com/education`.

4. Once you are logged in to your account, make sure that you are on the **Subscription** tab and then click on the **Download** button on the right-hand side of the screen for the operating system of your choice (I am using Windows).

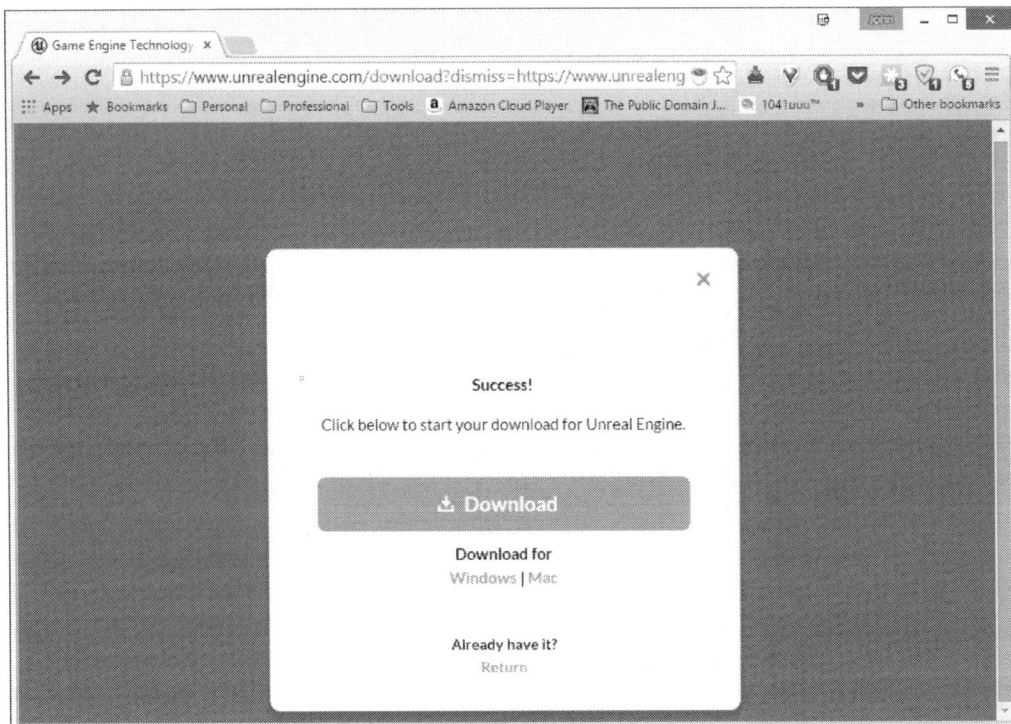

> If by chance you don't see the preceding screen, you can always get the latest version of the software at `https://www.unrealengine.com/dashboard`.

5. Next, once the installer has finished downloading, open it up and start the installation. If you see a security warning, click on the **Run** button.

6. Go through the installation process, but make sure that the destination folder you're installing it in has a lot of disk space as UE4 will take up around 8 GB of space for each version that you have installed. Once the installation is complete, the Epic Games Launcher should open. If it doesn't, open it from your desktop.

7. Once the launcher is open, fill in your e-mail and password and then click on the **Sign In** button.

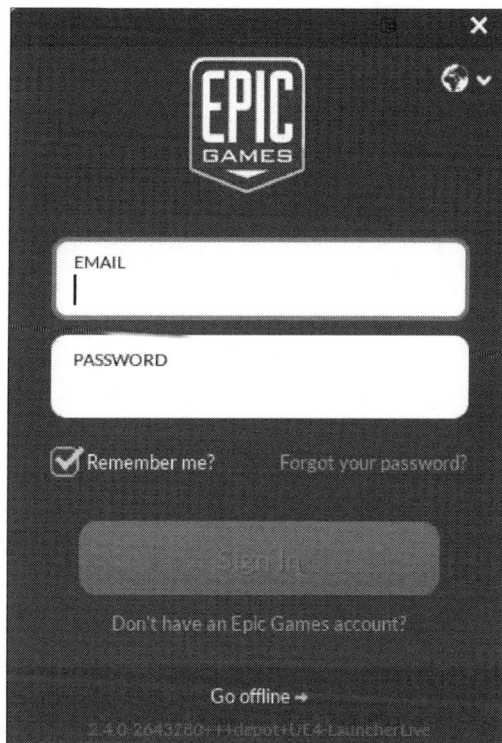

8. When you log in, the current version of UE4 will begin to download. Take a break as this will most likely take a while. Once the download is finished, you can see the **Launch** button lit up.

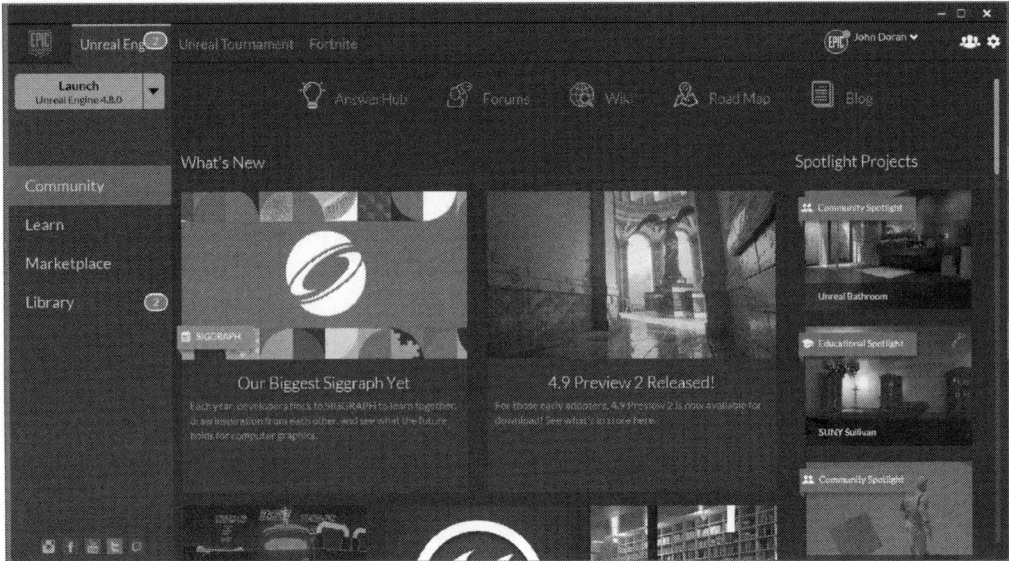

There's more...

Now that you have your UE4 installation completed, it's a good idea to see what actually has been installed. For a definition of what all of these folders are used for, please refer to `https://docs.unrealengine.com/latest/INT/Engine/Basics/DirectoryStructure/index.html`.

UI overview

One of the hardest things to understand when first starting out with a tool is knowing how to actually access all of the tools that are contained in the engine. Let's take a look at the interface of the Unreal Editor.

Getting ready

When you actually launch UE4 from the launcher, the first thing that you'll be brought to is **Unreal Project Browser**. Switch to the **New Project** tab, and you'll be given a choice of various templates to use for projects. For now, we'll stay with **Blueprint** visual scripting and will create a **Blank** project with starter content included so that we can see some stuff in the project. For the project's name, I have put UIOverview. Once finished, click on **Create Project**.

How to do it...

Now that we have our project set up, let's get started and see what the editor looks similar to:

1. Once the project is opened, close the tutorial popup that comes up (if it does). This new window that's opened is referred to as the level editor, which is the core of content creation in UE4. Here, you can see the default interface layout:

2. At the top-left of the editor, you can see the **Modes** tab, which contains various tool modes to allow you to put things into the world, such as BSP brushes, painting, and foliage and terrain. Below this, you can see the **Content Browser** tab, which contains all of the models, textures, and data that make up our game worlds. We'll be exploring this much more in *The Content Browser overview* recipe later in this chapter.

3. In the center, the largest window that you see is the viewport , which is the actual level that we are building. We will talk more about viewports in the *Navigating the viewport* recipe.

4. To the right of the window, you will see the **Scene Outliner** tab, which will display all of the actors within our level. This is a useful tool for being able to find actors easily as well as adding a parent/child relationship to objects. Below the **Scene Outliner** tab, you'll see the **Details** tab, which contains information about whatever object is currently selected in the level or the Scene Outliner tab. For each component on the object, it will display the functionality for it, such as the transform and the materials the object uses.

5. At the top, you'll see the tab bar, which will show the name of your project as well as a tab for the level that you currently have running with its name.

6. Below this, you'll see the menu bar that will provide access to general tools and commands:

    ❑ The **File** menu lets you save and open maps as well as projects. It also allows you to import/export actors.

    ❑ The **Edit** menu allows you to copy and paste actors as well as configure properties in the editor. In this menu, users can configure **Editor** and **Project Settings** as well. It is in these settings that let you create the icons for the game launcher, set up input actions for your game type, and so on.

    ❑ The **Window** menu allows you to toggle visibility of the various things that UE4 contains and save or reset your layouts.

    ❑ The **Help** menu has a number of additional resources to help make working in UE4 as painless as possible.

7. On the right-hand side of the menu bar, you'll see a search bar that you can use to look for help. The far right of the bar shows whether you are currently connected to source control through Subversion (SVN) or Perforce, which would be useful when you're in teams.

8. Finally, below this in the center is the toolbar that contains a group of commonly used shortcuts to make it easier to find certain things.

For more information on the default interface, check out `https://docs.unrealengine.com/latest/INT/Engine/UI/LevelEditor/index.html`.

Navigating the viewport

Now that we have an understanding of what the UI actually is all about, let's work with the viewport and learn how to move around and use it.

How to do it...

To get started, let's first try to move around in the game world a bit by using just the mouse:

1. Inside the viewport, with the left mouse button clicked and held, move your mouse forward and you should notice the level moving as well. If you move your mouse backward, you should notice that the camera is moving in the same way, and when we move the mouse to the left and right, the camera turns, it doesn't move.

2. Holding the right mouse button and moving the mouse will rotate the viewport camera in a similar manner to a **First-Person Shooter** (**FPS**) game. Moving the mouse up and down will make the camera loop upward and downward. And, when we move the mouse to the left and right, the camera behaves in the same manner.

3. Holding the middle mouse button (scroll wheel) and moving the mouse will pan the camera in the direction you move it as if it is on a track.

   You can adjust the speed with which the camera moves by modifying the **Camera Speed** property in the top-right of the viewport to increase or decrease the amount of movement you need to travel via the camera. Alternatively, holding the left or right mouse button and scrolling the middle mouse button (wheel) will also change the camera speed.

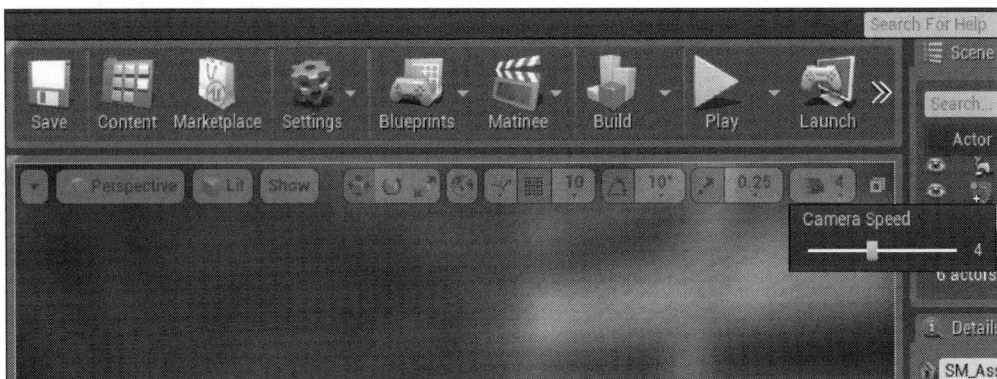

4. In addition to rotating the camera like an FPS game, when holding down the right mouse button you can also use the *W*, *A*, *S*, and *D* keys to allow you to move just like you would in an FPS in **Spectator** mode.

> If you're not a fan of the right mouse button, you can hold any other button on the mouse and move. If you aren't a fan of the *W, A, S,* and *D* keys, you can also use the arrow keys or *8, 4, 6,* and *2* keys on the numpad.

5. You can also use the *E* and *Q* keys in order to rise or fall in the air and the *C* and *Z* keys to zoom in and out, respectively, by changing the **field of view** (**FOV**). This change in FOV is only temporary though as when you release the right mouse button, it will reset back to normal.

6. The final way we can move through the viewport is very similar to how Maya users can move around their models. We activate this mode by holding the *Alt* key. If we click and drag, we will tumble around whatever is there in our current pivot in a similar manner as we orbit around the pivot. Clicking on the right mouse button and dragging will zoom the camera in and out of the pivot, while holding down the middle mouse button and dragging will move the camera in the direction of the mouse movement. We can change where our pivot is easily by selecting the object we want to move around and then pressing the *F* key to focus on it.

> For more information on moving around the viewport, refer to
> `https://docs.unrealengine.com/latest/INT/Engine/`
> `QuickStart/2/index.html`.

The Content Browser overview

The **Content Browser** is a central repository for creating, importing, and modifying all of the content that we use within UE4. This contains all of the assets that our project is made of, and it's important to have a good idea about how to use it.

Getting ready

This recipe assumes that you have a project open with the sample assets included. If you do not have that yet, feel free to follow the instructions in the *Getting ready* section of the *UI overview* recipe.

How to do it...

Now that we know how to move around the viewport, we will next want to get acquainted with the **Content Browser**, which is what we use in order to import or modify contents for our project:

1. By default, the **Content Browser** tab is docked in the lower-left corner of the main Level Editor interface, but it can be redocked anywhere within the Level Editor or floated as its own window. You can make it float as a separate window by clicking on the **Content Browser** tab and dragging it off. If you have a second monitor, having one for the **Content Browser** tab can often be a nice way to work as you'll often be grabbing things from there and bringing them into the world when building levels.

2. Close the **Content Browser** tab by clicking on the **X** button in the top-right corner of it. To bring it back, go to **Window | Content Browser | Content Browser 1**.

> Alternatively, you can also click on the Content shortcut icon above the viewport or press *Ctrl + Shift + F* to bring the **Content Browser** tab back.

3. You can snap the **Content Browser** tab back to where it was by dragging the tag over it and releasing. You can also create multiple **Content Browser** tabs to allow you to see multiple things at a time or to move assets between folders easily.

4. The interface of the **Content Browser** tab needs space to look nice. Move your mouse over to the edge of the Content Browser tab and drag to extend it. Do the same from the top. Next, double-click on the StarterContent folder to open it.

5. The top section is called the navigation bar. It allows you to create, import, and save assets on the left-hand side as well as to move through the different folders in a similar way to a web browser.

6. Below this on the left-hand side is the sources view. This contains a list of all the folders and collections inside the project, formatted in **Folder Hierarchy**. Extend the `StarterContent` folder in the view to see all the folders.

7. Below this is the **Collections** view, which provides easy access to your created collections. **Collections** are a way for us to organize assets into personally-defined groups, such as all characters or environment meshes for a level. Unlike being in a folder, you can think of all of the objects in a collection as being a reference or shortcut to that content. This can be collapsed if you're not using it by clicking on the icon to the left of the **Collections** text.

8. On the right-hand side, below the navigation bar, is the asset management area. This is used mostly for filtering out files or searching for a particular asset that we will see below in the asset view.

9. Below that is the asset view, which is the largest section of the UI. This is a grid displaying all the items that meet the filter requirements in the navigation bar's folder. Right-clicking on an asset or folder will show contextual options based on the objects. All of the assets you see can be dragged and dropped into a scene easily by clicking on the `Shapes` folder and dragging one of the objects into your scene.

10. You can also create new objects within the folder you have selected by right-clicking on some open space and then selecting the desired asset from the menu.

11. In the bottom-right corner of the **Content Browser** tab, you'll see **View Options**. Select it and notice that you can view these assets in three different styles. Go through each of them and note the differences. Each of them have their own advantages and disadvantages; it's good to know that they all exist. You can also change the size of the thumbnails and this may be helpful as the number of objects that you have increases.

In **View Options**, users can also see the game engine's contents by selecting **Show Engine Content**. This will allow you to see all of the content included in the engine, by default, which can be quite useful for creating content for the game projects of your own.

Importing your own content

Now that we have a good foundation on the Content Browser tab, let's start off by bringing in some of our own content into the game.

Getting ready

This recipe assumes that you have a project open with the sample assets included. If you do not have that yet, feel free to follow the instructions in the *Getting ready* section of the *UI overview* recipe.

In addition, this recipe uses assets from the example code provided for the book. If you do not have it, download it from the Packt Publishing site at `http://www.packtpub.com`

Downloading the example code

You can download the example code files for all Packt books you have purchased from your account at `http://www.packtpub.com`. If you purchased this book elsewhere, you can visit `http://www.packtpub.com/support` and register to have the files e-mailed directly to you.

How to do it...

Let's start off by importing a simple model from the **Content Browser** tab.

1. Make sure that the **Content Browser** tab is at the `Game` folder and then click on the **Import** button.

2. Once there, browse to the location where the example code of this chapter is placed and open the `Ship` folder. Select the `Ship.fbx` file and then click **Open**.

3. You'll be prompted with an FBX import dialog, click on **Import**, and you should see your new asset included in the **Content Browser** tab, accompanied by **Materials** that was created to be used for the `Ship` model.

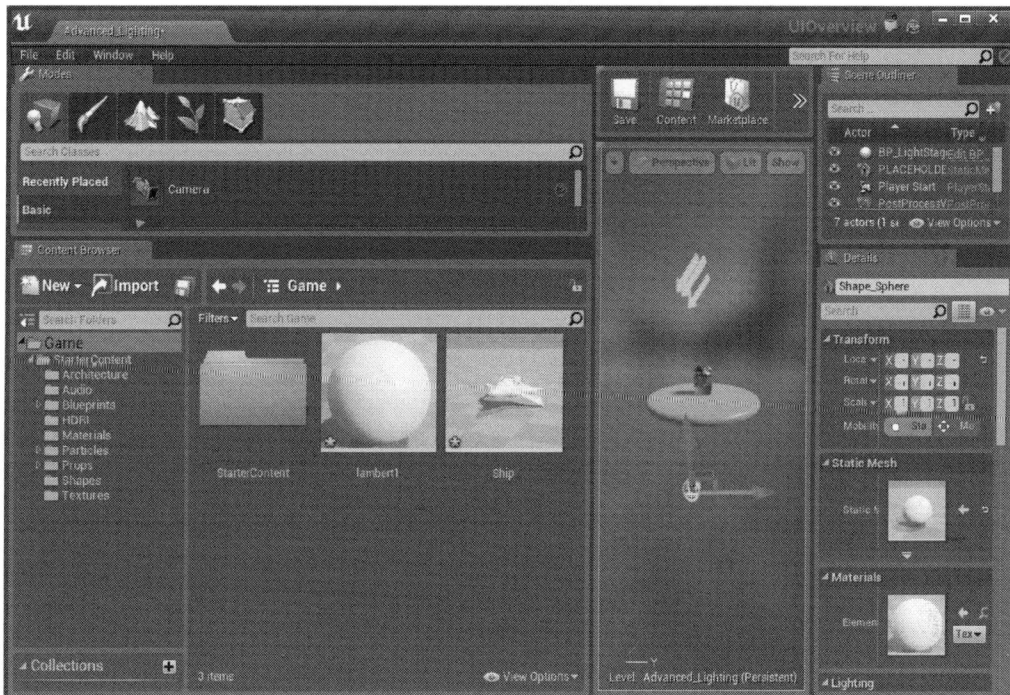

4. The other way to import assets is simply by dragging and dropping them into the **Content Browser** tab. Let's do this by opening up our `Ship` folder in our operating system and then dragging it onto the asset view of the **Content Browser** tab. You'll notice that textures (images) do not have a dialogue like the model did.

5. Currently, all of the objects have a * in the bottom-left corner of their images. This is because they are currently not saved to the project. Fix this by clicking on the **Save** icon (blue floppy disk) in the **Content Browser** tab.

   Alternatively, you may also right click within the **Content Browser** tab and then navigate to **Import to /Game** to import assets into your scene from whatever folder you are currently in.

2

Level Design – Building Out Levels or Greyboxing

In this chapter, we'll cover the following recipes:

- Building a room
- Building out a level
- Applying materials to geometry brushes
- Converting brushes to static meshes or volumes

Introduction

In the game industry, there are two main roles in level creation: **environment artist** and **level designer**.

An **environment artist** is a person who builds the assets that go into the environment. They use tools such as **3ds Max** or **Maya** to create the 3D model and then use other tools such as **Photoshop** or **Gimp** to create textures, including diffuse and normal maps.

A **level designer** is responsible for taking the assets that an environment artist creates and assembling them in an environment for players to enjoy. He/she designs the gameplay elements, creates the scripted events, and tests the gameplay. Typically, a level designer creates environments through a combination of scripting techniques and uses some tools that may still be in development. In our case, that tool is **Unreal Engine 4**.

> One thing that is important to note is that most companies have their own definitions for different roles. In some companies, a level designer may need to create assets, and an environment artist may need to create a level layout. There are also some places that hire someone to just do lighting or place meshes (called a **mesher**) because he/she is so good at it.

In this chapter, we will be exploring the topics that are relevant to the role of a level designer.

Building a room

Now that we have an understanding of the interface of UE4, let's start with creating one of the most basic things, a room.

Getting ready

Before we start working within the Unreal Editor, we will need to have a project to work with:

1. Open the Unreal Editor by clicking on the **Launch** button from the Unreal Engine Launcher.

2. Start a new project from the **Unreal Project Browser** window by selecting the **New Project** tab. Select **Third Person** and make sure that **With Starter Content** is selected. Give the project a Name (for this chapter, I am using Blueprints_ Chapter2). Once you are done, click on **Create Project**.

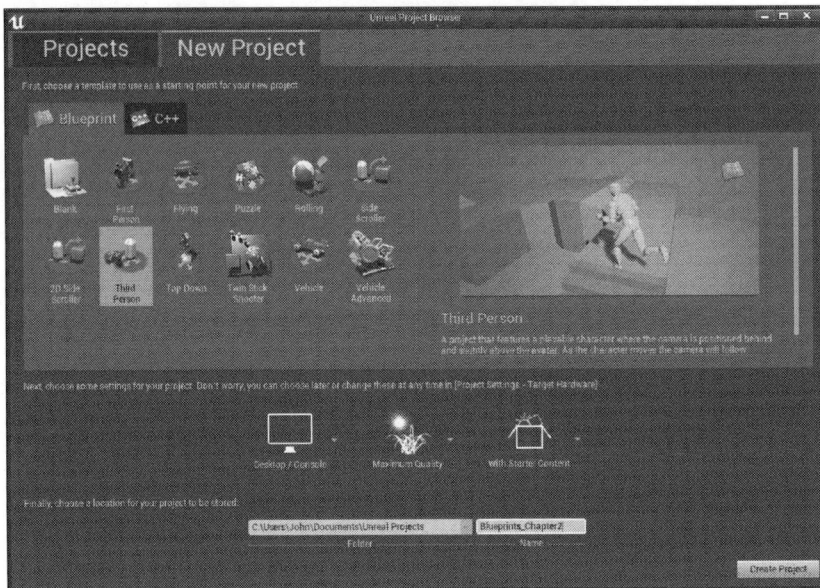

How to do it...

Now that we have our project set up, let's get started with building the room.

1. With the editor open, we will first create a new level for us to work in. To do that, go to the top-left corner of the screen and go to **File | New Level...** or press *Ctrl + N*.

2. From here, the **New Level** window pops up. Click on the **Empty Level** template, and you will find an empty level to work with.

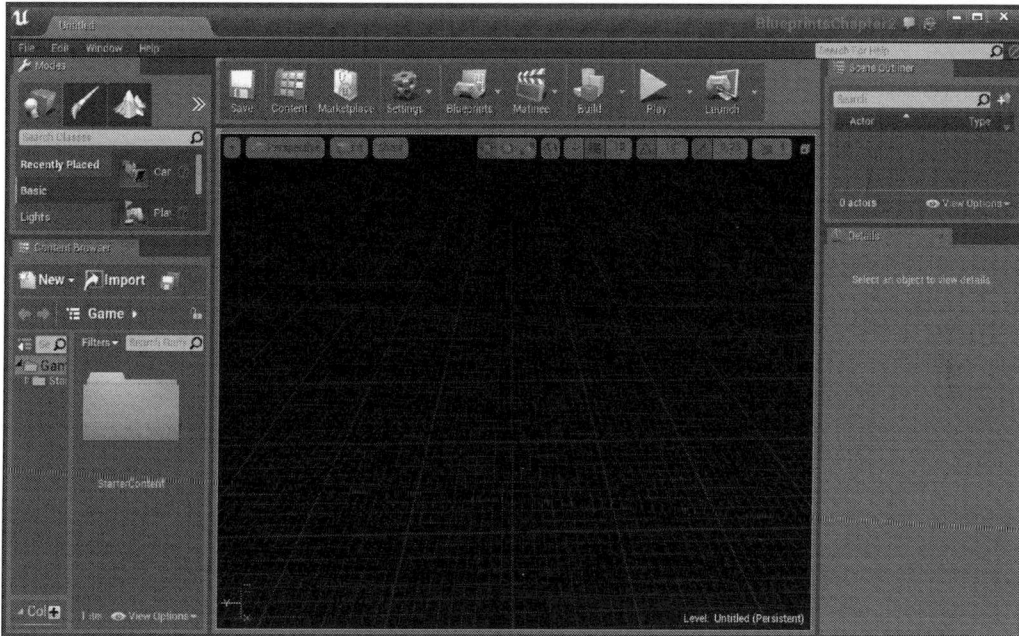

If you look closely and tilt downward, you should see a never-ending grid that fades into the distance. This is a guide to help show you distances and make it easier to work within a 3D environment.

3. Next, we will want to place some geometry into the world in which we can build out our room. To start out with, we will create a box. To do so, under the **Modes** tab, in the top-left corner, click on the place icon (the one on the far left that resembles a cube and lightbulb) to switch to the **Place** mode if not there already.

> For more info on the **Place** mode, refer to `https://docs.unrealengine.com/latest/INT/Engine/UI/LevelEditor/Modes/PlaceMode/index.html`.

4. Now select the **BSP** category on the left-hand side, below the mode icons. From there, click and drag the **Box** button into the world. You may see it show up as some red lines initially, but give it a minute, and you'll see the box appear on the screen, as shown in the following screenshot:

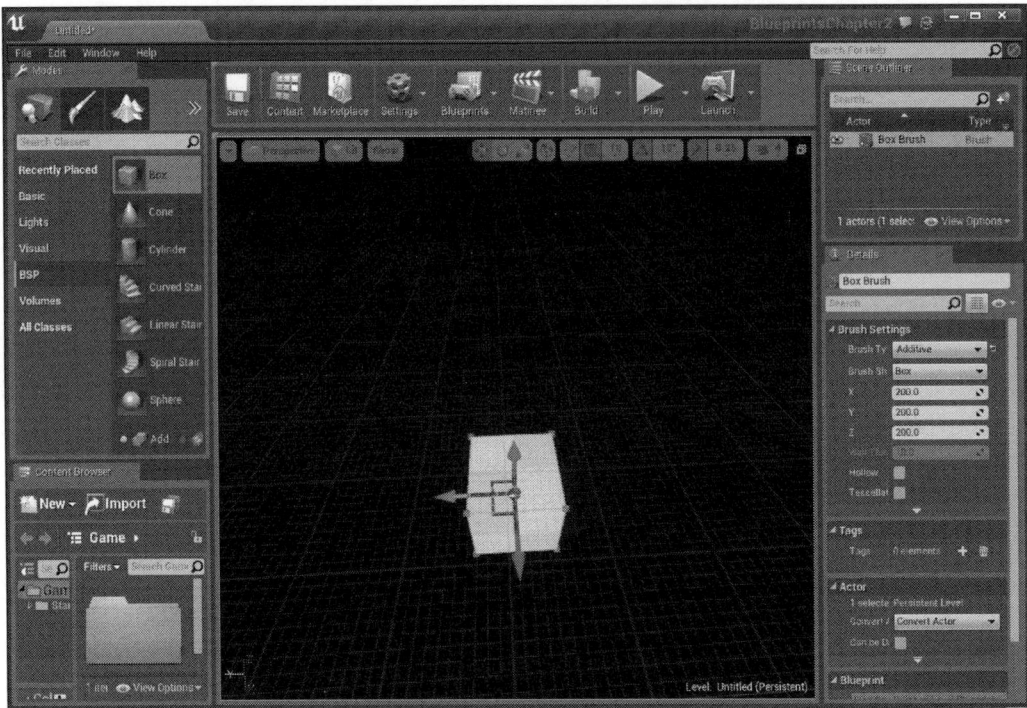

> If you don't happen to see the box, that's because, by default, UE4 has the default lighting mode set to **Lit**, and as there is no light, everything will be just black once the lighting is built. You can switch to **Unlit** mode by going to the top-left area of the **Level** window and clicking on the **Lit** button and then selecting **Unlit** from the dropdown, or just using the hotkeys—*Alt + 3*, for **Unlit** and *Alt + 4* for **Lit**.

Once the box is created and selected, note the **Details** tab on the right-hand side. This tab contains all the information about this brush that can be modified. If you know what size your brush will be, this can be very useful.

5. From **Brush Settings** under the **Details** tab, change the **X** and **Y** values of the brush to `1000` and the **Z** value to `25`.

   This will create a room that is about 10 x 10 m with a width of 25 cm. Be sure to note that it is **Z** that is the vertical axis inside the Unreal Engine. The **X** and **Y** values define how large we want our room to be, but I used a **Z** value of `25` because inside normal buildings, the joists or horizontal foundation supports between levels are about 10 inches (approximately, 25 cm) thick.

   > By default, 1 unit in Unreal Engine is equal to 1 cm. If you'd like to change this or customize this value, you can go to **Settings** | **World Settings** and modify the **VR** | **World to Meters** value to `100` (1 m is equal to `100` cm).

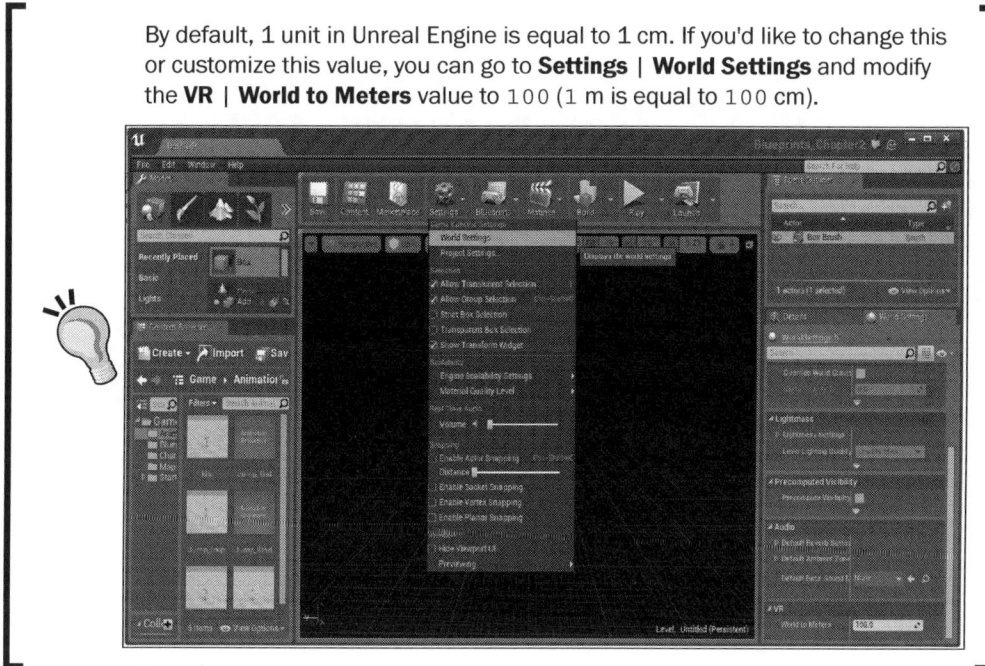

6. Now that we have a floor created, let's add a reference for us to work with. Under the **Content Browser** tab on the bottom-left, go into the `Character` folder and drag and drop the `HeroTPP` skeletal mesh onto the scene.

   Having a character reference in the world makes it a lot nicer for us to see how the sizes of objects relate to our player.

7. If we were to run the game now, we won't be able to see anything due to lack of light. Let's fix this. Under the **Modes** tab, change the section to **Lights** and drag and drop **Directional Light** into the level.

A directional light acts similarly to the sun; no matter where it's placed, it will modify the objects in the area.

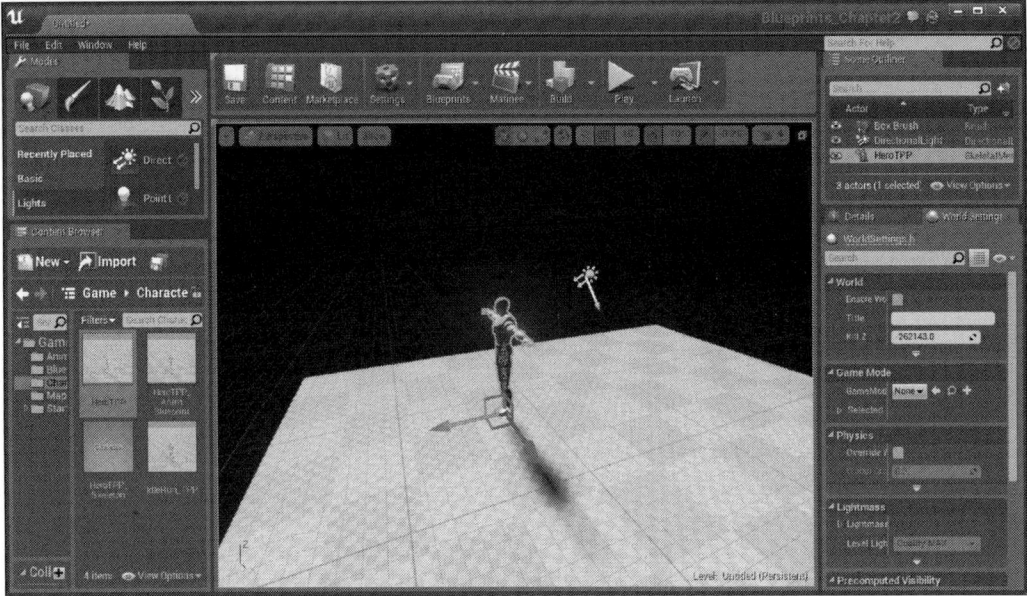

Effect of a directional light

8. The next thing we are going to do is to create walls for this room. To do this, let's first drag another box into our world, this time placing it above our floor. Once created, inside the **Details** tab, under the **Brush Settings** section, set **X** to 10, **Y** to 1000, and **Z** to 300.

> Creating levels based on real world locations can be an excellent exercise for a budding level designer. Should you want to do that, the real world walls normally have a thickness of 12 for interior walls and 16 for exterior walls.

9. Once finished, select the wall and use the transform gizmo (the three arrows) to move the object over the ground of our room (if you don't see the arrows, press the *W* key, and if you still do not see it, toggle Game Mode by pressing the *G* key) Once over it, press the *End* key, and you should see the brush fall down to hit the floor. Once this is finished, move the wall in the **X** and **Y** axis using the transform tool until it is flush with the edge of the level, which is to say they should be placed next to each other.

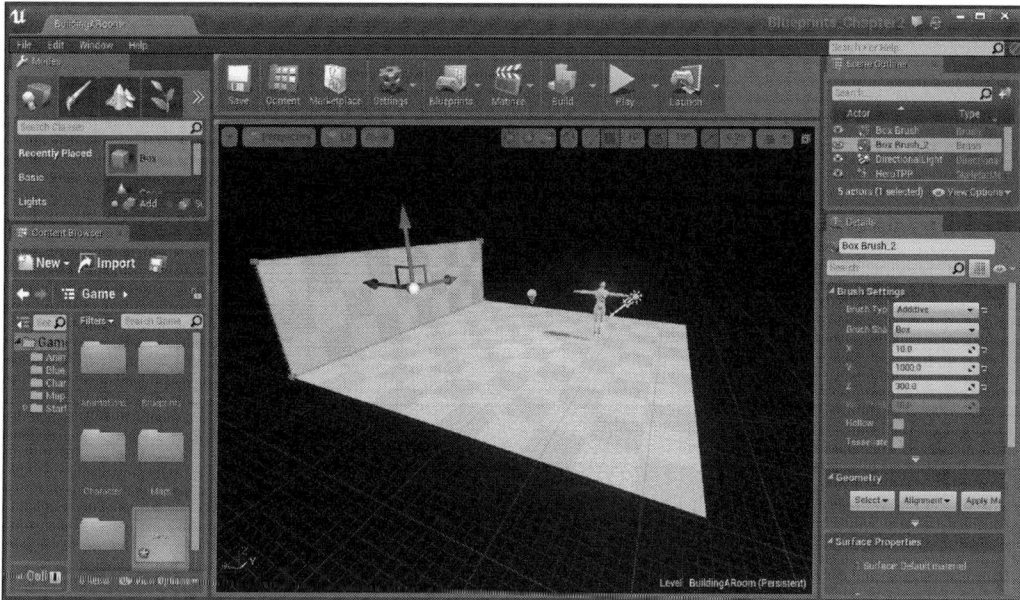

Creating walls for a room

10. We can add a ceiling to our room very easily. Click on the floor that we've created, hold down the *Alt* key and then drag the item by the blue arrow to be flush with the top of our wall that we created previously.

You'll notice that with the ceiling placed, there are now shadows covering a good portion of our level. If we want to be able to see in the room, we will need to add a new light, a **Point Light**.

11. Back in the **Modes** tab in **Place** mode, go down to the **Lights** section and select it. Once selected, you should see the **Point Light** option on the right-hand side.

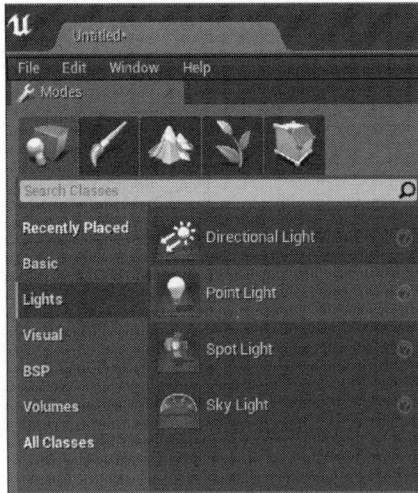

12. Drag and drop **Point Light** into the center of the room. You'll see that we can see in the room now!

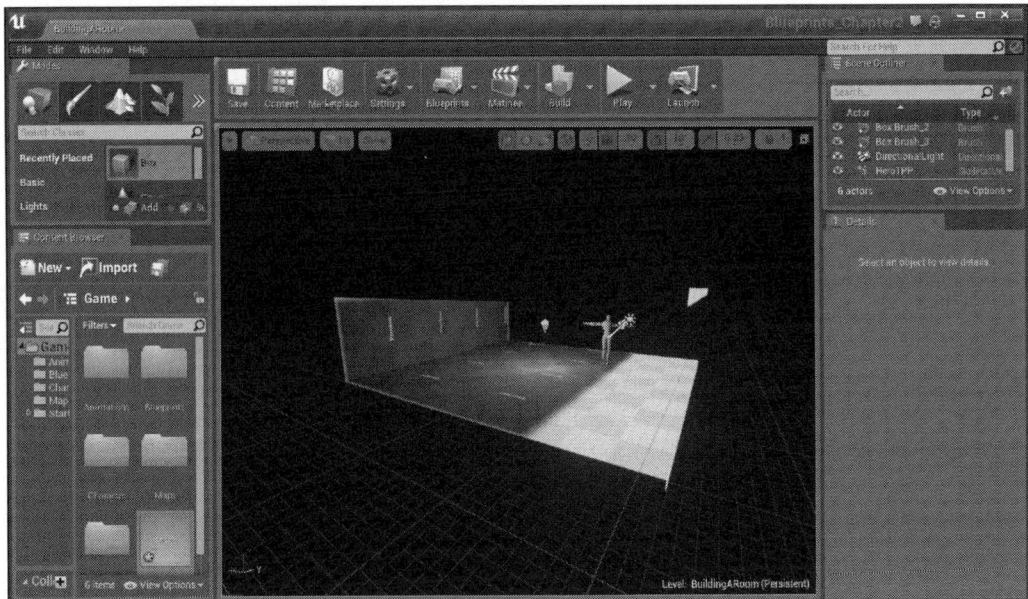

A **Point Light** works similar to how a lightbulb does in the real world, shining equally in all directions from a single point.

> Alternatively, you can create a point light by holding the *L* key and clicking on the center of the room.
>
> For more information on point lights, refer to `https://docs.unrealengine.com/latest/INT/Engine/Rendering/LightingAndShadows/LightTypes/Point/index.html`.

13. Next, let's close this room. With the wall selected, create a duplicate to go to the other side of the room by holding the *Alt* key and dragging it to the other side.

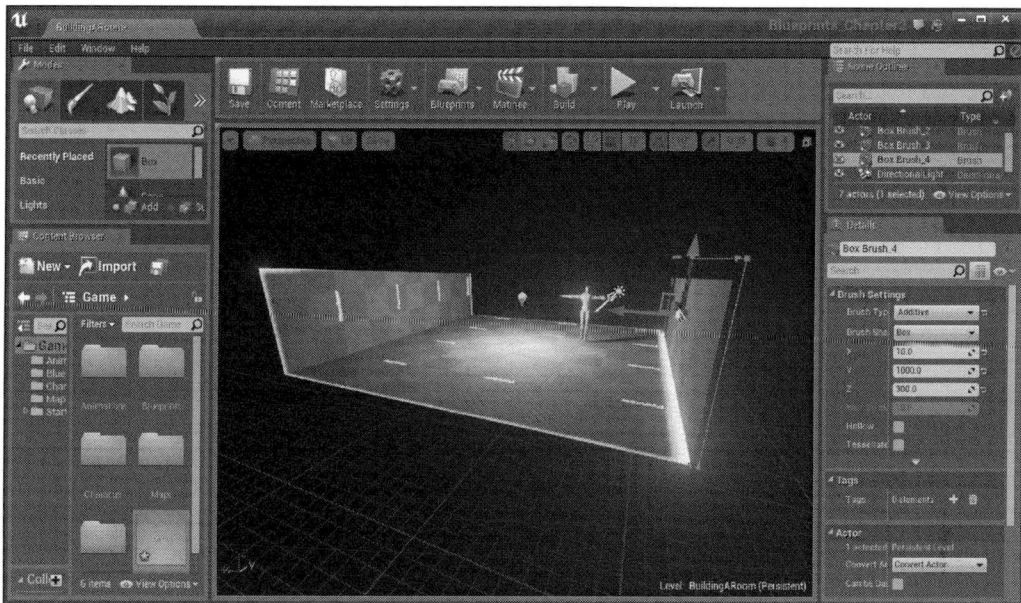

14. Next, we will place the other two walls. We could create another box like the one we created before and give it different values, but in this instance, we will use the rotation tool instead. Select one of the walls and hold the *Alt* key and drag the item in the **X** axis (red). After that switch to the rotation tool (*E*) and then rotate the wall 90 degrees along the **Z** axis (blue).

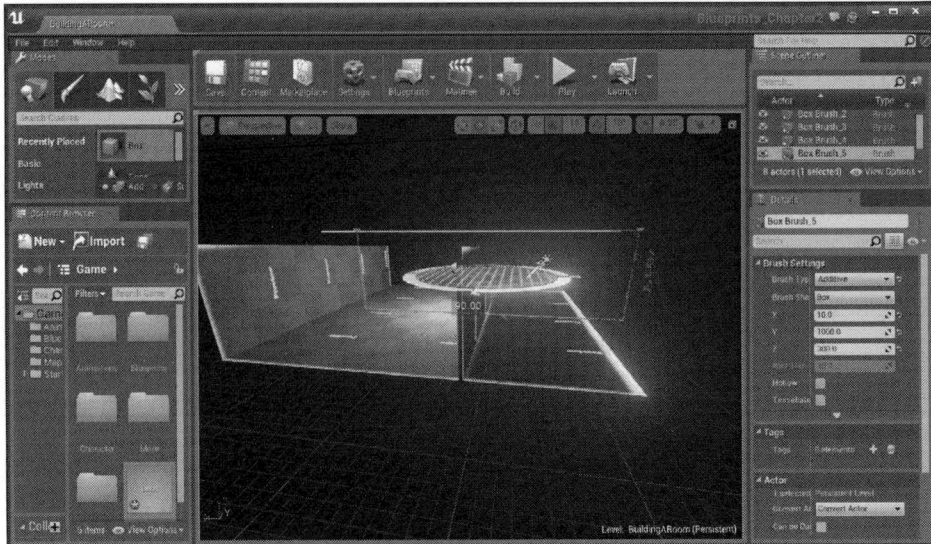

The original wall has been duplicated and rotated

15. When you let go, change back to the Translate tool (*W*) and then move the wall to fit the empty slot.

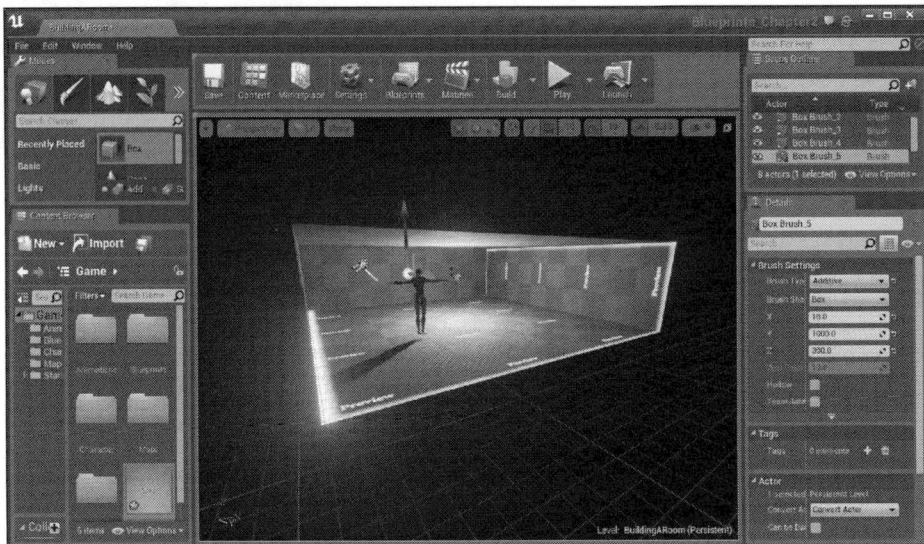

You can also use spacebar to toggle through the transform, rotation, and scaling widgets. You should be able to tell which is which, based on the gizmo that shows up, and can just hit the spacebar until you find the one you want.

16. Then, duplicate this newly created wall in order to close the gap. Now, to see what's going on in the level, you'll need to move into the map. Once inside, right-click on the floor and select **Play From Here**.

With that done, you now have a room that we can walk into!

If, by any chance, you fall from the edges of the surface, press *Esc* to exit the game, switch your view from **Perspective** to **Top**, right-click on one of the objects (walls or surface), press *F* to focus on that object and then, finally, switch your view back to **Perspective**.

Alternatively, you can also double-click on any object in **Scene Outliner** to zoom the camera to it.

It is also possible to create a room by creating a box with a size of 1010, 1010, and 300 with **Hollow** enabled and a **Wall Thickness** of 10, but you will lose a lot of control for larger areas.

Building out a level

When I started using Unreal Engine, it took me a long time in order to create any type of new level. I would keep placing static meshes to hide areas of geometry that I missed or added in blocking volumes to make it actually possible to go through certain places. One of the key reasons I had problems with this, is because I didn't know how to create a good workflow and the key to mapping things very easily by using brushes in the **Geometry Editing** mode.

Getting ready

Minimize the **Perspective** viewport by clicking on the button in the top-right corner of the viewport (circled in the following image):

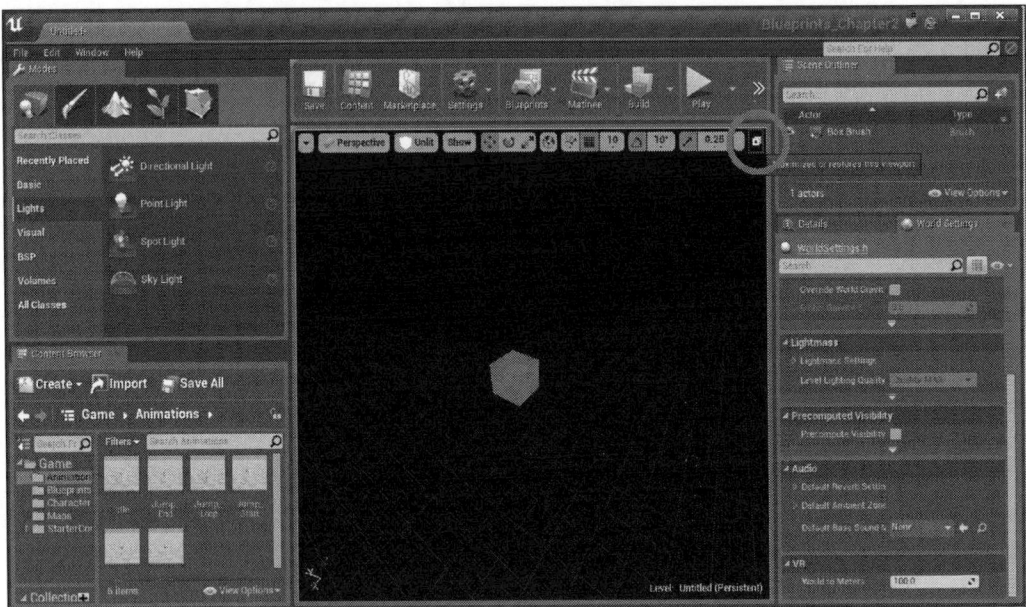

You will then see four windows and notice a grid of sorts in all the other viewports.

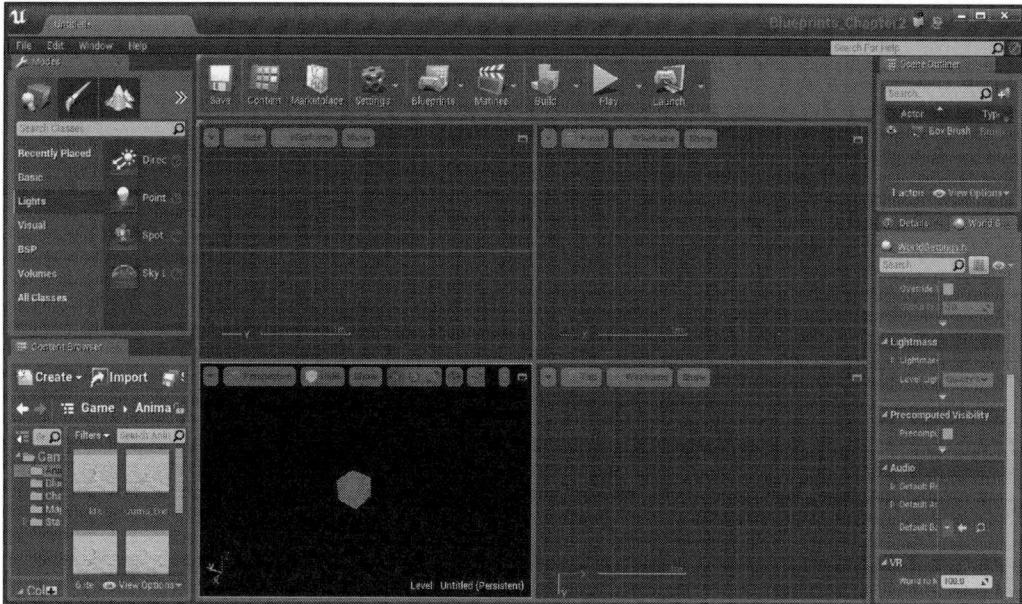

> You can click on the same button in the top-right corner of any of the four windows to maximize it.
>
> When in a different viewport, controls work a bit differently. Most importantly, right-clicking and dragging will pan the camera. For more information on the differences, refer to `https://docs.unrealengine.com/latest/INT/Engine/UI/LevelEditor/Viewports/ViewportControls/index.html`.

We will be using the grid as a guideline in the creation of our levels in the same way that we use paper to draw things out, which is something some level designers do to get the general feel of an area. Starting to build a general area needs to have planning ahead of time to have a general idea of how you want to place buildings and guide the traversal of the player.

Some keyboard tips

Holding the left mouse button and dragging will allow you to select all the objects that are contained within it, which we refer to as a **marquee selection**. If you are in the Geometry mode, this will let you select individual/overlapping vertices, allowing you to increase or decrease the size of your brushes very easily which we will be using to create our environment.

Another useful tip is if you press *Ctrl* and hold and drag the left mouse button anywhere in a viewport, it will move the brush, actor, and/or vertices that you have selected from any position. This is a good way to move objects that may not be far away or not have to move the screen and don't want to use the widget that is usually by the object.

If you hold *Ctrl + Shift* while moving an object, your camera will move with you as well. This can be really useful for repeating things in a certain direction.

Also, you can select multiple objects by holding *Ctrl* and then clicking on multiple objects.

Seeing double – duplicating elements

Duplicating things that we have already created, such as walls or buildings, are an effective way of blocking out an environment very quickly.

> I did this in the setup of the previous recipe by duplicating the room that we created in the first section.

As what we care about most here is creating the best gameplay possible. We pay less attention to fine details here and basically, want to just block out an area so that we can iterate as quickly as possible. After all, you're a lot more willing to get rid of or change a huge box than a ridiculously detailed office building.

After placing a single brush in our level, you don't really need the builder brush again. Unless you are creating something other than a box, you can just duplicate brushes and mould them using the Geometry Editing mode to quickly shape out areas that usually makes it much quicker to build.

How to do it...

With the knowledge of how to start a workflow, we can create a level:

1. Create a new level by going to **File | New Level...** and from that window, select Default.

2. The floor that currently exists in the game is actually a static mesh. We don't need this, so let's get rid of it by selecting it and then pressing the *Delete* key.

3. Next, we are going to the **Restore Viewport** button on the top-right of the viewport to get the four viewport split screens.

4. Once there, let's add a box for our foundation. Go to the **Modes** tab and select the **Place** button and go to the **BSP** section. Once there, drag and drop the **Box** to the viewport to bring it into the world. Once created, go to the **Details** tab and change the **Brush Settings—X** to 5000, **Y** to 3000, and **Z** to 300.

> I intentionally made this really tall because later, I will decrease the value of this brush to create a little area that my player can safely get around, and thus, I will not need to worry about them falling out of the world.

You may have noticed that when we move brushes around, they snap to certain positions. This effect is known as **grid snapping** and the amount of space moved is dependent on the **Grid Snapping** variable in the top-right of your viewport (by default, it's 10).

5. Increase the grid size to 50 by clicking on the grid icon on the top-right of any viewport and selecting 50 for the **Snap Sizes** value.

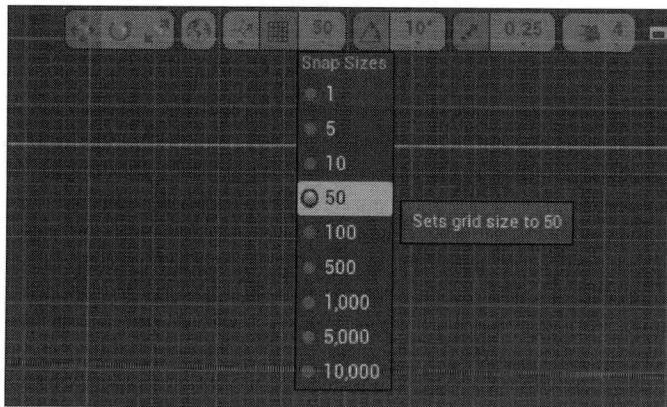

Another way to modify the grid space is by pressing the *[* and *]* keys in the editor that will decrease and increase the grid snap points, respectively, making the level more or less detailed in your brush placement. Some people will want to use a smaller area, but I argue that when blocking something out, we really only care about the big picture and getting the overall feel of the area.

In case your brush is not aligned to the grid, you can right-click on the vertices, and it will automatically snap it onto the grid. Working with the grid is a fundamental way of making sure that you don't get any holes and/or overlays of your brushes while creating a level.

6. Now duplicate our current brush by selecting it and holding the *Alt* key and then from the **Front** viewport, drag it one step (50 units) upward.

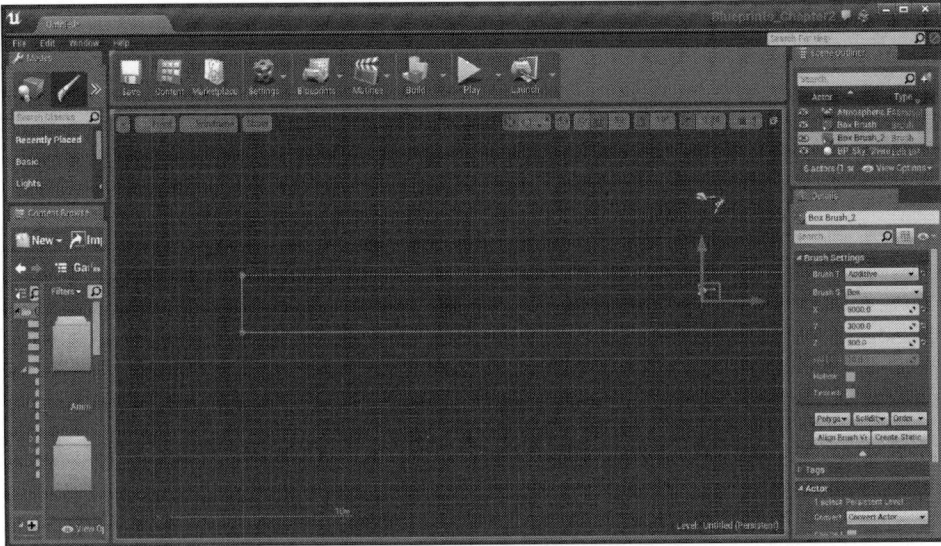

Duplicating the current brush upwards

7. Now, under the **Modes** tab, select the **Geometry Editing** mode, which is the furthest on the right. You'll notice that the edges or vertices of the selected brush will be larger than they were earlier. Select the two vertices on the left-hand side of the **Front** viewport and drag it one step (50 units) inward.

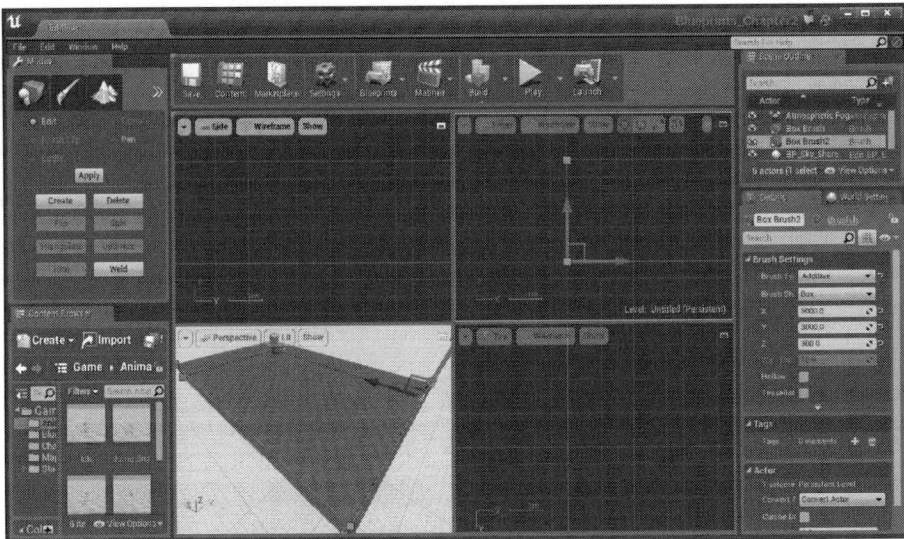

Selecting vertices via Geometry Editing mode

8. Do the same thing for the right side and the top of the brush. To do this for the top, which is much larger than the others, zoom out, select them both and then zoom in to do the movement.

9. Finally, we will need to move to the **Top** viewport. To do this, click on the **Front** selection and select **Top** and then drag the top and bottom vertices one step inward from here.

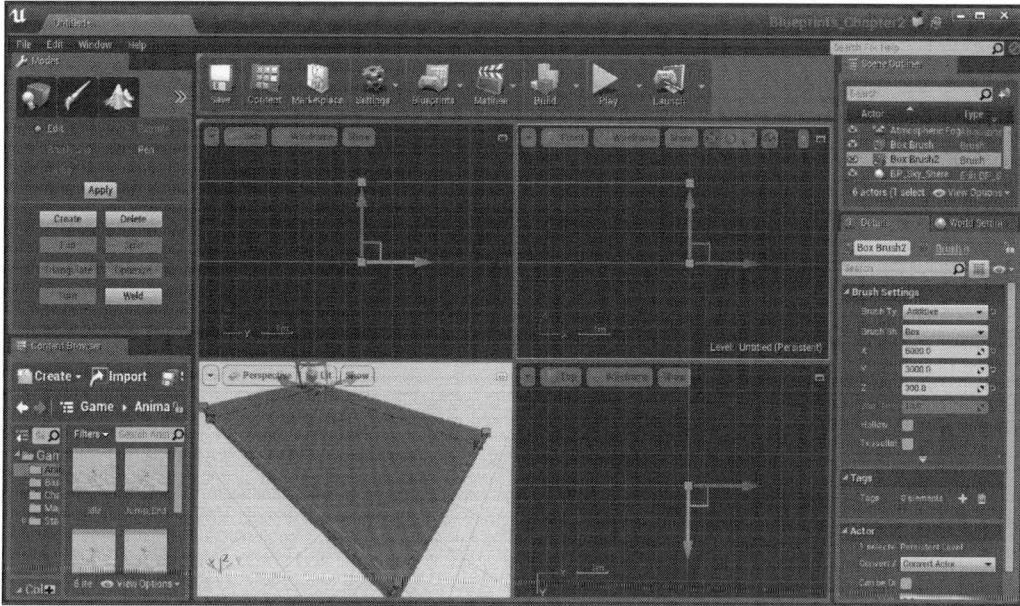

10. Finally, move back to the perspective view to see things clearly. Under the **Details** tab, change **Brush Type** to **Subtractive**.

A **subtractive brush** is used whenever you want to remove solid space, such as when you want to create a door or window. A nice change from Unreal Engine 3 is the fact that subtractive brushes only carves out space from the earlier created additive brushes so that we can place additional brushes on top of it.

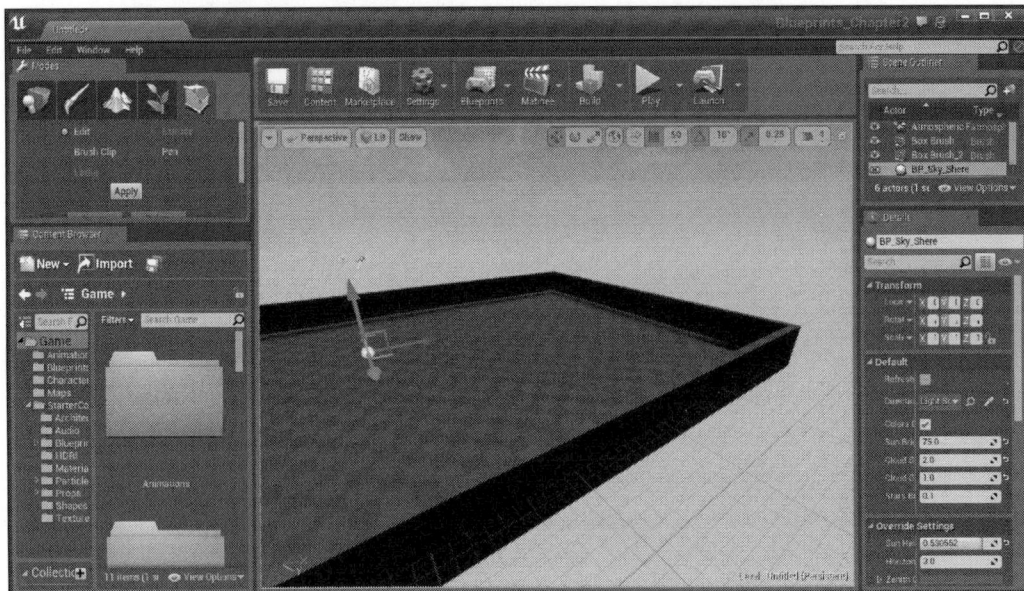

The use of the subtractive brush

With this, we now have an area that our player can inhabit. The player can jump on things that are approximately 200 pixels high, so we need to keep that in mind when developing our platforms as these walls are 250 pixels tall.

11. Go to the **Scene Outliner** tab on the top-right of the screen and then double-click on the `Player Start` object to center your camera on it. This is where the player will start the game from, so let's translate it to one of the edges of our map, pressing the *End* key to make it land on the ground.

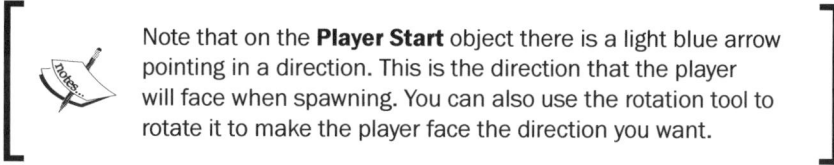

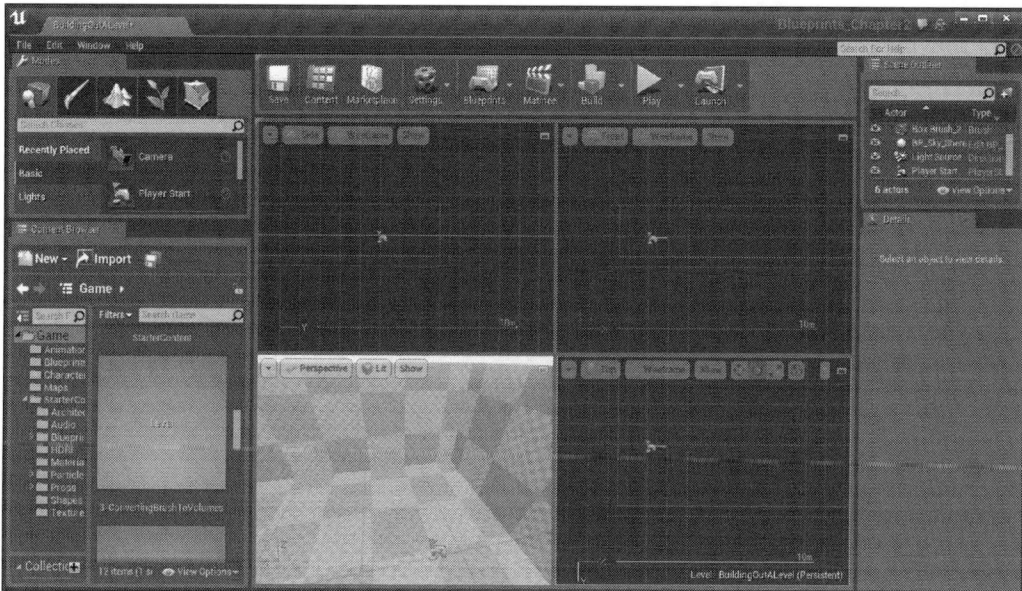

> Note that on the **Player Start** object there is a light blue arrow pointing in a direction. This is the direction that the player will face when spawning. You can also use the rotation tool to rotate it to make the player face the direction you want.

12. Now, we want to give the player some guidance on where to go, so I'm going to close off some areas inside the level. Drag and drop a new box into the level. Give it a size of 20, 200, 300 and put it flush up against the wall.

13. Once this is done, create another duplicate and leave some space to create an opening for the player to walk through. Finally, duplicate the brush again, rotate it 90 degrees in the **Z** axis and then use the **Geometry Editing** mode in order to have it fit the room by selecting the vertices using a marquee selection and then using the translate tool to move them into place.

> As a reminder, to do a marquee selection, click and drag some empty space on your screen and create a box that will hold the vertices you want to select. If you have a brush selected and you are in the Geometry mode, it will only select vertices from there.

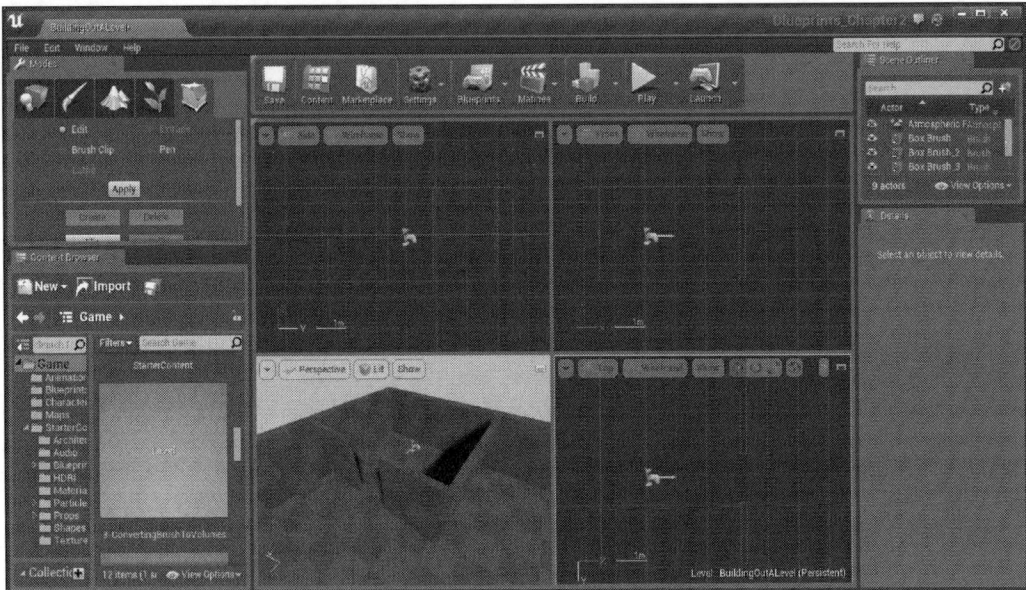

Creating walls with openings for a player to walk through

14. Next, let's build something a little more interesting, a staircase. We can do that by going into the **Modes** tab, selecting **Place**, going to the **BSP** section and then selecting **Linear Stair** and dragging it into the world and finally, placing it onto the ground.

> By default, there are 10 steps and each step is 20 units tall, so by default, the stairs are 200 units tall.

15. From this staircase, we are going to create a path to a tower. Create another box to create a walkway along the staircase. Make this walkway 1100 units long. Duplicate the brush, rotate it 90 degrees along the **Z** axis, and have it go down only 700 units.

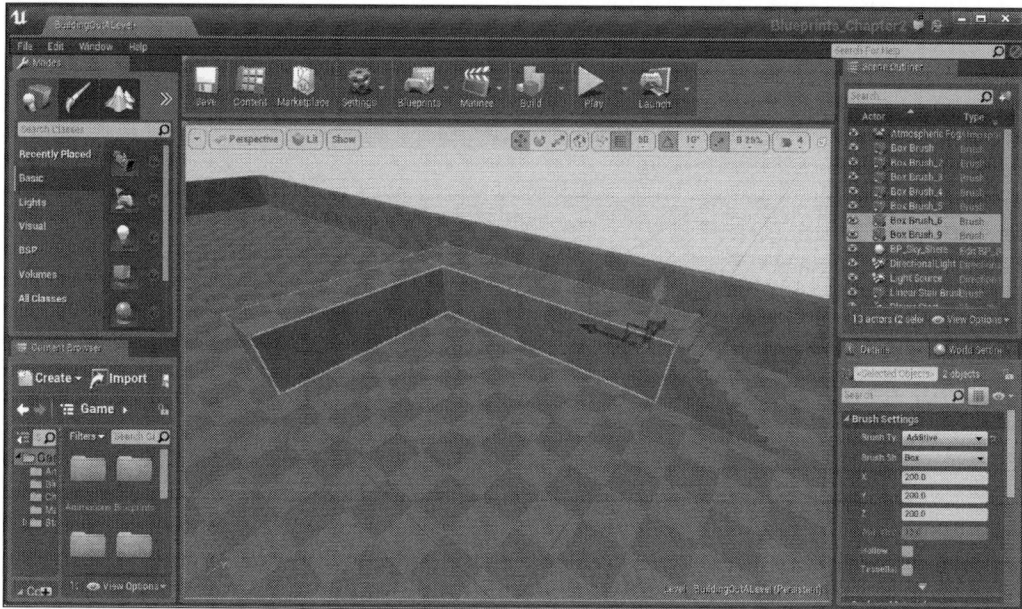

16. Duplicate the walkway again and have it only 500 units long. In the little 500 x 500 x 600 area, we've created a box to fill that hole.

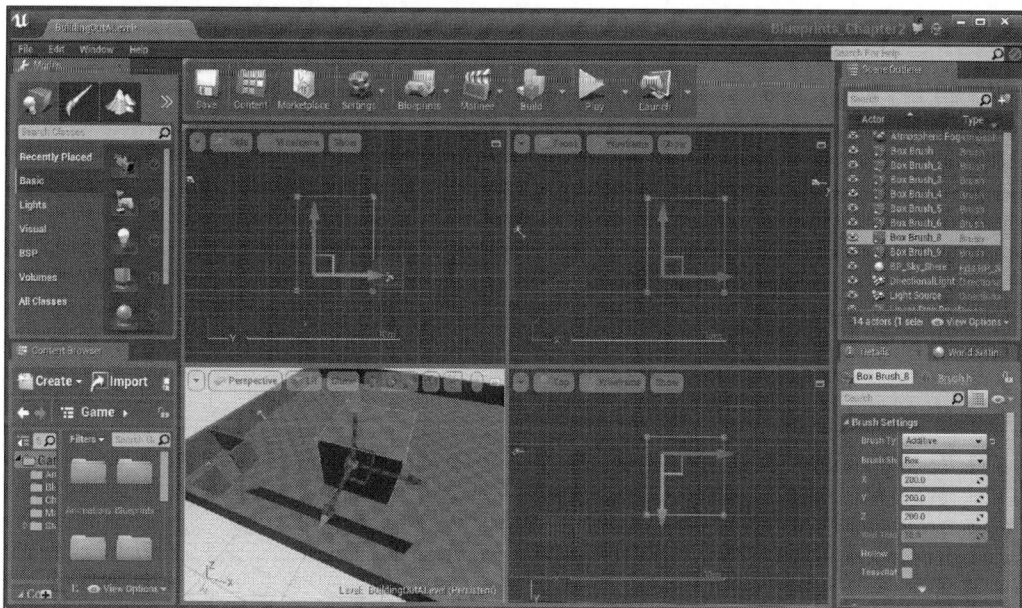

17. To create a path for the player to get up there, on the last created walkway, click on the left-hand side vertices from the Front viewport and drag it up to match the new tower. It should look similar to a ramp heading up there, making it easier for people to add one final walkway to get up to there.

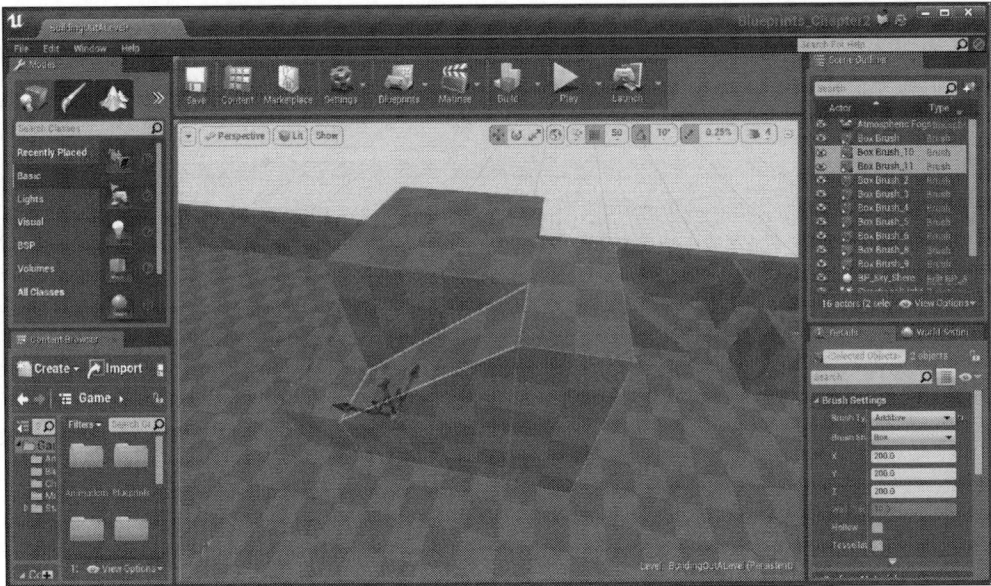

18. Once it's all put together, we should have something that looks similar to the following image:

19. In the **Perspective** viewport, it may be a bit hard to see what's going on. To help with this, place an additional **Directional Light** into the world with its rotation in the opposite direction of the **Light Source** object that is already there so that we can see where the shadows are. With this in the **Details** tab, change the **Light's Intensity** to 1. This is what's referred to as a **fill light**.

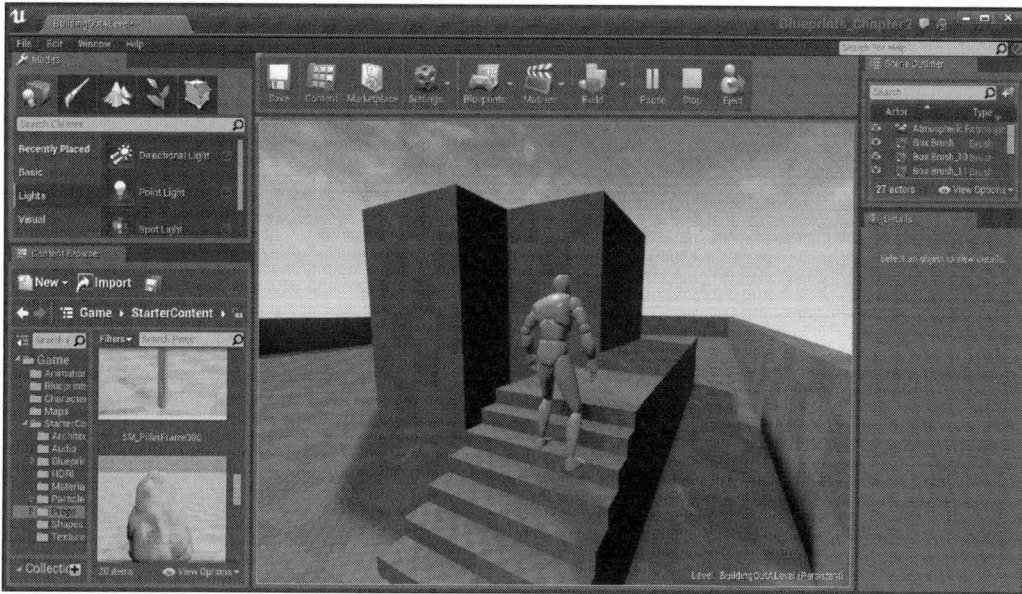

Placing an additional Directional Light as a fill light

We now have a firm basis with which we can build even more complex and interesting levels!

Applying materials to geometry brushes

Once you have your level blocked out, you'll probably want it to look better than just some greyboxes. We can very simply add some life to our world by adding **materials** to the surfaces of our brushes. Let's do this now.

Getting ready

This recipe assumes that you have a project open with the Sample Assets included as well as a room created with Geometry Brushes (BSP). If you do not have that yet, feel free to follow the instructions for the *Building a room* recipe.

How to do it...

Now that we have our room created, let's add some materials to it:

1. Inside the **Content Browser** tab, go to the `StarterContent/Materials` folder. Here, you'll see a number of materials that we can apply to the surfaces in our world. Select the `M_Wood_Floor_Walnut_Polished` object and drag it onto the floor of our room.

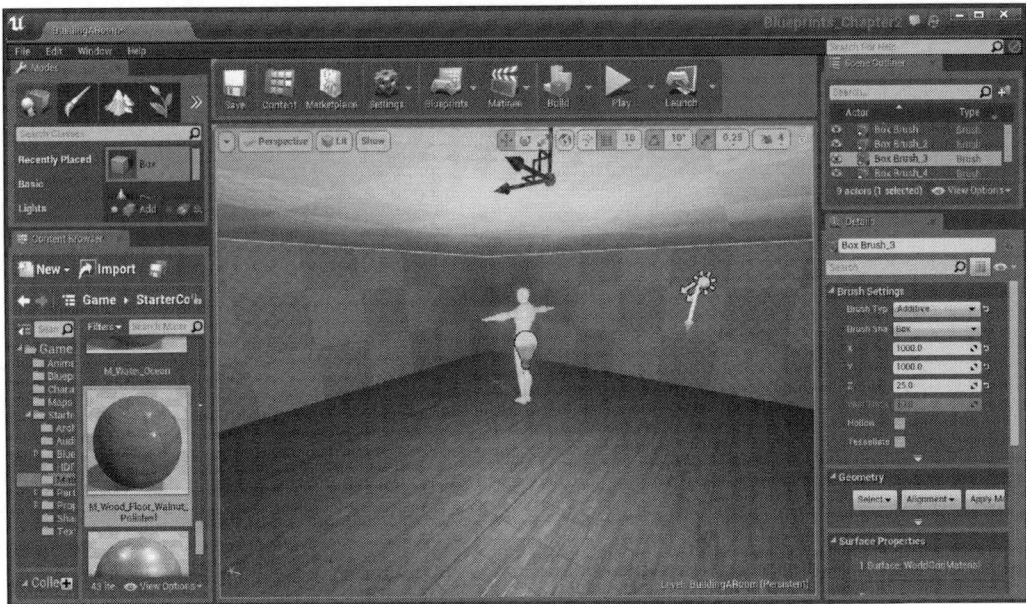

You can already see how its making the room look a lot nicer. This works well for a one-time event, and technically, we can do the same thing for the walls, however, it can become quite tedious over time. Thankfully, there are some tools we can use to make our lives easier.

2. Select one of the walls inside our room. Once there, go to the **Details** tab and under the **Geometry** section, click on the **Select** dropdown menu and then select **Select All Adjacent Wall Surfaces**.

3. You should see lines along all of the walls in place. After this, let's select a material to use for the walls (I am using `M_Basic_Wall`) and then back at the **Details** tab under **Geometry**, click on the **Apply Material** dropdown menu and then select **Apply Material: M_Basic_Wall**.

4. Finally, we will want to add a ceiling to our world. Select the `M_Concrete_Tiles` material and drag it onto the ceiling.

   This is a great starting point, but there are some other features you may want to be aware of. For instance, this wooden floor looks fine, but maybe you want the planks of wood to be larger. You can very easily do this by going into the **Details** tab, and under **Surface Properties**, modifying the **Scale** value to `2.0` in the **U** and **V** directions and then clicking on **Apply**.

You may also want the planks to face horizontally instead of vertically. To do this, click on the **90** button in the **Rotate:** section. You can also move the textures a little at a time in order to get it perfect using the Pan option.

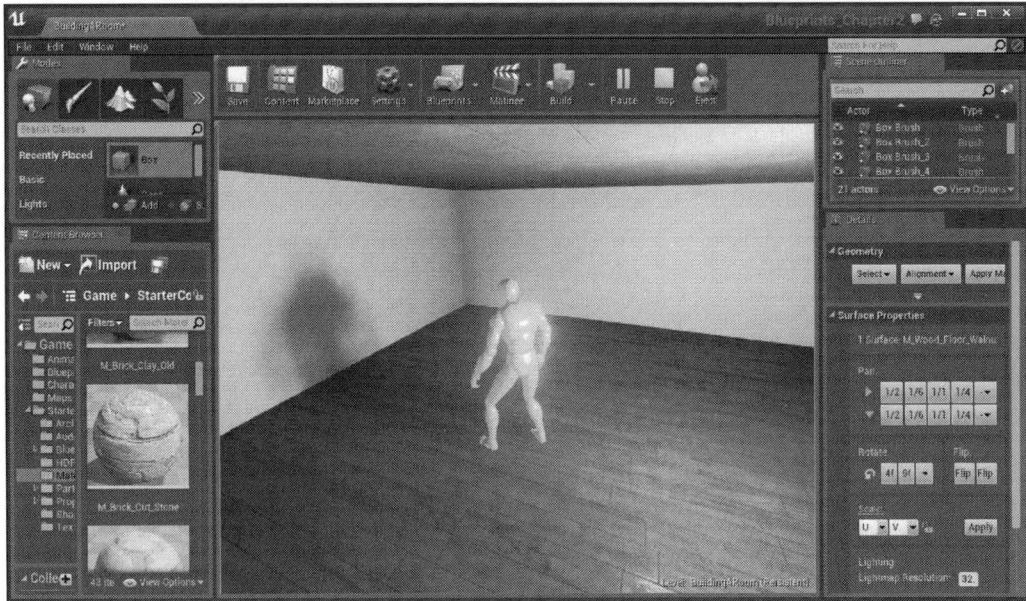

We can now work with materials on our brushes.

Converting brushes to static meshes or volumes

As level designers, we will often greybox our levels to playtest and make sure that a level is fun and works correctly. Once we get to a point where the level is not going to change very much, we give our environment artists a model with the environment and then they can go in and make everything pretty with complex meshes or create pieces for us to build it out modularly. The first thing we will be doing in this recipe is creating the mesh that we can give to our artists. The second thing we will be learning is how to convert brushes into volumes. As you may be aware, the high-poly meshes that our environment artists would create could be very computationally expensive to check against collision with other objects at runtime. A trick that we will often use is to convert the brushes into a blocking volume that will still have the collision as we've been using and then filling the world with meshes to look the best it can.

In addition, you may have something like a doorway, and when you enter the hall, you want something to happen. We can use a Trigger volume for this. Rather than creating a trigger volume and then scaling it, it would be much easier to just use the doorway brush as a base.

Getting ready

This recipe uses a level of two rooms connected via a hallway with a subtractive brush opening the way, which should be easily completed if you followed the *Building out a level* recipe. If not, you can open the **3-ConvertingBrushToVolume (Persistent)** setup level and use it for this task.

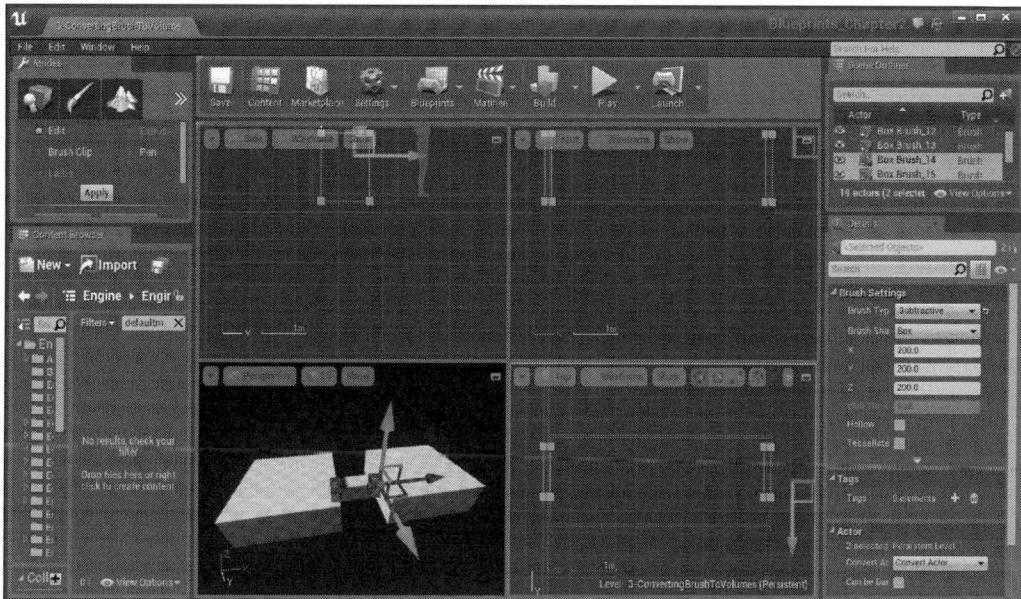

How to do it...

Let's first export one of these rooms so that we can give them to our artist to work with:

1. If you have not already, minimize the Perspective viewport by clicking on the top-right minimize button in the viewport to go to the four-window default view. With this done, select all of the brush actors in the right room by doing a marquee selection. You may have to unclick on an object, such as a point light by holding the *Ctrl* key and then clicking on them. Once you have only brushes selected, in the **Brush Settings** section under the **Details** tab, click on the downward facing arrow to open up the advanced options and then click on **Create Static Mesh**. You'll be given an option to name it (I am putting `Room_StaticMesh`). Then, click on **Create Static Mesh**.

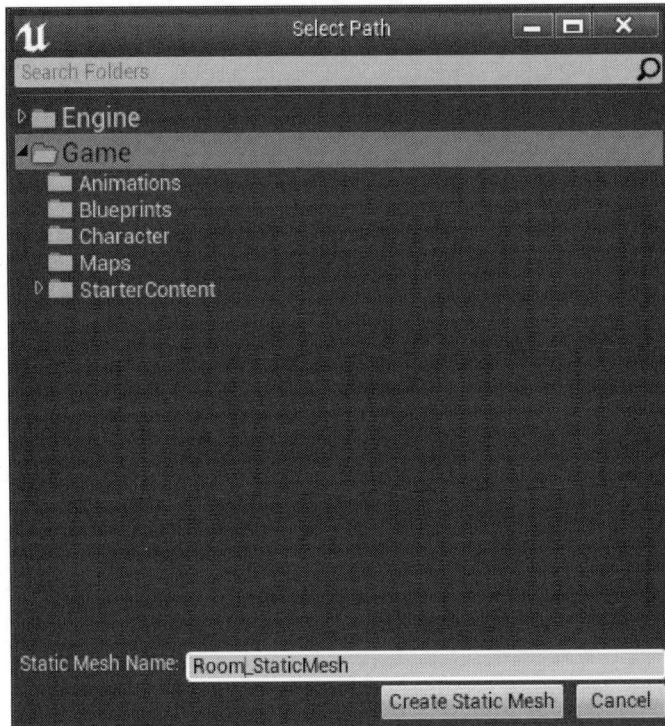

2. Once this is done, if you go into the **Content Browser** tab and the Game folder, you should see your Static Mesh there! Finally, we need to export it so that our artist can open it. Right click on the mesh and then select **Export** and save it as an FBX file!

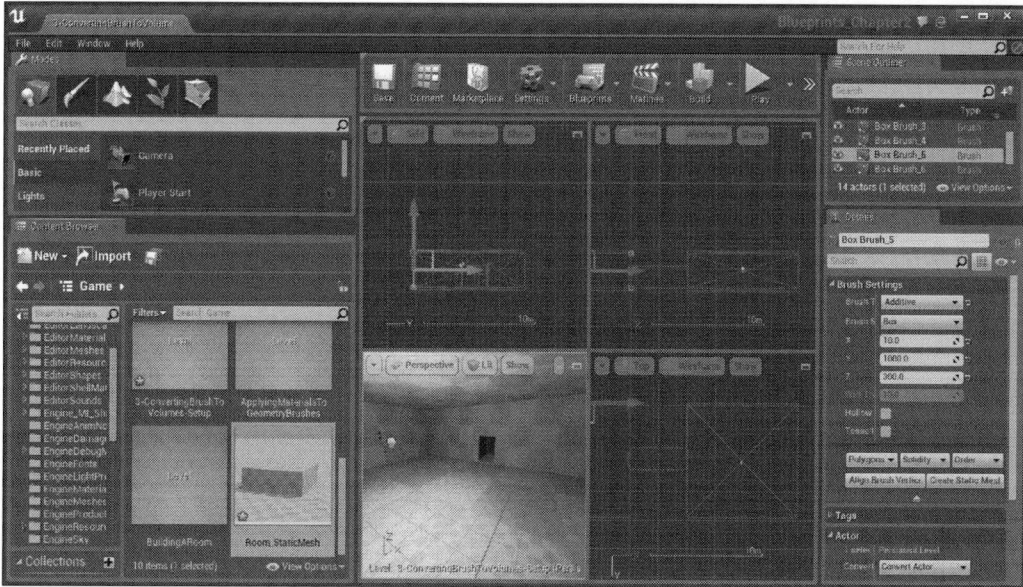

After this, you can give the model to your artist, and they will know the size of the area that you've created!

> It's important to note that after you turn something into a static mesh, you cannot convert it back to brushes again, so before doing this, I always suggest saving a copy of the level.

Another thing that we may want to do, is for something to happen when we enter the hallway, so we will want to have a trigger volume in the position. Rather than creating one from scratch, let's use our subtractive brush as a base.

3. Inside of the hallway you want to add the trigger to, click on a wall created by the subtractive brush.

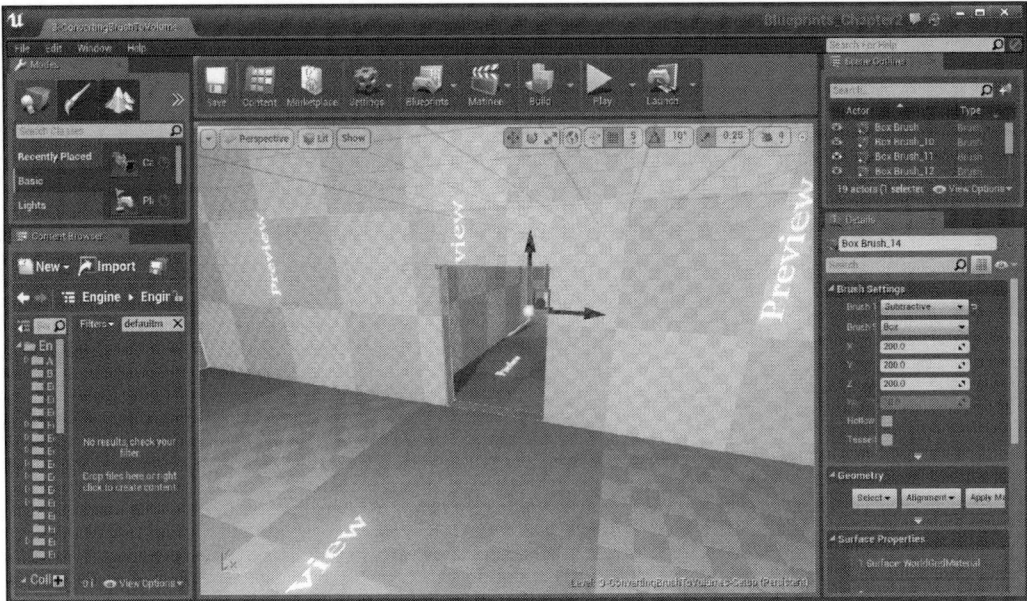

Selecting the subtractive brush

4. Next, create a duplicate of this brush by holding the *Alt* key and then dragging it out somewhat on the **X** axis (red).

5. In the **Details** tab under the **Actor** section, go to the **Convert Actor** action and select **Trigger Volume**. After a few seconds, you'll see that it's converted to have green edges and is of the same shape of brush as what we had beforehand!

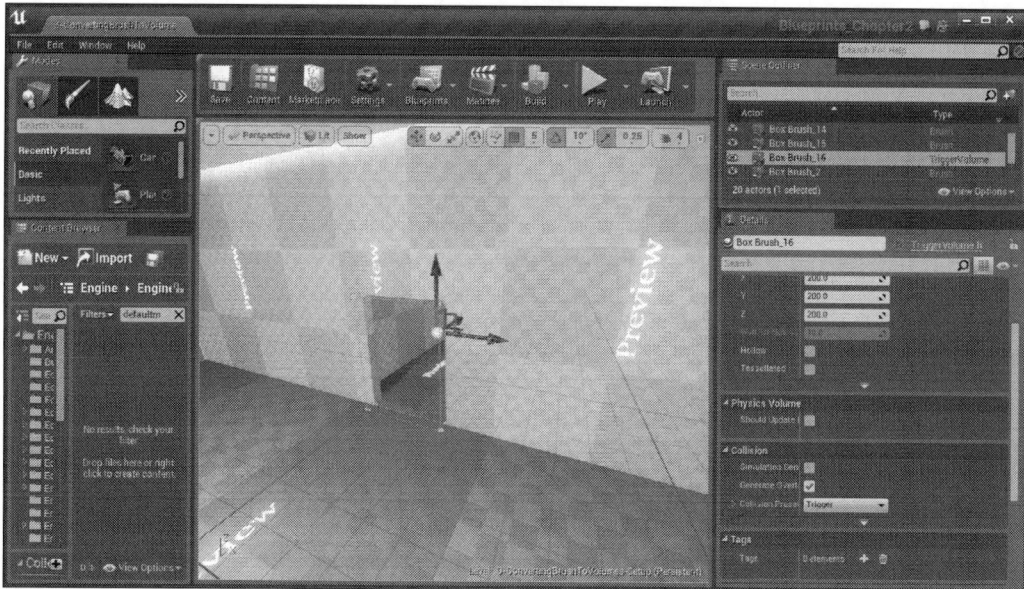

With this, we now have a good idea on how to convert brushes into other brush-like things!

If you are interested in learning what Trigger Volumes are and how they can be used, check out the *Using Trigger Volumes – opening a door using Matinee* recipe of *Chapter 8, Blueprint Scripting – Level Effects*.

3
Creating Quality Interior Environments

In this chapter, we'll cover the following recipes:

- ▶ Placing static meshes
- ▶ Placing a particle system
- ▶ Using Groups
- ▶ Meshing an example map
- ▶ Adding life to static meshes

Introduction

Continuing with the theme from the previous chapter, once we have created a level and have it playtested, only then we will want to make it look nicer.

In fact, level designers will often pass off the level geometry to an environment artist to recreate the level with new art assets.

Here, we will talk about the various ways in which we can polish our game to make the insides of buildings look great. Meshes will fill up a scene and give some depth to help with the suspension of disbelief, which is very important in game development.

Placing static meshes

Once we have our level at a point where it needs to be polished, one of the first things we can do is add meshes to decorate the level and make it feel more lived in. It's actually quite simple to do, so let's get started!

Getting ready

This recipe assumes that you have a project open with the Sample Assets included as well as a room created with Geometry Brushes (BSP). I have provided a sample level that will be used for this demonstration (ModernHouseBase), which is included in the Example Code that you can access from Packt's website at http://www.packtpub.com. If you are not familiar with building levels using BSP, feel free to follow the instructions for the *Building a Room* recipe from *Chapter 2, Level Design – Building Out Levels or Greyboxing*.

To open up the level files, create a new project with **Starter Content** included and then move the Maps folder (or just the .umap file) into your project's Content folder. You can easily access this folder from the Unreal Editor by going to the **Content Browser** tab and then right-clicking on the Game folder and selecting **Open with Explorer**.

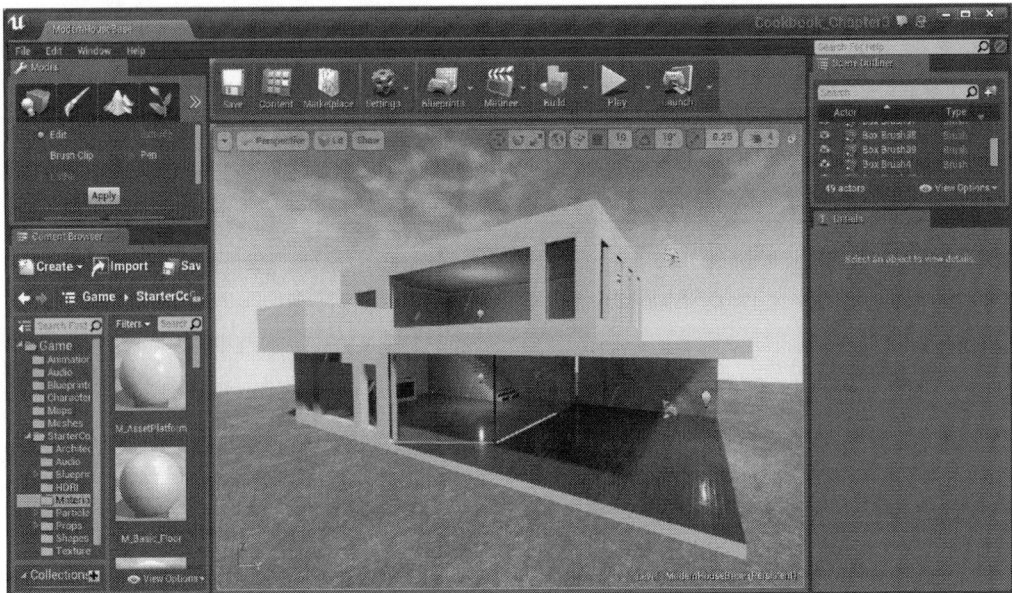

How to do it...

Now that we have our level open, let's start off by placing a single static mesh into our level:

1. Open the **Content Browser** tab. We first need to find the mesh that we want to use. If you have **Starter Content** added, the meshes are located in the `StarterContent\Props` folder.

   With the folder open, you'll see a preview of all of the meshes that you can work with, with a light blue border around them.

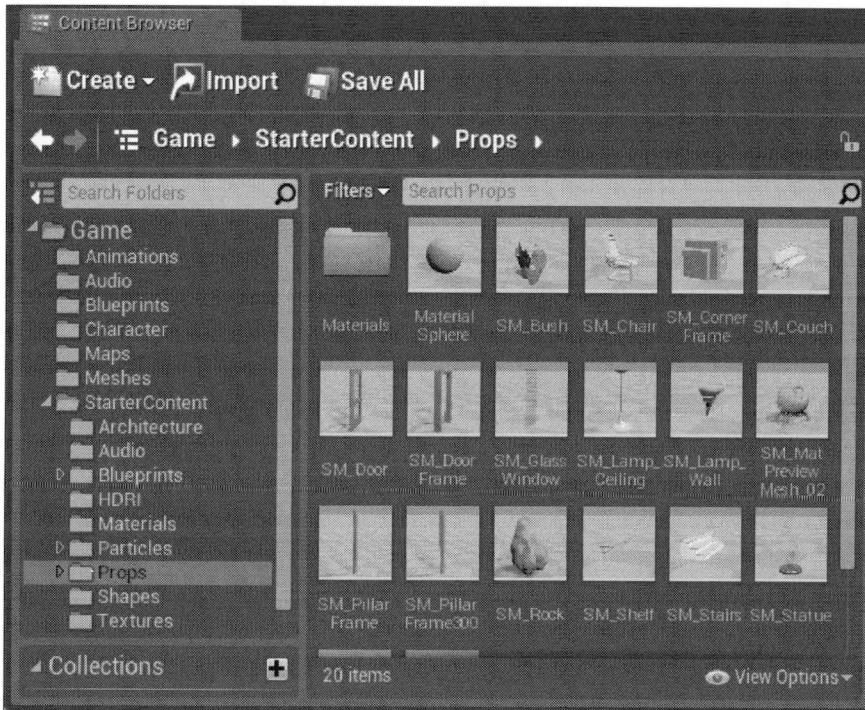

> You can modify the size of the images by going to **View Options** and modifying the **Scale** slider. There are a number of other options that you can use as well to customize the Content Browser tab to your liking, such as changing **View Type** of the contents from the default **Tiles** to **List** or **Columns**.
>
> For more information on customizing the Content Browser UI, refer to `https://docs.unrealengine.com/latest/INT/Engine/Content/Browser/UI/index.html`.

2. Click on the `SM_Chair` mesh and then drag it into the level on the wooden floor of our level. Once here, release it to place the mesh into the world.

Placing a chair mesh on the level's floor

3. Let's add one more mesh to our level in another way. Select the `SM_TableRound` object in the **Content Browser** tab and then right-click inside the level, near the table. From here, go to **Place Actor | SM_TableRound**.

With this, we've learned two ways to add a static mesh to our level!

Note that just like working with brushes, whenever an object is selected, the **Details** panel will fill itself with information about the actor that was added. From here, we can modify the **Scale**, **Location**, and **Rotation** values of the added meshes and can also change the Mobility of that mesh from Static to Moveable, which we will use later.

Placing a particle system

In a designer's toolbox, one of the most effective tricks used to make things look stunning are particle systems. We can spawn a large number of particles which are small simple images or meshes, without much of a performance hit. Particle systems control these particles and their display and movement. They are very useful for elements such as liquid, smoke, clouds, magic, and in this instance, fire, as we bring life to our house's fireplace.

Getting ready

This recipe assumes that you have a project open with the Sample Assets included as well as a room created with **Geometry Brushes** (**BSP**). I have provided a sample level (ModernHouseBase), which will be used for this demonstration. It is included in the Example Code, which you can access from Packt's website. If you are not familiar with building levels using BSP, feel free to follow the instructions for the *Building a Room* recipe of *Chapter 2, Level Design – Building Out Levels or Greyboxing*.

How to do it...

Now that we have our level open, let's start off by placing a particle system into our level:

1. With the level opened, move your camera to the fireplace on the bottom story.

2. Adding particle systems is very similar to adding a static mesh. Open the **Content Browser** tab, and we will first need to find the particle system that we want to use. If you have the Starter Content added, the particle systems are located in the StarterContent\Particles folder.

   With the folder open, you'll see a preview of all of the particle systems that you can work with, with a white border around all of them.

3. Click on the P_Fire system and then drag it into the level into the fireplace. Once here, release it to place the particle system into the world.

4. Now, starting off the particle system will be too large for our fireplace, but just like working with the Geometry Brushes, we can also modify the properties here under the **Details** tab. Change **Rotation** to `-90, 70, -90` and **Scale** to `.5` in all the axes.

> A quick way to scale all of the axes together at once is by going to the **Details** tab with the object selected and then, from the **Transform** component, clicking on the lock button to the right of the three parameters of the **Scale** property. Once we've locked the axes, we can then put in a `.5` value in one of the parts and the other two will change as well. This will make the object always maintain its proper shape.

At this point, we now have an idea of just how easy it is to make our level look much nicer!

> For more information on creating custom particle systems of your own refer to `https://docs.unrealengine.com/latest/INT/Engine/Rendering/ParticleSystems/index.html`.

Using Groups

When working on large projects, it's important to keep all of your content organized. With that in mind, it's a good idea to keep your levels organized as well. In this section, we will learn how we can use Groups to make your life easier. This will allow you to easily manage multiple Actors at once.

Getting ready

This recipe assumes that you have a project open with a level created. I have provided a sample level that will be used for this demonstration (`ModernHouseBase`). It is included in the Example Code that you can access from Packt's website at `http://www.packtpub.com`. If you are not familiar with building levels, feel free to follow the instructions for the *Building a Room* recipe from *Chapter 2, Level Design – Building Out Levels or Greyboxing*.

How to do it...

Let's see just how easy it is to create a group:

1. The first group we are going to make is for the second floor of our house. With that in mind, go back to the four viewport view by clicking on the top-right minimize button.

2. From the Front (also seen as **World Outliner** in future version of UE4) viewport, click and drag from the top-left of the house to the floor of the second floor/ceiling of the first floor. Once finished, hold the *Shift* button and select any items you may have missed in either the viewport or in **Scene Outliner** (also seen as **World Outliner** in future version of UE4), and remove the two brushes used for the fireplace as well as particle systems.

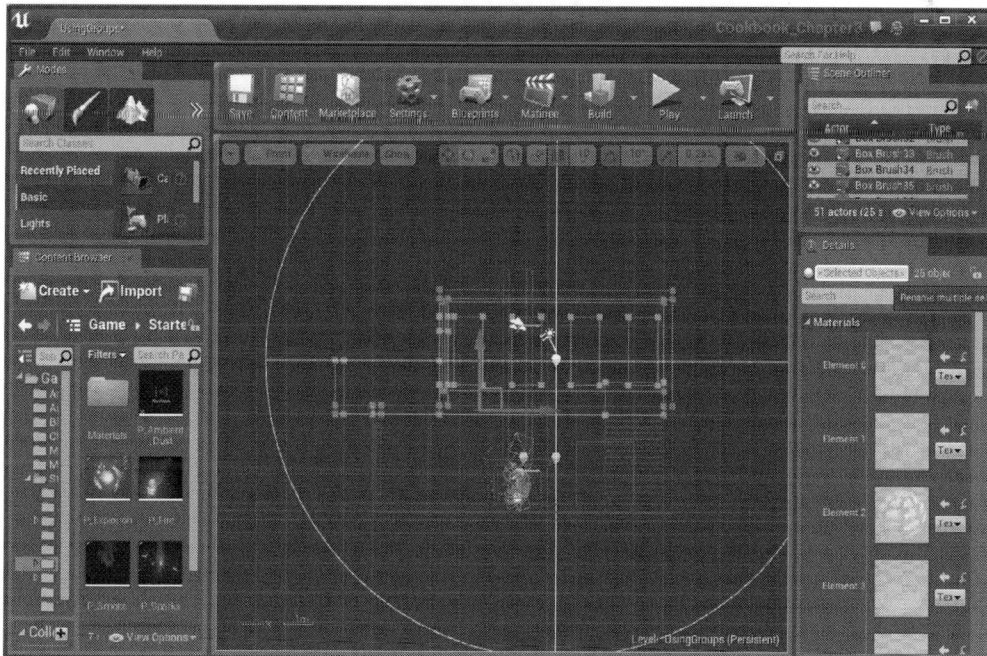

Selecting items on the second floor

> [💡 While selecting objects, you can also hold *Ctrl* and click to select or deselect the unwanted brushes or objects that were selected.]

3. With the items you want to create selected, right-click and select **Group** or press *Ctrl + G*.

4. Now deselect the items and then click on one of them again. You'll notice now that all of the objects are selected if you select any of the items.

> [💡 If you do not see the **Group** option on the context menu, make sure that **Allow Group Selection** is enabled from the **Settings** menu located on the top toolbar.]

When you create a Group, an object of the GroupActor type is created inside the **Scene Outliner** (in our case, it's named GroupActor5, but it may be a different number in your case). Just like selecting any of the objects in the group, selecting the GroupActor object will automatically select all of the others as well.

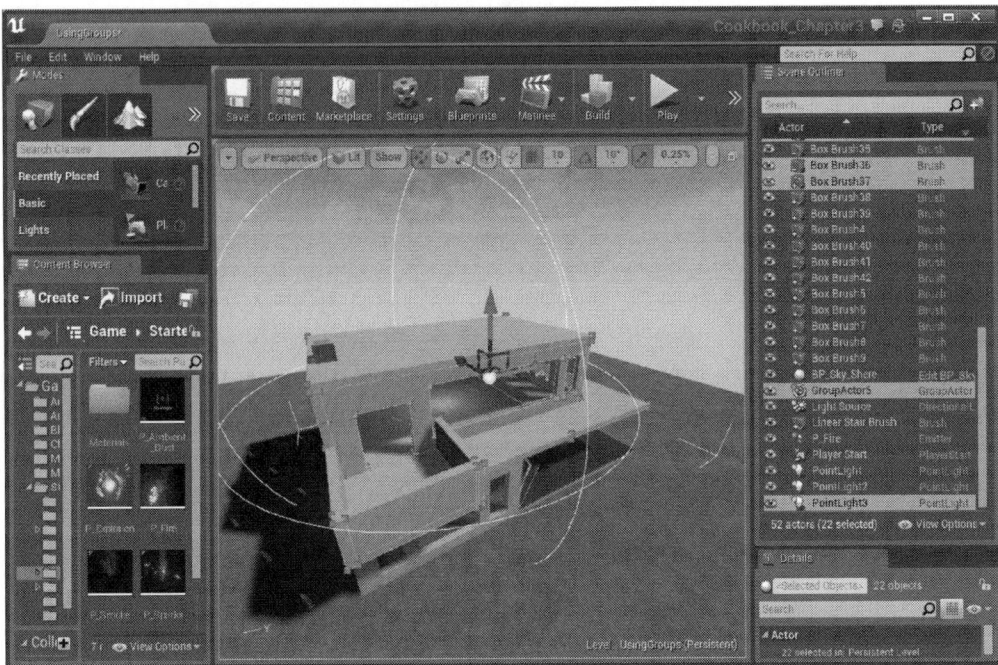

5. One of the useful properties of having a group is that you can hide the meshes by hitting the *H* key or pressing the eye icon to the right of the actor's name in the **Scene Outliner** or by right-clicking and navigating to **Visibility | Hide Selected**.

> You can click on the closed eye icon in the **Details** panel or press *Ctrl + H* to unhide all the objects that are currently hidden.

6. Another thing that you can do to make it easier to tell which group objects are attached is to rename the objects as the name of our group. To do this, go to the **Details** tab and select those brushes. Then, at the top, change the name of the objects to 2nd Story by either double-clicking on the name in the **Scene Outliner** tab or selecting the object/objects in it. After that, press *F2* and edit the name. You can also rename the objects via the **Details** tab at the top:

Renaming objects as name of a group

With this, we now have a good foundation of how we can use Groups to make our levels nicer!

> For more information on Grouping, refer to https://docs.unrealengine.com/latest/INT/Engine/Actors/Grouping/index.html.

Alternatively, you may also create a folder in the **Scene Outliner** tab and put levels inside that. That way you can organize scene contents in whichever way you'd like.

Meshing an example map

Watching a single mesh being placed is nice and all, but actually watching an example workflow is one of the best ways to see some of the tricks you can use to really polish a level up. In this section, we will be doing just that.

Getting ready

This recipe assumes that you have the example project and the level I provided (`ModernHouseBase`) opened that is included in the example code which you can access from Packt's website.

How to do it...

Let's first export one of these rooms so that we can give them to our artist to work with:

1. Let's first add in a door. Move your viewport to the first floor of the house to the right of the deck where you can see the glass opened up.

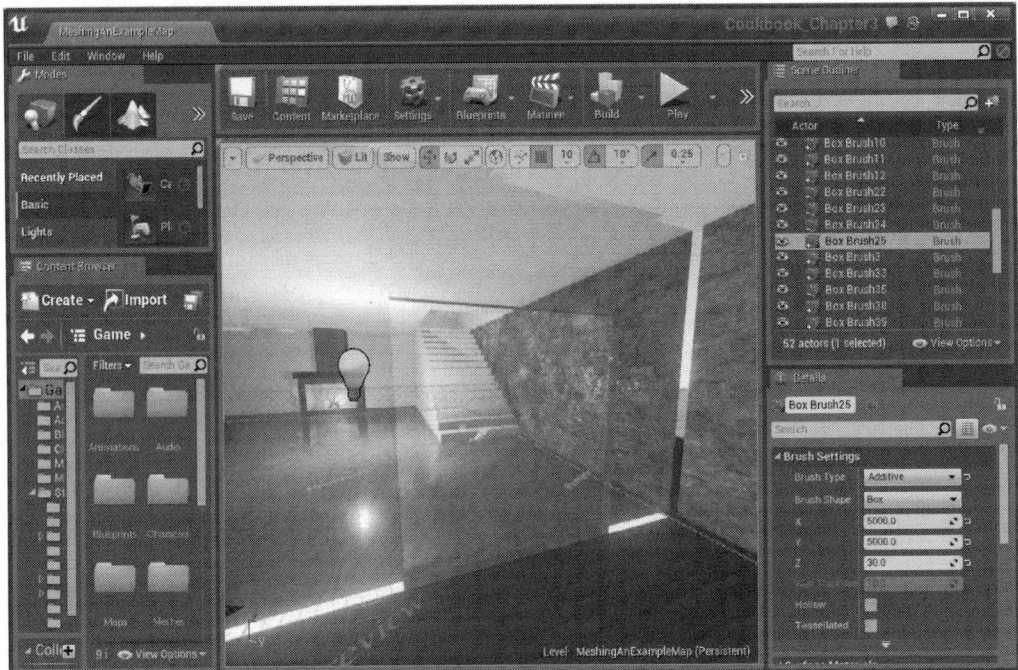

2. Once there, let's access the `StarterContent/Props` folder and select the `SM_Door` object and drag it into the world. Once placed, it will need to be rotated to face our doorway (`-90` degrees). After this, use the **Translate** tool to move the door into the doorway, leaving **10** units of space in the **Z** and **X** directions, as shown in the following image:

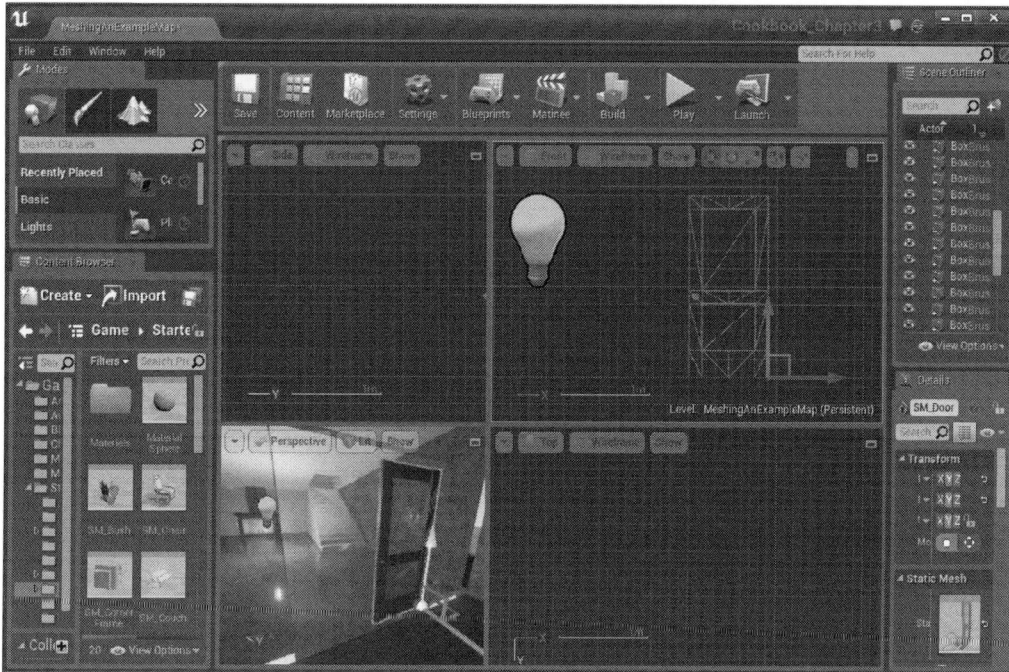

Placing a door

3. Now select the door and duplicate it from the **Front** viewport by holding down the *Alt* key and dragging it in the **X** axis. We don't want the doorknob to be on the same side, so we will want to flip the door by right-clicking and navigating to **Transform | Mirror X**. Then, move the door over to be flush with the other one so that they are touching each other.

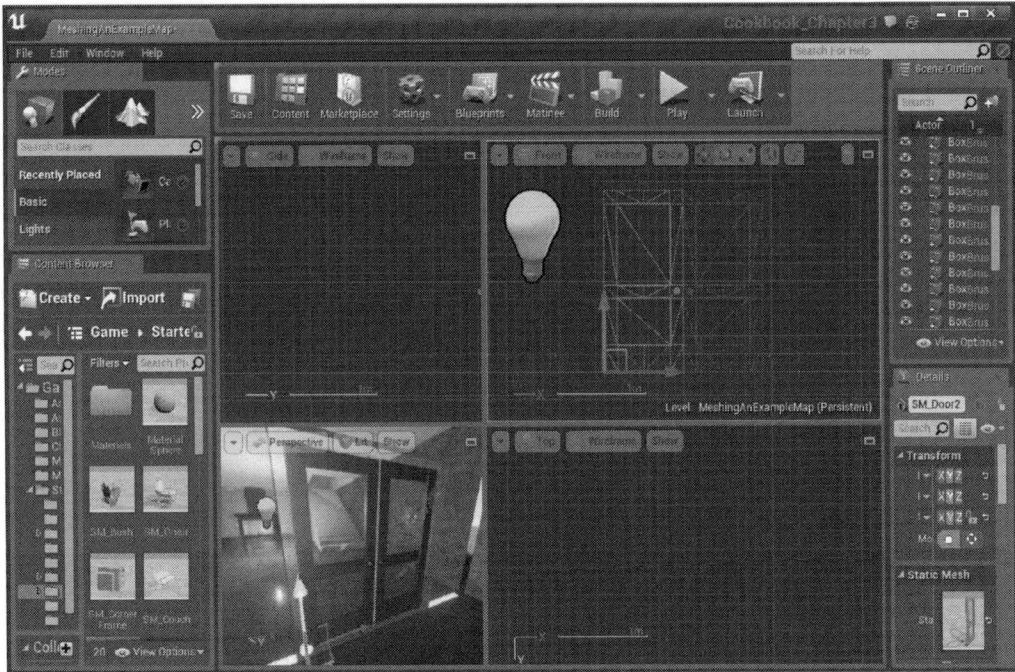

4. Next, let's add in the doorway. From the **Content Browser** tab, select SM_DoorFrame and drag it into the world.

5. It's initially created to only support one door at a time, but we can fix that with some slight changes. In the **Details** tab, change the **Scale** value in the **Y** axis to 2.0. After this, rotate the door to fit our doorway.

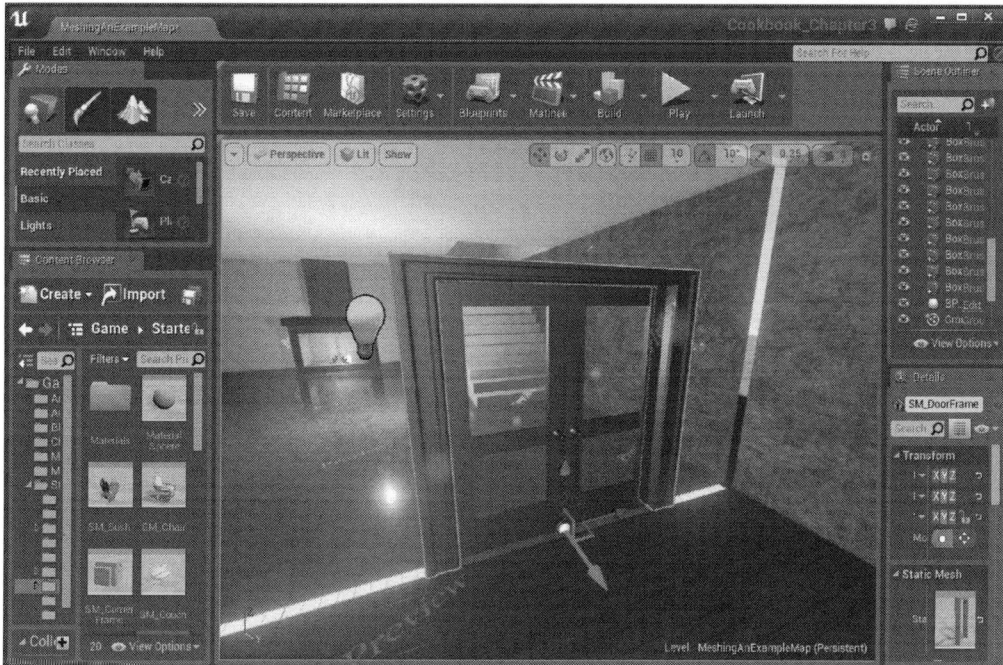

6. The next thing you may notice is the edges on our glass look strange. Rather than creating some additional brushes to fill it in, we can use some additional meshes to make our level look much nicer and more detailed, and cover up these tiny issues that occur. In the **Content Browser** tab, select the SM_FillarFrame300 object and then place it to cover our wall (rotated) so that it can face the glass. In order to fix the mesh in the middle of the glass, you may need to temporarily change the snapping to 5.

As a reminder, to change the snapping of the grid you can press the left/right bracket keys (*[/]*), which will decrease and increase the snapping respectively, otherwise, you can adjust the snapping by clicking on the dropdown menu next to the grid icon at the top of the main viewport window.

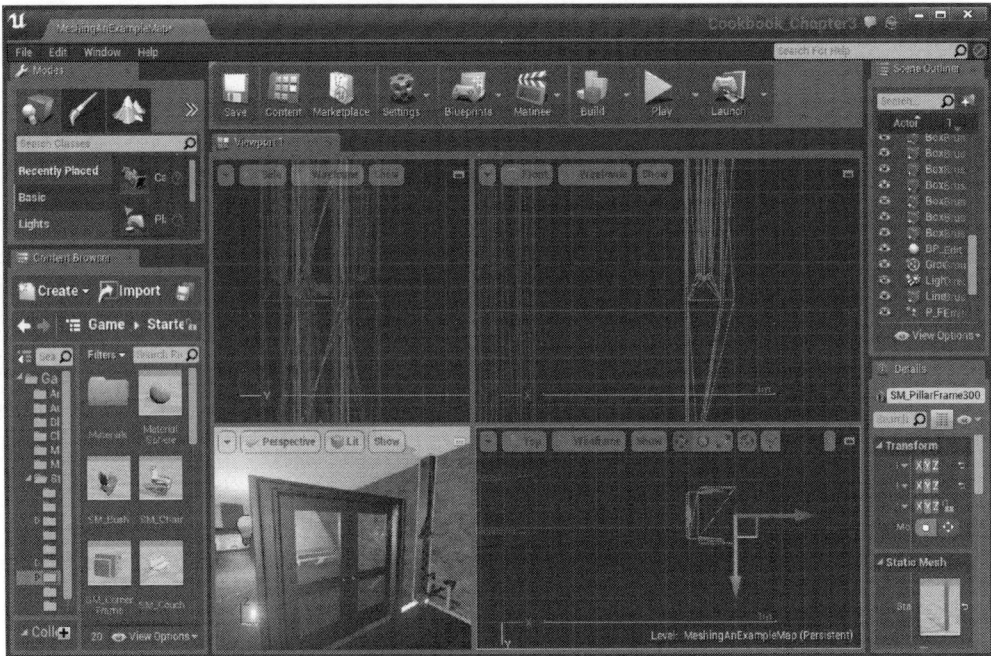

7. After this, we will duplicate the frame to fit it at an approximately equal distance from the door as the first frame for symmetry. Then, we will place the frame at the edges of the glass doors to help make the glass feel more realistic.

8. Next, we will need to take care of the tops and bottoms. From the **Content Browser** tab, select SM_PillarFrame and rotate it down along the **Y** axis so that it faces the floor. Once you complete that, scale it to 1.2 in the **Z** axis and place it between the door frame and the edge of the glass.

9. After this, duplicate it upwards with a scale of 1.95 to fill up the top and then duplicate it once more with a scale of .2 to fill the gap on the other side of the door. When you're done, it should look similar to this:

Scaling the objects to fit the frame

10. Next, duplicate the bottom once again and rotate it -60 degrees in the **X** axis with a scale of .9 in the **Z** axis. Then, bring it up to finish the window!

11. Now that we have this section down, we can move over to the right to tackle the windows. With this, we can select the `SM_WindowFrame` and drag it into place with the smaller slot. Just like earlier, we can scale the object to fit it in the whole we've created. In this instance, we will set it to `(1.2, 1.1 and 1.7)`. To fit the larger middle window, increase the **Y Scale** until it fits (I am using `3.5`).

12. With this knowledge, we can also fill out all of the windows and the door on the second floor:

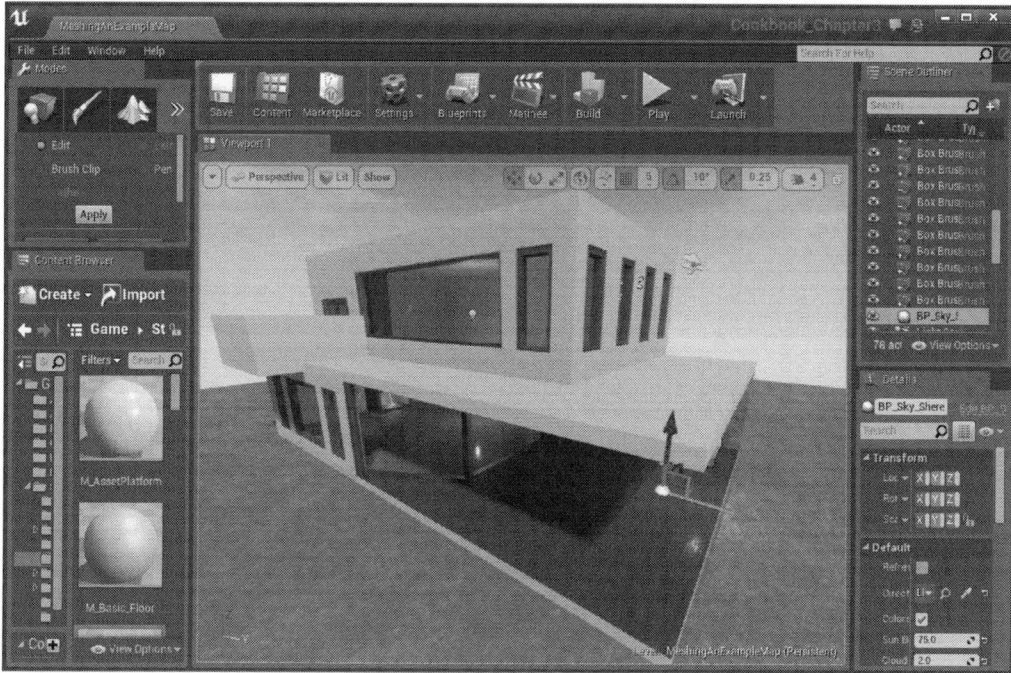

13. Next, let's create a little decor inside the actual house. Move back to the fireplace and place a `SM_Couch` object in front of it. After that, place two chairs on each side, making sure to rotate them a little bit toward the fire. Giving some difference in angle will help to make the world seem more realistic because objects in the real world that humans interact with are almost always not at a fixed angle (except architecture).

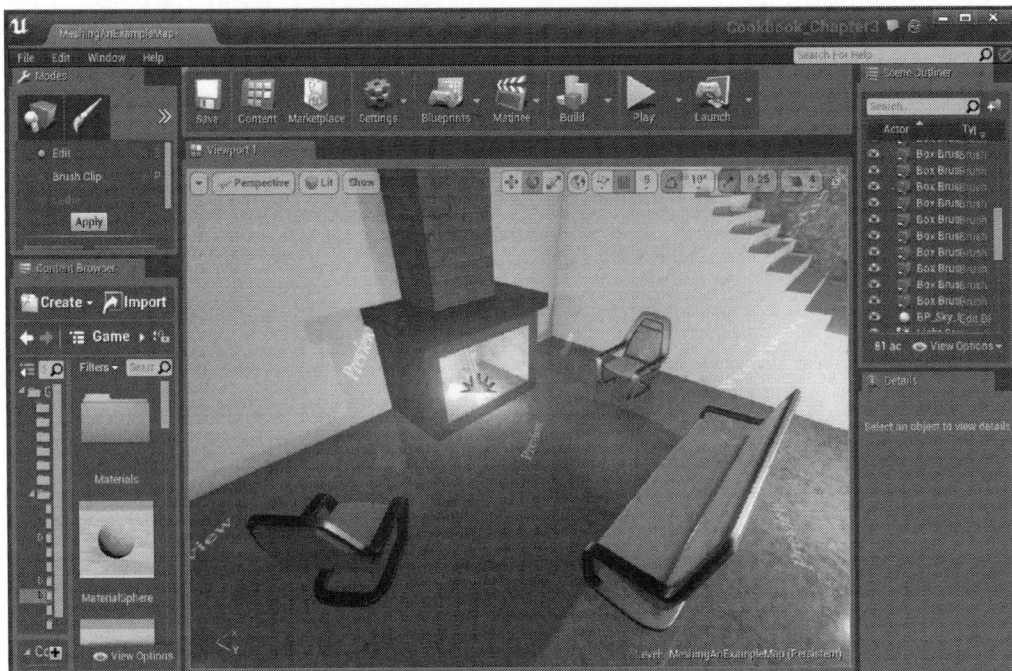

And with this, we have a good idea about how to add meshes to a level to add life and realism to it!

Adding life to static meshes

Though it is nice having a level with a lot of static meshes (this is by default), they don't move at all (hence, they are called static). Static meshes are used for efficiency's sake, but there comes a time where you want the player to be able to interact with those objects, such as moving crates or shooting at things.

Getting ready

This recipe assumes that you have the example project and the level I provided (MeshingAnExampleMap) opened.

How to do it...

With that in mind, let's learn how we can breathe some life into our static meshes:

1. Select a static mesh inside your level, such as the SM_Chair object we have placed in the fireplace.

2. Once selected, go to the **Details** tab and under **Physics**, check **Simulate Physics**.

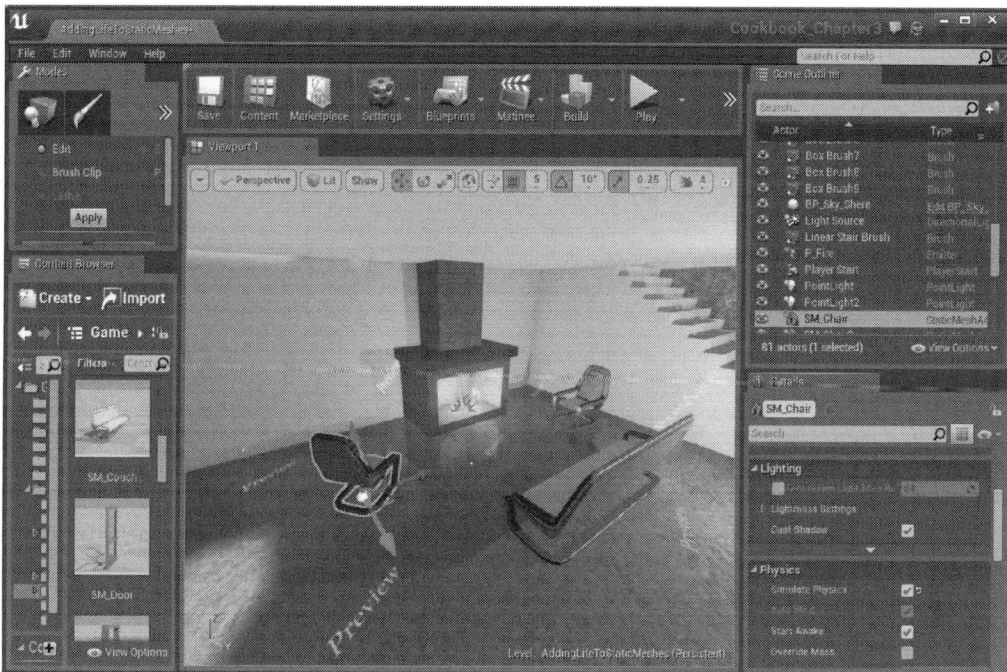

3. Once finished, go in and play the game.

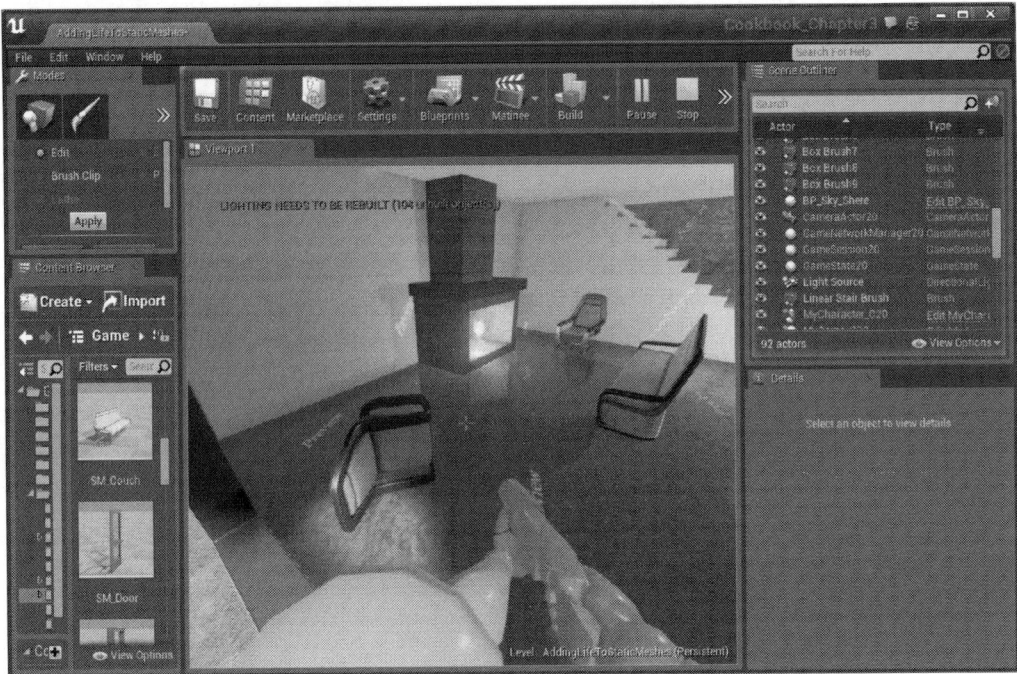

At this point, if you run into the chair or shoot at the object, they will react correctly, according to physics.

> You may also want to make a static mesh movable for something such as moving platforms and the like using **Blueprints**. To enable that functionality, in the **Details** tab, change the **Mobility** property to **Movable**.

In the preceding image, you'll notice that it says, LIGHTING NEEDS TO BE REBUILT. This is said anytime the world has changed in such a way that the current way the lighting data has will not show the most up-to-date version of the level. To get a full appreciation of the level and to have a better representation of how our light will be in the game, build your lighting by going to **Build | Build Lighting Only** and wait for it to finish (when the popup on the bottom-right says, "Lighting build completed").

> For more information on lighting, refer to https://docs.unrealengine.com/latest/INT/Engine/Rendering/LightingAndShadows/QuickStart/index.html.

4
Building the Great Outdoors – Exterior Environments

In this chapter, we'll cover the following recipes:

- Creating a landscape
- Building an exterior level using the Sculpt mode
- Creating rivers with the Flatten tool
- Placing trees and rocks using the Foliage tool
- Streaming levels

Introduction

We've seen how to build levels using BSP and meshes. This is really great for man-made structures, such as office buildings, houses, and floors, which are all made of things that look similar to each other. However, things outdoors are very chaotic, with changes in elevation and randomness everywhere. To help facilitate that, Unreal has tools such as Landscapes that allow us to create massive worlds that our players can interact in.

Creating a landscape

One of the first things that we will need to do to work with build terrain is to create a landscape through Unreal Engine's **Landscape** mode, so let's get started!

Getting ready

Before we start working within the Unreal Editor, we will need to have a project to work with:

1. First, open up the Unreal Editor by clicking on the **Launch** button from **Unreal Engine Launcher**.

2. Start a new project from the **Project Browser** tab by selecting the **New Project** tab. Select **First person** and make sure that **With Starter Content** is selected. Give the project a Name (Cookbook_Chapter4). Once you are done, click on **Create Project**.

How to do it...

Now that we have our project set up, let's get started with building a landscape:

1. With the editor up, we will first want to create a new level for us to work in. To do this, go to the top-left of the screen and select **File | New Level...** or press *Ctrl + N*.

2. From here, you'll have the **New Level** window pop up. Click on the **Default** template, and you will have an empty level to work with.

3. Since we are going to create everything from a terrain, we don't need to have the default floor. So, select the SM_Template_Map_Floor mesh and delete it by going to **Edit | Delete** or pressing the *Delete* key.

4. After this, we will need to access the **Modes** tab on the top-left of the screen and click on the icon that looks like a mountain to change the game to the **Landscape** mode.

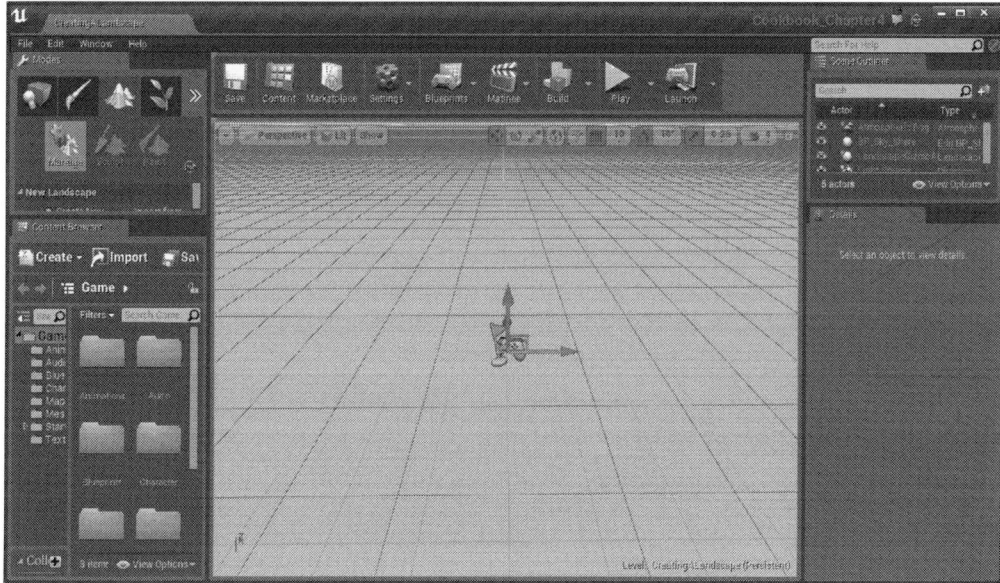

You'll know that we're in the **Landscape** mode when you can see a green grid showing up inside the level.

> You can also access the **Landscape** mode by pressing *Shift + 3* on your keyboard.

Under the mode image, you'll notice that the properties have changed to show three modes, with two grayed out and the first one, **Manage**, selected. When selected, the **Manage** mode allows us to create new landscapes and modify the properties that we have already created. We will learn about the other modes later in this chapter.

Right now, we'll only see the **New Landscape** section. Now, we don't actually have a landscape created yet, but let's first set up some properties to make this seem more realistic:

1. Go into the **Content Browser** tab and the `StarterContent\Material` folder. Once here, drag and drop the `M_Ground_Grass` material into the **Material** property under the **New Landscape** section. This will make our landscape use this material on all of the terrain, by default. Alternatively, you can also select the material in the **Content Browser** tab and then within **New Landscape**, click the arrow to the right of the **Material** variable and apply the material to the landscape.

> It's possible to have multiple materials in your landscape to help create cool effects. For details on this, refer to `https://docs.unrealengine.com/latest/INT/Engine/Landscape/Editing/PaintMode/index.html`.

There are a number of properties (that we can change at this point), which will alter the landscape such as **Location**, **Rotation**, and **Scale**. There are also some new properties that will affect the size and quality of the landscape. The default values are balanced for quality and build time, so we're going to use them for the most part.

> For more information on the New Landscape properties, refer to
> `https://docs.unrealengine.com/latest/INT/Engine/`
> `Landscape/Creation/index.html#creatinganewlandsc`
> `apeusingthelandscapetool.`

2. Continuing in the **New Landscape** section of the **Modes** tab, change the **Z** property of **Location** to `-10` to place it below our character's starting point (the **Player Start** object that looks similar to a hole in one with a gamepad controller to its next).

3. Finally, at the bottom-right of the **New Landscape** section, click on the **Create** button to place the landscape into the world with our specifications.

Creating a landscape

4. When it's first created, you may notice these dark lines in grids everywhere. This is because we haven't built lighting yet, so let's go ahead and do this by selecting the **Build** section's drop-down menu from the top toolbar above the level and selecting **Build Lighting Only** or by pressing *Ctrl + Shift + ;* on your keyboard. Wait for a few seconds, and the lighting should complete, however, there is a popup, which will display a warning:

This is alerting us to the fact that we should add **Lightmass Importance Volume** around the important parts of the level. Being a warning, it is something that we could technically avoid. As game developers, it's important for us to remove warnings wherever possible. To fix this, follow these steps:

5. Switch back to the **Place** tab, go under **Volumes**, and scroll down to the **Lightmass Importance Volume** option. Drag and drop it into the center of the world. Once the option is created under the **Details** tab, change the **X, Y**, and **Z** properties to 50000. To check that everything is contained, restore the viewports and maneuver as needed to get the yellow lines to fit in your level.

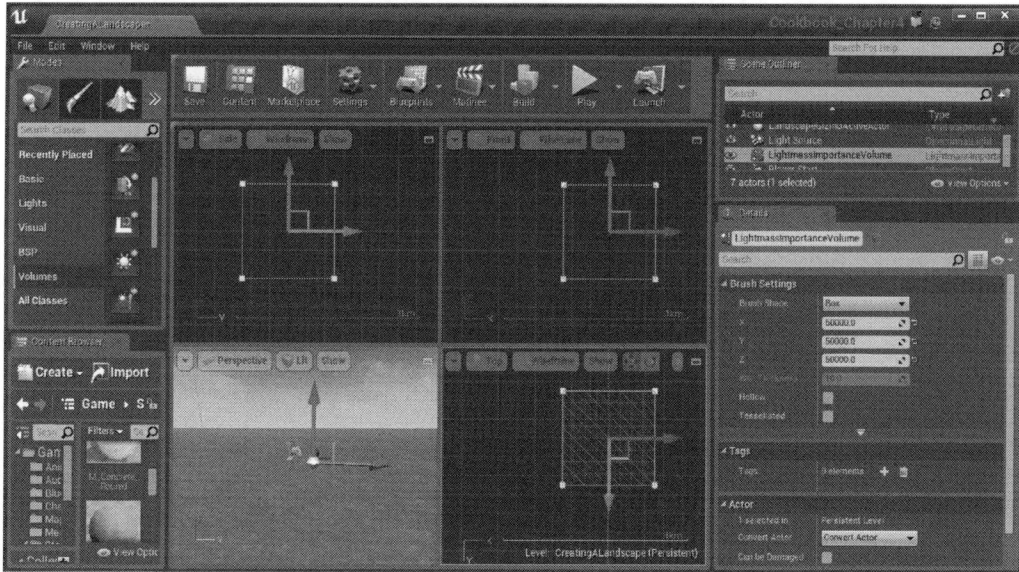

In my example, I made the volume as big as needed to fit the terrain, but you may make it smaller to fit with just what your level contains.

6. Build the lighting in the same manner as before, and everything should be set up correctly!

> For more information on creating landscapes and what all of the properties mean, check out the Unreal documentation at `https://docs.unrealengine.com/latest/INT/Engine/Landscape/Creation/index.html`.

Building an exterior level using the Sculpt mode

Of course, creating a landscape on its own looks just the same as a flat plane. In this section, we are going to explore the foundation of building a level by making use of the **Sculpt** mode of the **Landscape** tool.

Getting ready

In order to follow this recipe, you will need to have a landscape created. If you need assistance with this, check out the *Creating a landscape* recipe earlier in this chapter.

How to do it...

With the knowledge of how to start a workflow, we can now apply that by quickly creating a level:

1. With our landscape created, make sure you're in **Landscape** mode and select the **Sculpt** option (to the right of the **Manage** icon) to go into the **Sculpt** mode.

This will bring us to options for modifying our terrain in many different ways. Currently, the **Sculpt** tool is selected and if you move your mouse over the level, you'll notice a light gray circle moving around with the mouse pulsing on and off; this is the brush for our terrain creation and where we will either rise or fall.

2. Clicking will raise the terrain into the air. Click around the edges of the world to create some hills that we can work with. Changing the **Brush Size** setting will increase or decrease the size of your brush, and the **Brush Fallout** setting will determine how smooth or rough the brush will be. The **Tool Strength** setting will make things go up quicker. Holding down *Shift* while clicking will lower the terrain instead.

> Similar to setting the grid size, when working in the **Landscape** mode, you can use the *[* and *]* keys to increase or decrease the radius of your brush.

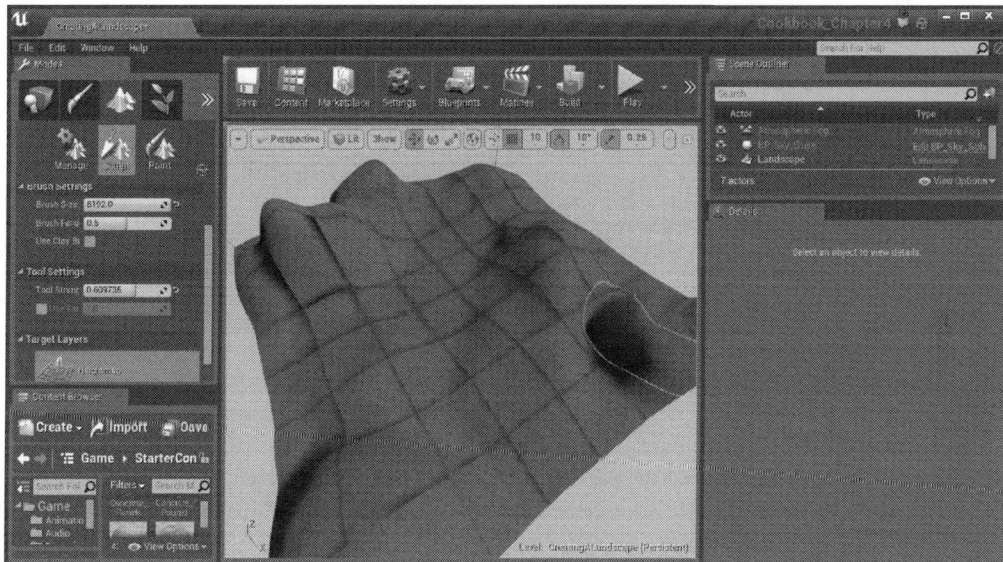

Adding height variation within our terrain

Make sure that your **Player Start** object is above your terrain or else you will fall through the world. If this does happen, drag the player to start up on top of the terrain and hit the *End* key for it to fall.

> When creating hills, it's a good idea to look at the multiple angles so that you can make sure that none are too high or too short. Generally, you want to have taller hills the further back you go or else you cannot see the smaller ones since they're blocked.
>
> To move your camera around, you can hold down the right mouse button and drag it in the direction you want the camera to move around, pressing the *W*, *A*, *S*, and *D* keys to pan. The scroll wheel can be scrolled to zoom in and out from where the camera is.

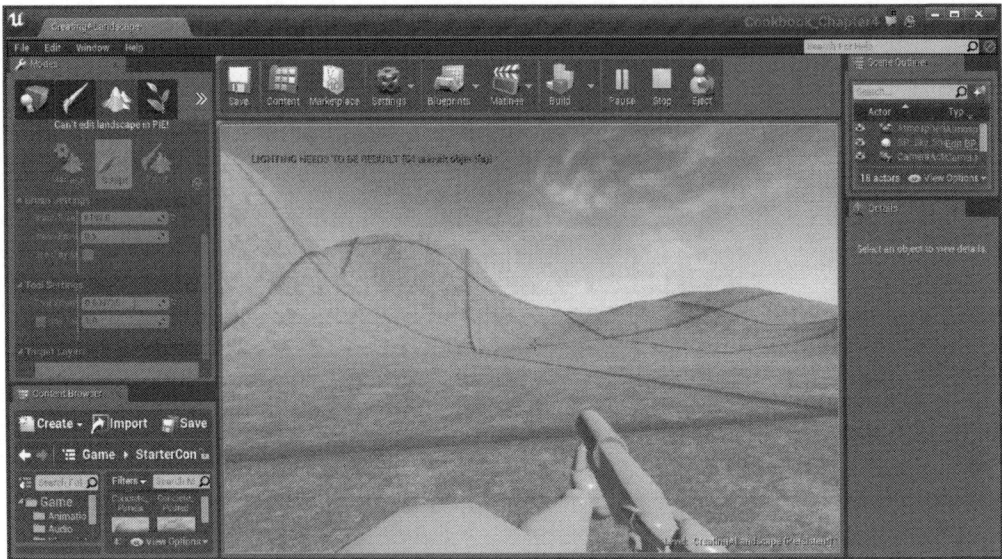

Playing the game after placing the Player Start object on the terrain

With this, we have added some hills to the world!

Creating rivers with the Flatten tool

Now that we have some hills going on, let's add some holes, making use of an additional tool, the **Flatten** tool.

Getting ready

You will need to have a landscape created for this recipe. If you need assistance with this, check out the *Creating a landscape* recipe earlier in this chapter.

How to do it...

With the knowledge of how to start a workflow, we can now apply that by quickly creating a level!

1. In the **Landscape Mode** tab, click on the **Sculpt** tool tab and select the **Flatten** tool.

2. Check the **Flatten Target** selection and put in -100. By default, the **Flatten** tool will flatten to the middle of the map, but this allows us to pick a new position for it to go to.

3. Next, we want to increase **Tool Strength** to .8 to make it easier to dig out the river by clicking and dragging around wherever we want water to be placed.

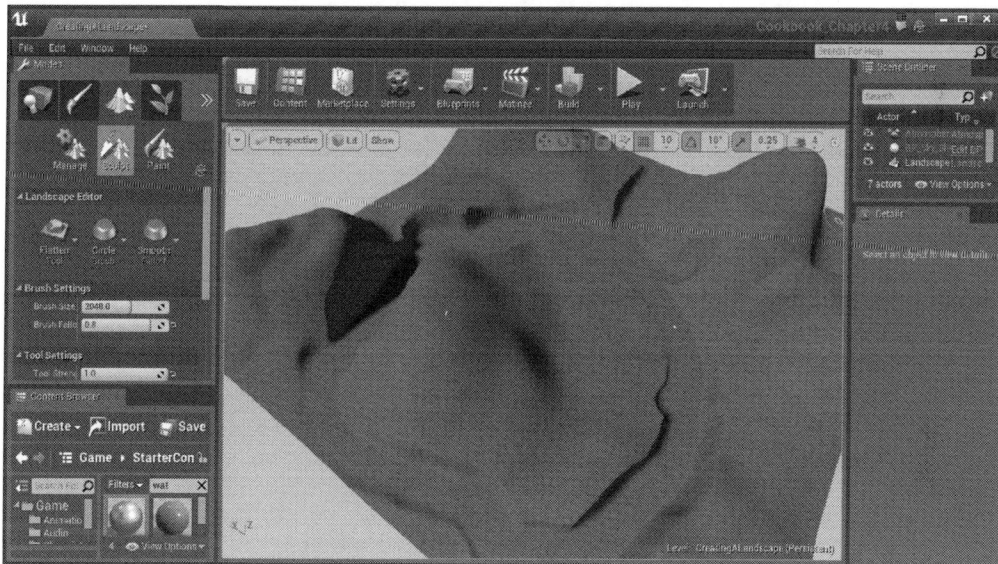

> There are a lot of other sculpting tools that can be used for other own purposes, but we don't have enough room to cover them all. For more information on all of the **Sculpt** mode tools, refer to https://docs.unrealengine.com/latest/INT/Engine/ Landscape/Editing/SculptMode/index.html.

4. Now that we have the ground for the river to be placed, we need to get our water placed in the world. In the **Modes** tab, select the **Place** mode and drag and drop a BSP `Box` object into the world. Under the **X** and **Y** axis, set the size to `50000`, just like our terrain, and shift it so that it is centered in the world, being above the water but below our normal terrain.

5. Then, go to the `Materials` folder and drag and drop the `M_Water_Lake` material to the **Details** tab under the **Element 0** property of **Surface Materials**.

> One thing to note is that if you have a material selected before you create a BSP box, the material will automatically be applied to it once it is brought into the world.

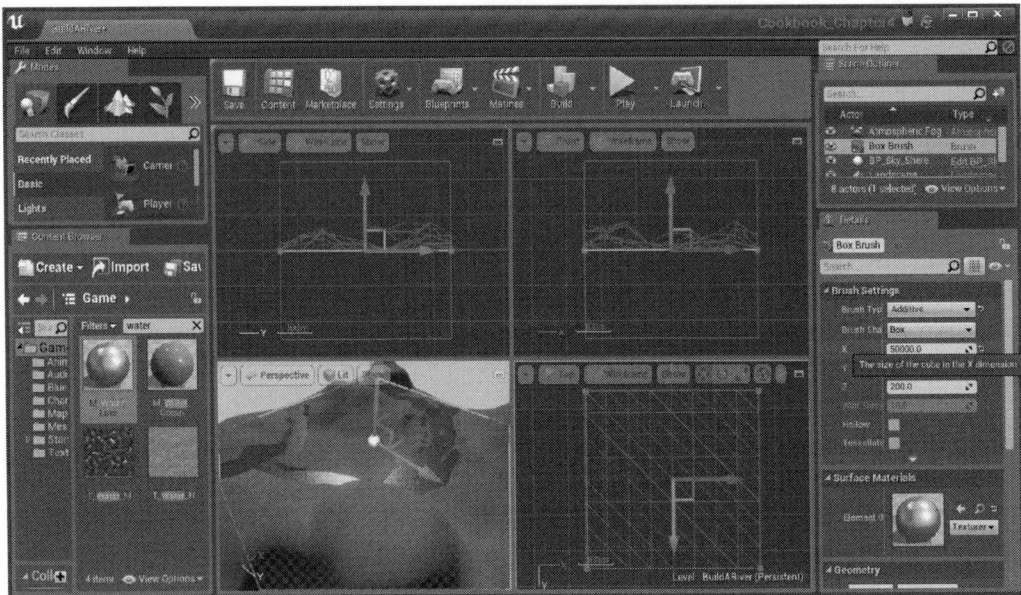

6. Play the game and move over the water.

Playing the game with water in the world

7. This is looking really nice, except that we can currently walk on water. That's because brushes always have collision. But, we can fix this by converting the BSP into a static mesh.

8. Select the `Box Brush` object from the **Scene Outliner** tab and under the **Details** panel, go to **Brush Settings** and click on the little arrow at the bottom of the part to show the extended options. Once here, click on the **Create Static Mesh** option.

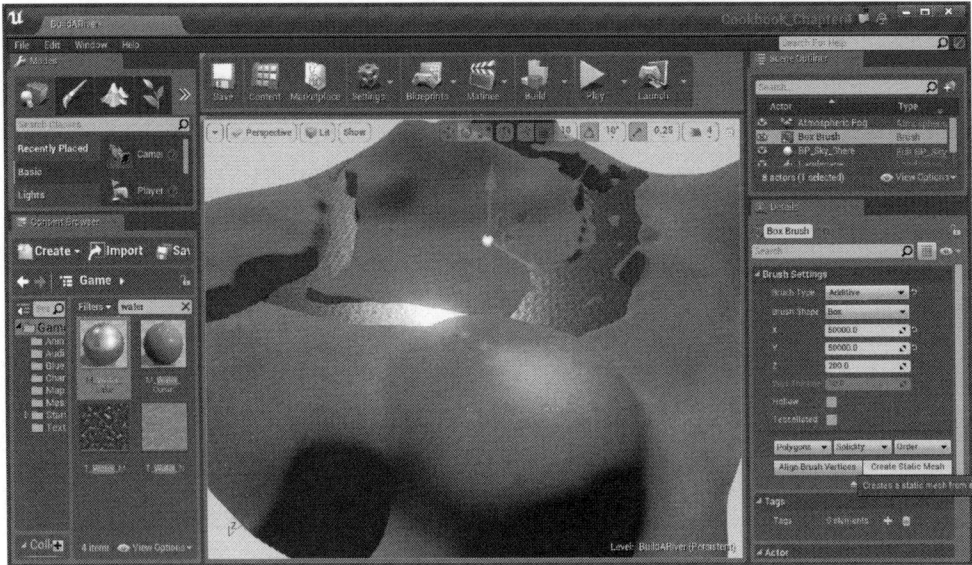

Option to convert object into a static mesh

9. It will ask where you want to save it. Click on **Create Static Mesh** once again and it will finally convert the object into a static mesh.

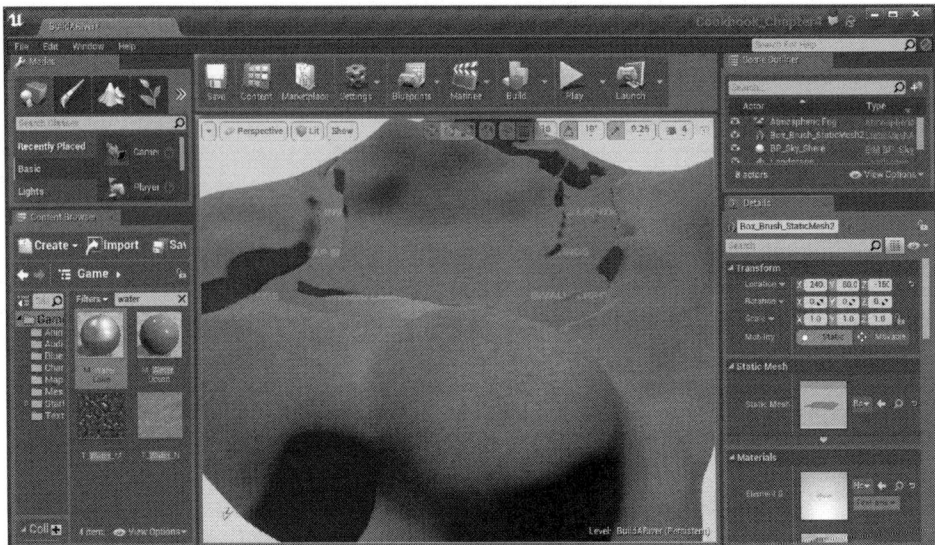

The river object is now converted into a static mesh

But you will see that on the geometry, it says `Invalid Lighting Settings`, as seen in the preceding image. To fix this, go to the mesh's location in the **Content Browser** tab and double-click on it to open up the **Static Mesh Editor**.

10. Inside the **Static Mesh Editor**, in the **Details** tab, go to the **LOD Settings** section and expand **Build Settings** if it isn't expanded already. From here, uncheck the **Generate Lightmap UVs** option and then click on **Apply Changes**:

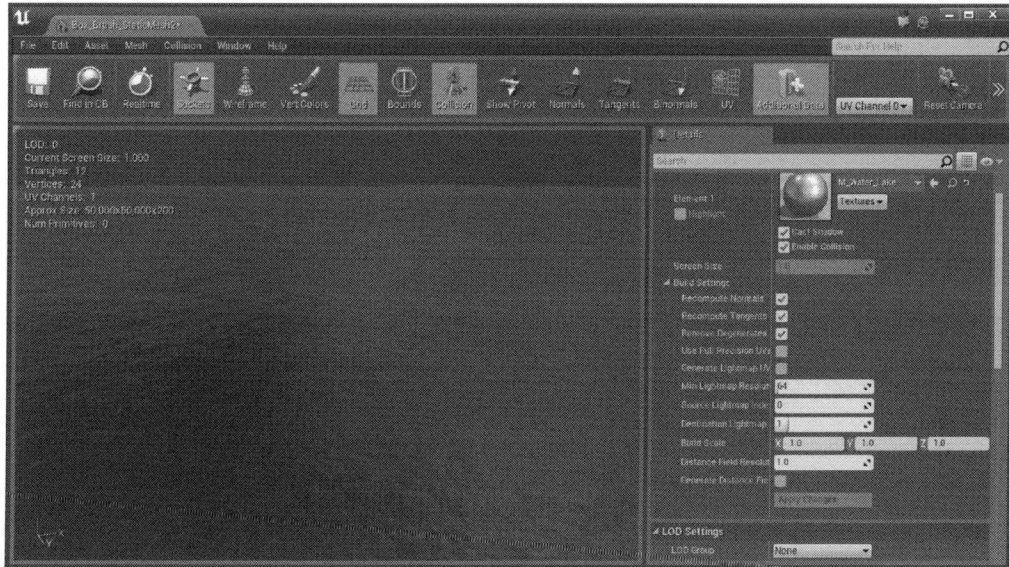

11. Finally, exit the **Static Mesh Editor** and go back into the Unreal Editor and select the mesh once more. From the **Details** tab, change **Collision** to `NoCollision`.

> Alternatively, in the **Static Mesh Editor** for the mesh, you can also go to **Collision | Remove Collision**, but this will make it so that all the objects with that mesh will not have collision, whereas the **Details** tab is only for that specific object in your level.

Playing the game with the removed collision allows the player go down into the water

Now you can go down into the water with no issues! It's looking pretty awesome!

> Another cool way of creating rivers is making use of the Landscape Splines tool. You can learn more about it at `https://docs.unrealengine.com/latest/INT/Engine/Landscape/Editing/Splines/index.html`

Placing trees and rocks using the Foliage tool

Now that we have a world basis for our level, we want it to be more than just land and a river.

Getting ready

This recipe assumes that you have a project open with the sample assets and landscape included. If you do not have that yet, feel free to follow the instructions in the *Creating a landscape* recipe.

How to do it...

Now that we have our room created, let's add some materials to it.

1. Under the **Modes** tab, click on the flower icon to open up the **Foliage** mode:

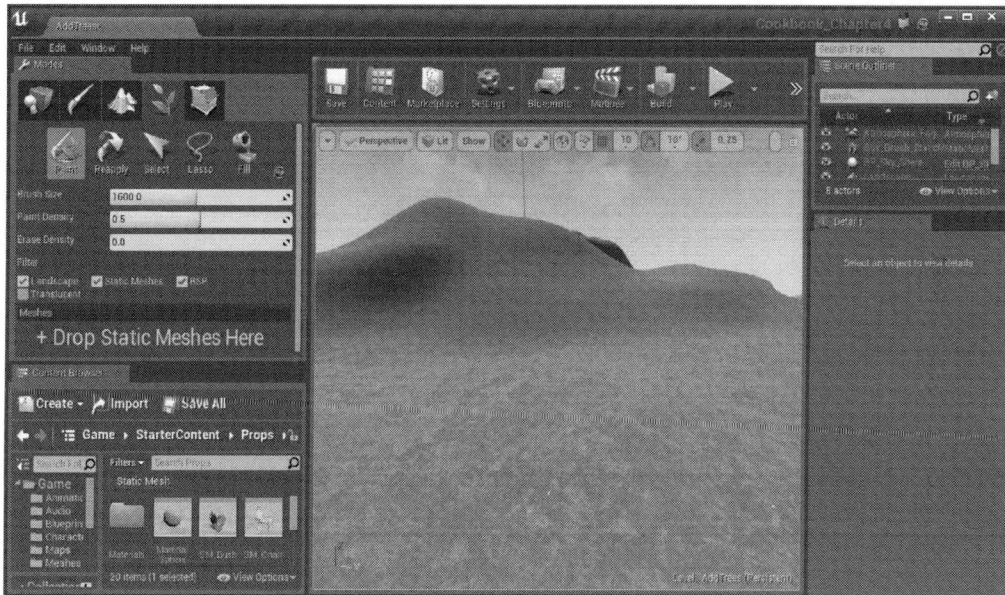

2. This should look fairly similar to the **Landscape** tool. But this time, there is a **Meshes** section at the bottom with the text **Drop Static Meshes Here**. With this in mind, go into the `StarterContent/Props` folder and drag a `SM_Rock` object into there.

3. At this point, there is a variety of options that can be used to modify how the rocks will be placed as well as how they will be drawn. First of all, if you draw on the level, you will see far more rocks than you need to have drawn.

Placing rocks all over the level

This is nice for something like grass, but not at all for rocks.

4. Press *Ctrl + Z* to undo what we did before. To lessen the amount, modify the **Paint Density** property up at the top of the **Foliage Mode Paint** section to a much lower number such as `.006`.

5. Now they're showing up at a nice rate, but they all look very similar. This is fine for something like trees, but rocks are much more random. To fix this, under the **Meshes** tab, make sure that **Show Painting settings** is up and change **Max Angle +/-** and **Random Pitch +/-** to 100.

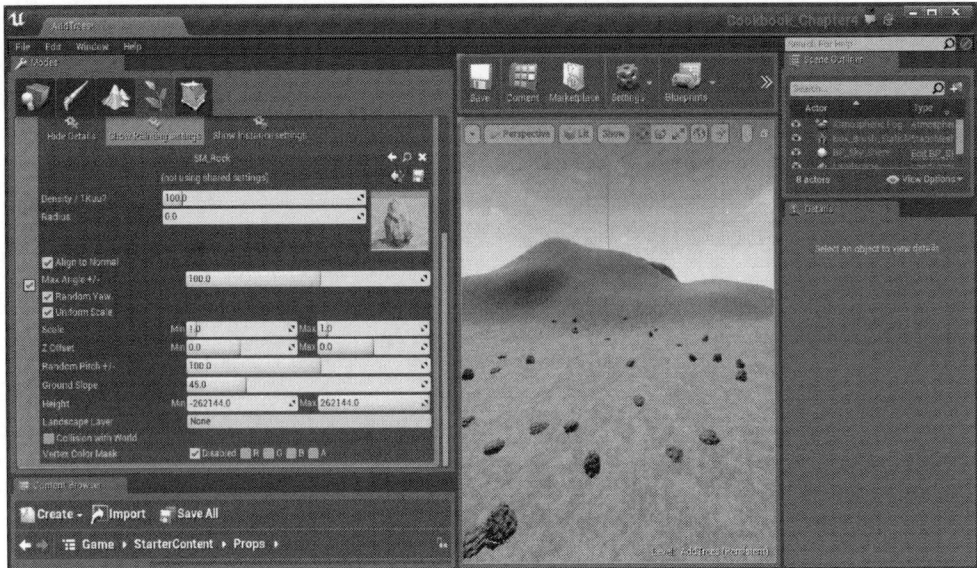

6. They look even better now, but they're all of the same size. To adjust this, change **Scale Min** to .5 and **Max** to 2.0.

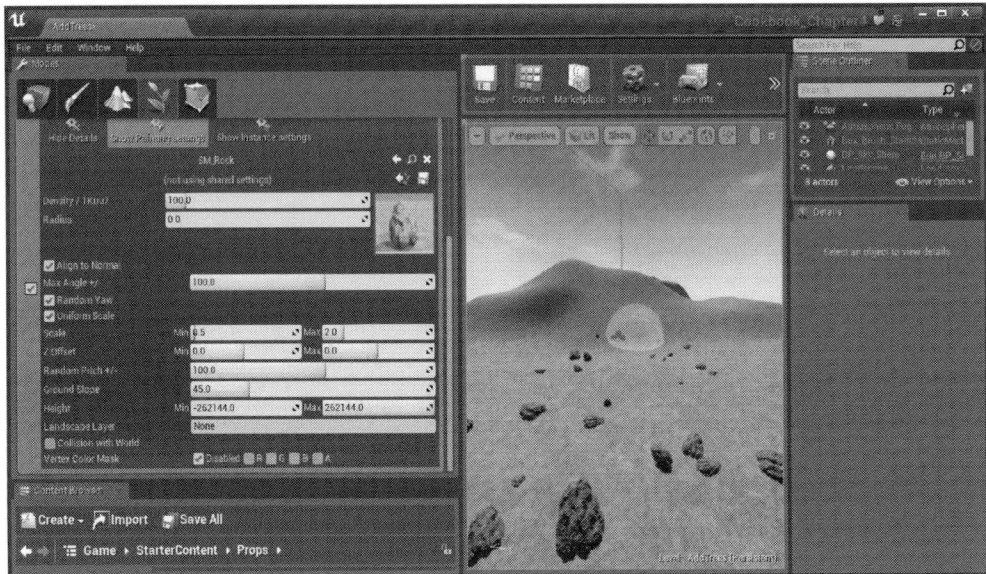

7. Finally, by default, foliage has no collision, but rocks need to collide so that the players can collide when they touch the rocks. To fix this, go to the top of the **Meshes** section and select **Show Instance settings**. Afterward, go to **Collision** and under **Collision Presets**, select **BlockAll**.

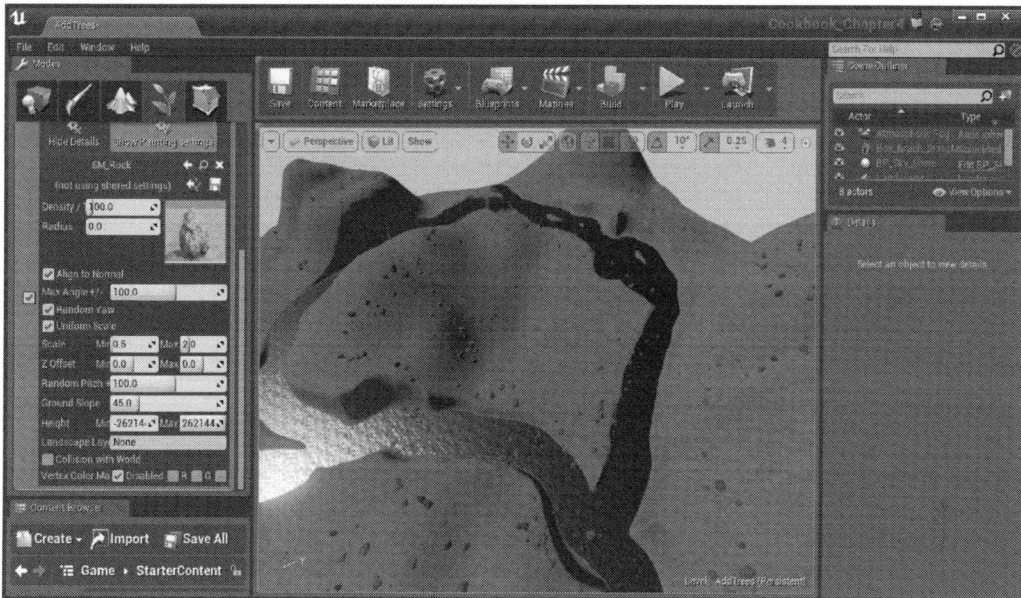

It's nice! At this point, we now have painted rocks all over the level

For some users, the **Show Instance settings** option may be hidden due to the **Modes** tab not being wide enough, so expand it if that is the case.

8. Of course, this is nice to work with now, but in the real world, we have other things, such as trees, which will be a lot more up above the ground. But, by default, Unreal does not give us tree meshes to work with. However, `SpeedTree` has some sample trees that are free to download at `http://store.speedtree.com/unreal-engine-4/`.

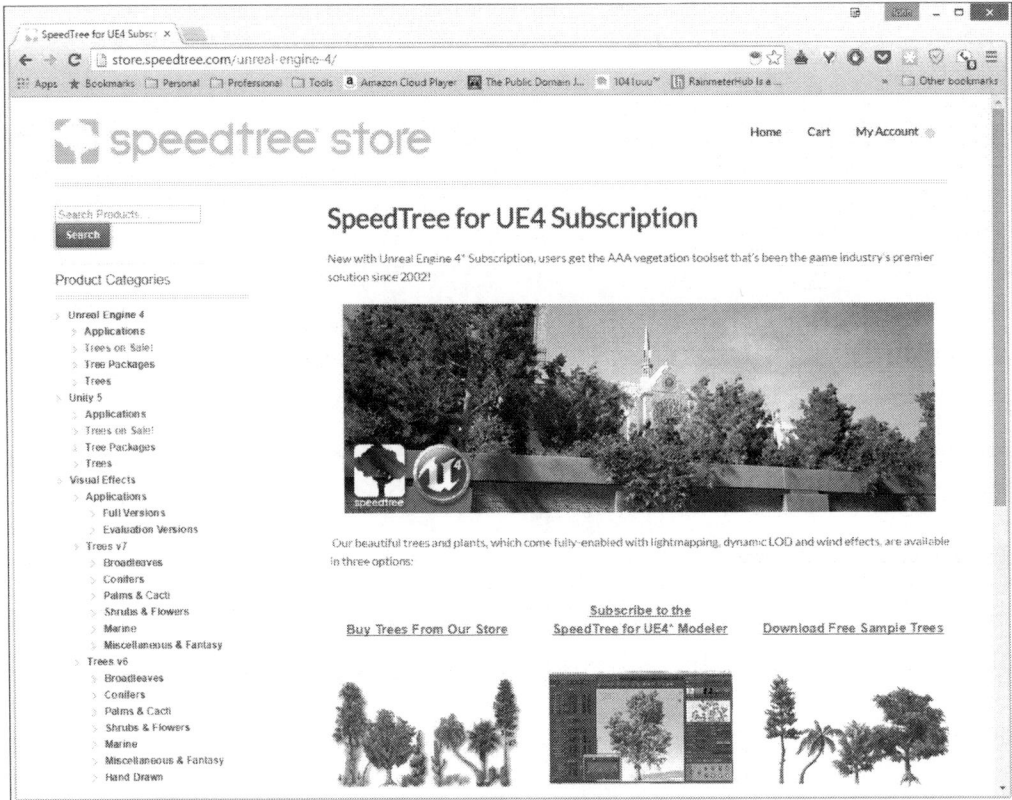

9. At the bottom-left of the website, there is a section that says you can download it directly; do that. Once it finishes downloading, go to the ZIP file and unzip it. Next, rename the folder to `Trees`.

10. We will be moving a large amount of stuff into our game, so first save your project and then drag and drop the `Trees` folder into the `Game` folder from the **Content Browser** tab, and it will start to import the content into your game. You'll see options popping up from time to time; hit **Import** each time to complete the process.

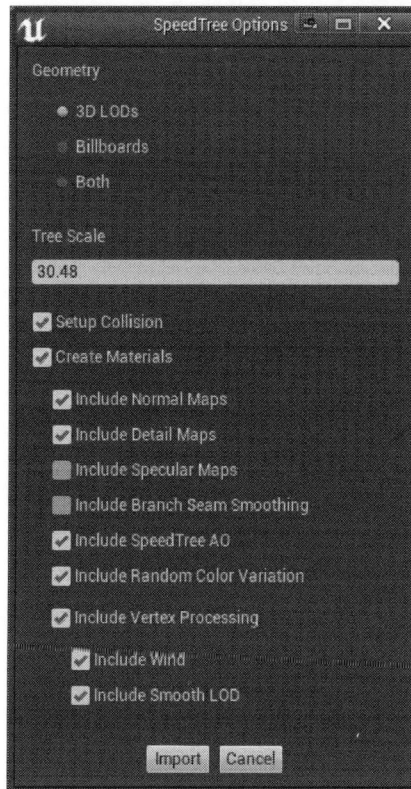

11. Now that everything is imported, you can save it by clicking on the **Save All** button and selecting **Save Selected**.

12. Next, drag and drop the `Broadlead_Desktop` static mesh into the **Foliage** tool. Go into **Show Instance settings** and add collision to the object as we described earlier.

13. Afterward, we want to add some distance between each tree, so switch back to **Show Painting settings** and change the **Radius** property to 200. After this, start painting once again around the level where you want trees to be.

Adding trees to the map

14. Finally, build all this again and start up the game. You may notice that the build time for lighting is probably going to take a lot longer than it has previously.

Final view of the terrain with trees and rocks

With this, we now have a much nicer looking level!

Streaming levels

As levels get more and more complex, they can sometimes get quite unwieldy. One of the tools that we have as designers is the ability to break our levels apart and load them in at runtime. This is also incredibly useful for working in teams, where one person can work on one part of the game and bring it all together later.

We will look at the easiest way to load in a level instantly, which is to have the level always being loaded.

Getting ready

This recipe assumes you have two levels you'd like to have loaded at the same time. I will be using the levels created in the *Placing trees and rocks using the Foliage tool* recipe in this chapter and the *Meshing an example map* recipe from *Chapter 3, Creating Quality Interior Environments*.

How to do it...

Let's first export one of these rooms so that we can give them to our artist to work with:

1. Open up the level that will be considered your base level. In our case, I will be using the map that contains our completed landscape.

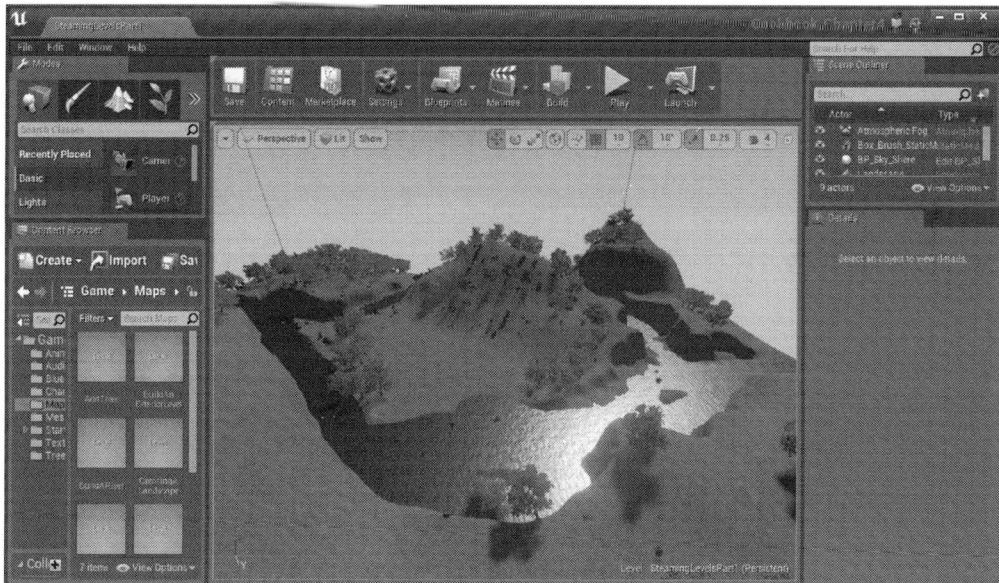

2. Under **Window**, select **Levels** to open up the **Levels** window.

3. From **Levels**, click and select **Add Existing...**.

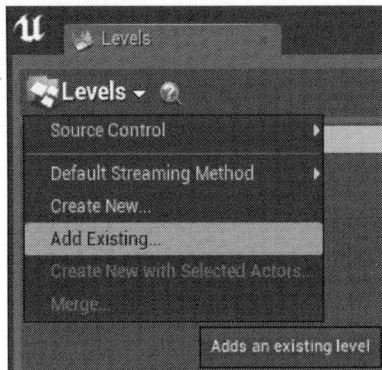

4. From here, you'll be brought to the **Open Level** dialog box. From there, select the map you want to be brought into the world. I selected the **MeshingAn ExampleMap** level. After you have the level selected, press the **Open** button.

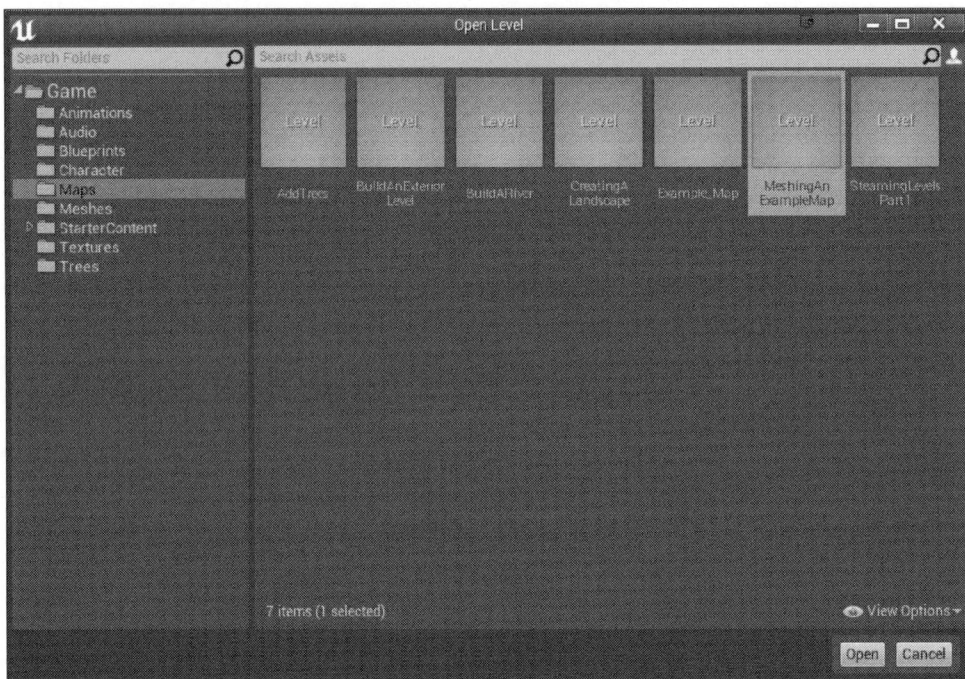

5. Now if you planned ahead, your house and terrain will fit together nicely.

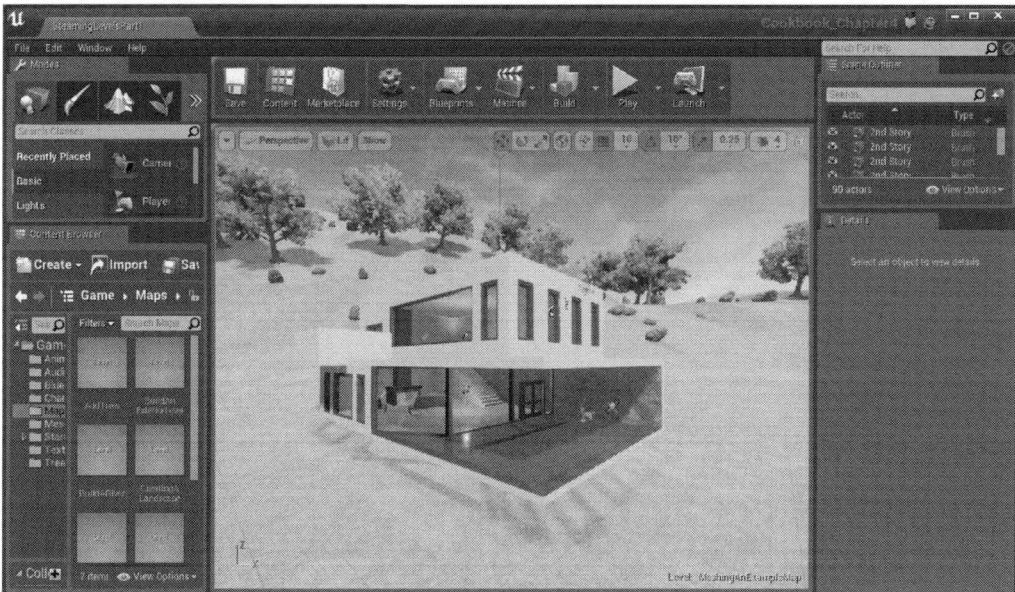

Final view of the house and the terrain

If this is not the case, go to the **Levels** window and right-click on one of the levels and select **Select Actors**. Then, move the level to fit where you want it to be placed. Of course, this assumes that you have some flat terrain somewhere. If not, use the **Flatten** tool on the **Foliage** tab to flatten the area to make it easier for people to see.

6.   Of course, it seems like we are done now, but if we play the game, we won't be able to find the house. There's actually a really good reason for this; the level isn't actually loaded.

7.   To fix this, from the **Levels** window, right-click on your house level and go to **Change Streaming Method | Always Loaded**.

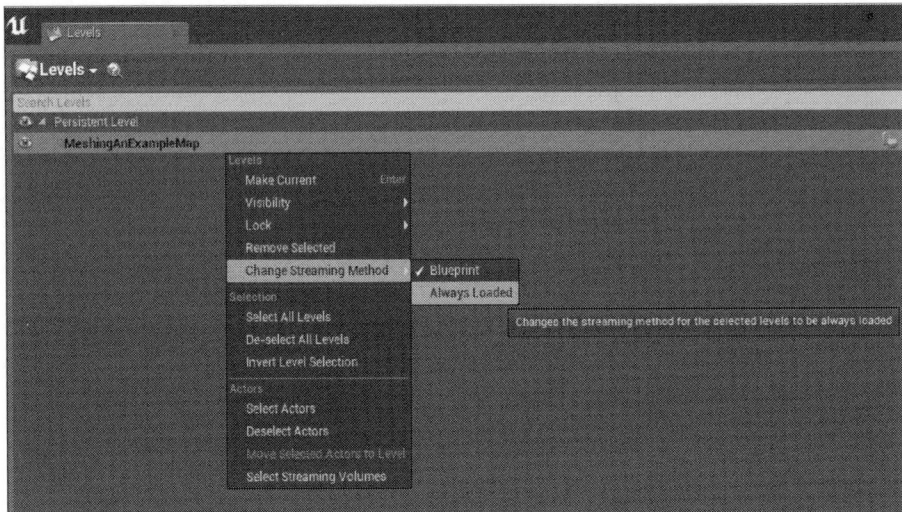

> If for some reason the method is grayed out, check to make sure your level isn't locked. If it is, click on the lock on the right-hand side to enable changes on the level. This is also a good tool to use if you want to make sure that you're only modifying one level at a time.

8. Now let's build our lighting again and run the project!

Now, we can see our levels loaded together!

> For those interested in having levels load dynamically over time rather than all at once, you can use blueprints to have levels stream in and out to create what seems like a seamless world. To see how to do this, refer to https://wiki.unrealengine.com/Blueprint_Manual_Level_Streaming.

5
Lights, Camera, Action – Cinematics

In this chapter, we'll cover the following recipes:

- An introduction to Matinee
- Creating an opening cutscene
- Playing a Matinee via Blueprints
- Preventing a player from moving via cinematic mode

Introduction

Now that we have an understanding of creating environments, let's take some time to dive a little deeper into creating cinematics that we can use to give our titles even more depth.

An introduction to Matinee

The Matinee tool is the driving force behind all the cinematic scenes within the Unreal Engine. It gives users the ability to be the director within your game, giving you control over the camera, the actor's movement, sound, as well as different cuts and animation effects. Think of any moment in an Unreal game where you didn't have direct control over the character, like in a cutscene. Chances are that was done in Matinee. However, Matinee can be used for many other things, which we will discuss at the end of the chapter.

In order to create a Matinee, we will use the (aptly named) **Matinee Editor** that can be accessed from the toolbar at the top of the screen.

Getting ready

Before we start working within the Unreal Editor, we will need to have a project to work with:

1. First, open up the Unreal Editor by clicking on the **Launch** button from the Unreal Engine Launcher.

2. Start a new project from the **Project Browser** tab by selecting the **New Project** tab. Select **Third person** and make sure that **With Starter Content** is selected and give the project a Name (`Cookbook_Chapter5`). Once you are finished, click on **Create Project**.

3. You should see a level similar to this:

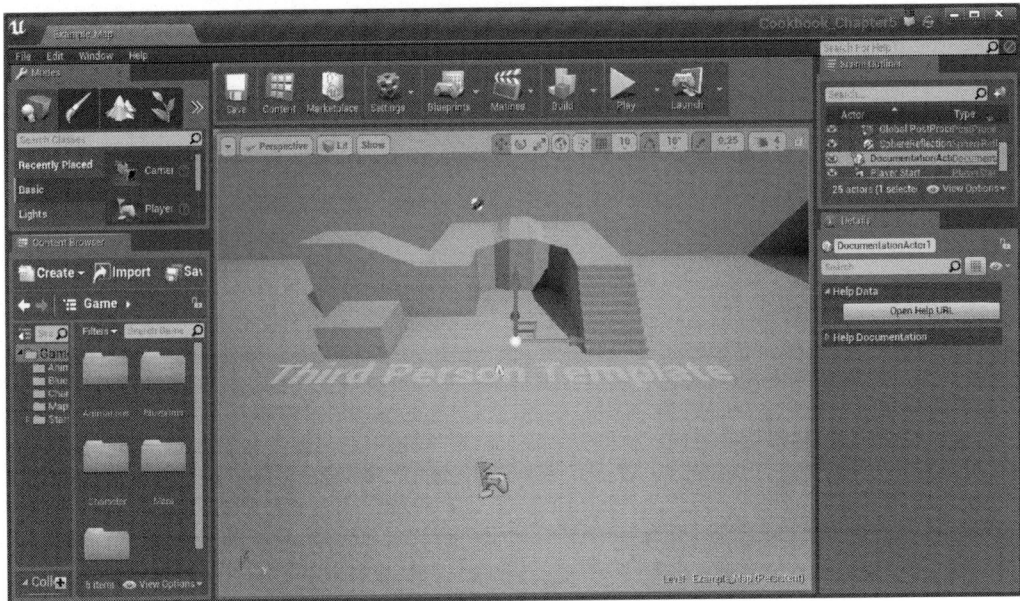

How to do it...

Having defined what Matinee is used for, let's begin using it.

1. With our level opened up, let's create our first **Matinee** by going to the top toolbar and selecting **Matinee** and then clicking on the **Add Matinee** option.

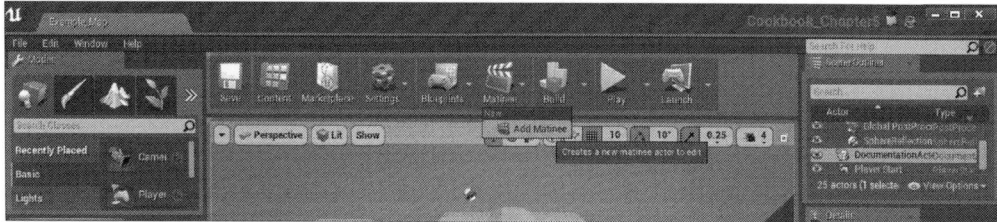

2. From here, you'll be brought to the **Matinee Editor** window.

> You can also create a Matinee by going to the **Modes** tab and then going to the **Place** mode (*Ctrl + 1*) on the far left if you aren't there already and then clicking on **All Classes** and finding the **Matinee** selection from there. Afterward, drag and drop it into your level and once it's there, click on the **Open Matinee** button.

Now, there are a lot of things up here currently and it may be confusing to look at them first, so let's briefly go over these windows:

1. **Toolbar**: The item at the very top is the toolbar; it contains various tools that we can use to check on our animations.

2. **Curve Editor**: Below the toolbar, we have Curve Editor, which is used to have fine control over properties that change over time (properties that make use of Distributions). Mainly, this'll be the key frames that you create. In order to see something on Curve Editor, you'll need to click on the gray box toggle button from the **Tracks** tab.

3. **Details**: On the right-hand side, we have the Details tab that will tell you the details about whatever key we have selected, such as whether it is active or how the key should move.

4. **Tracks**: Here is where we will manipulate objects and where the bulk of your work will be done. For those who have worked with video editing or animation software, this will be very familiar as a timeline of the changes we want to take place over time.

Creating an opening cutscene

Now that we have an understanding of what Matinee is, let's start building our first cutscene!

Getting ready

Before we start working, you should have a level opened and entered the Matinee Editor. For assistance with this, check out the *An introduction to Matinee* recipe.

How to do it...

In order to create a cutscene, you need to perform the following steps:

1. Matinee animates movable objects over time, but it needs to know what objects to animate and what properties of them to change. Under the **Tracks** tab on the left-hand side, right click and select **Add New Camera Group**. Once there, it will ask you for the name of your group; we will call it Camera01.

   When doing this, a camera is automatically created in the scene at the current position of the user camera within the editor.

You can also create a camera actor in the scene by right-clicking and navigating to **Place Actor | Camera Actor**. Once placed in the scene, with the camera selected, you can create a Camera group using that camera within Matinee.

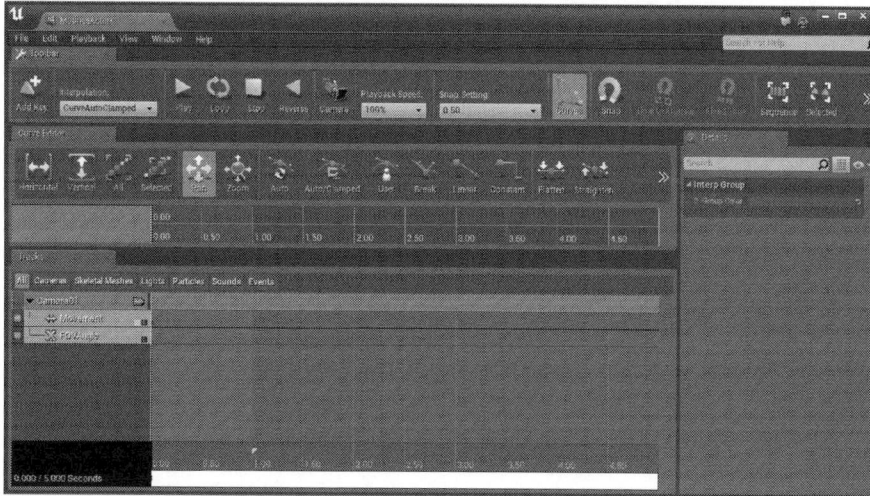

Camera group added to the Tracks tab

At the bottom of the track, you'll notice a series of numbers separated by lines. This represents the time that has passed from the beginning of the animation. Use the mouse wheel, scrolling in and out, to zoom/rescale the timeline.

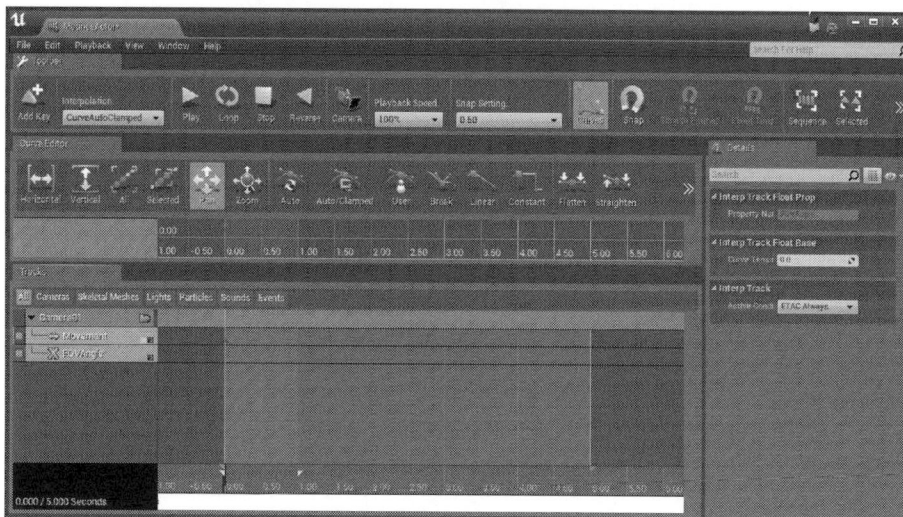

Rescaling the timeline

The bright red triangles at the bottom symbolize the size of the entire animation and you can click and drag them to modify its length. The green ones are used to determine which part will you see when you play in the editor.

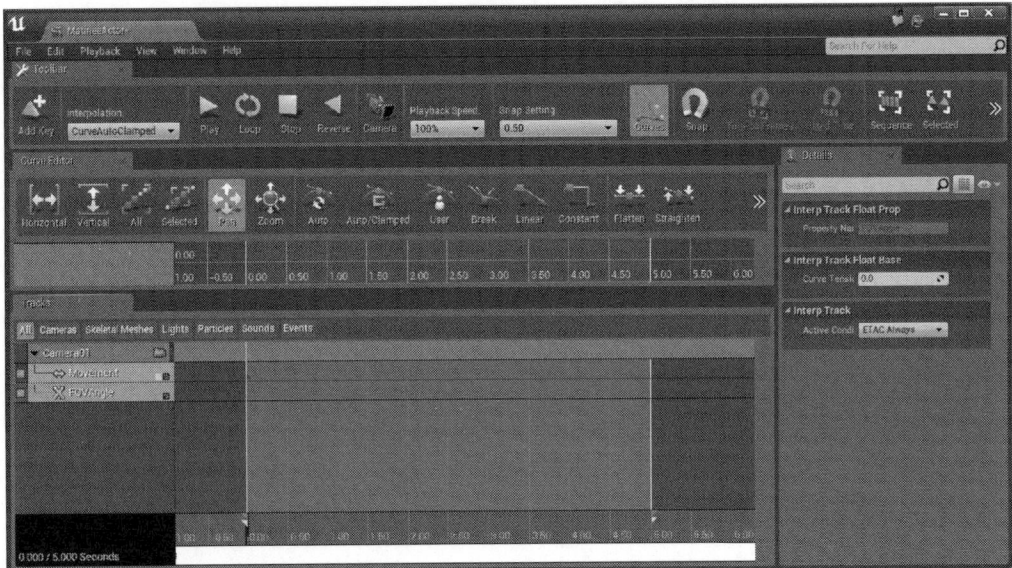

Dark red triangle showing key frame

Next, you may notice the dark red triangle at the 0.00 time marker under the **Movement** row in the tracks. This is known as a key frame, which is a point in time at which we want our Actor to be at a certain value. The first one is automatically created for us, and basically stands for the starting point.

2. Now drag the time bar to the 2.00 second mark so that we can add a key there. Then, click on the **Movement** part of our **Camera01** group and then press the **Add Key** button on the top-left of the **Toolbar** tab to add a key.

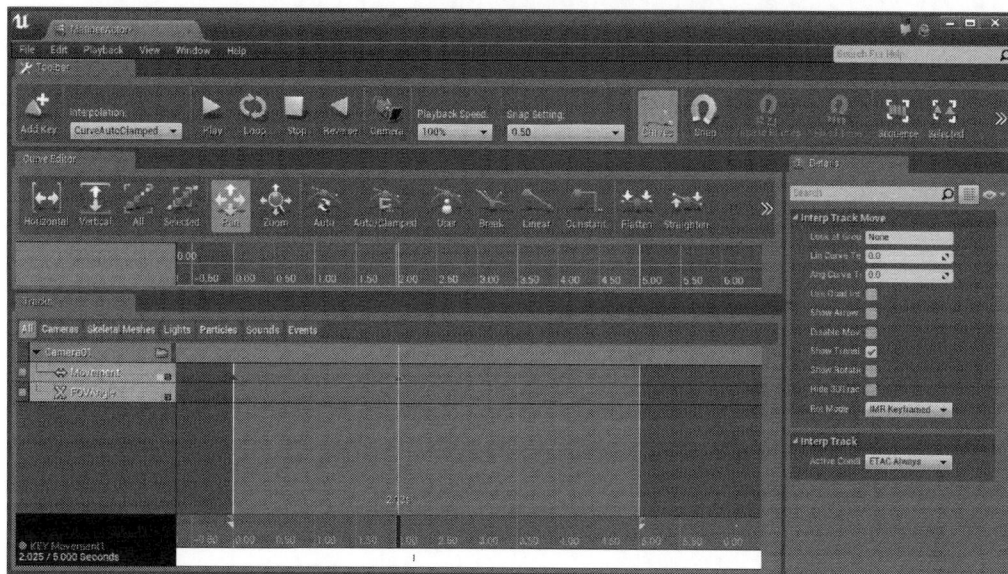

You can also press *Enter* to create a key.

3. With the key selected (it is outlined), minimize the Matinee Editor and move back to the main editor.

4. You will notice that you have `CameraActor` selected in the **Scene Outliner** tab. Either way, double-click on it inside the **Scene Outliner** tab to zoom to its position. At this point, we can move our camera to modify its position. I will move the actor down in the Z axis, and you should notice a line moving to show the transition between the two.

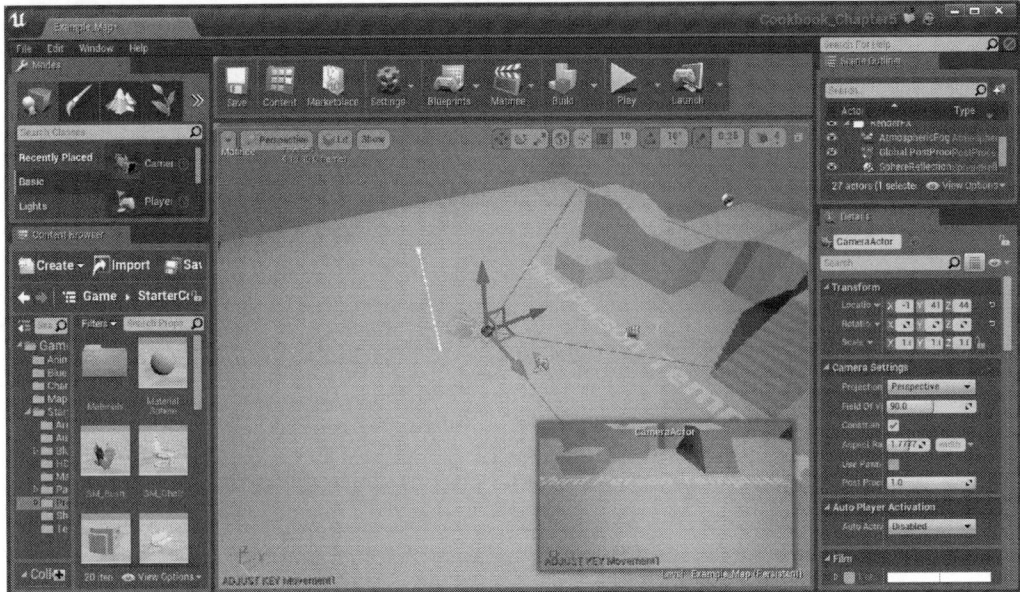

Modifying position of the CameraActor object

5. We can also modify the rotation, which we will do next to make it seem like we are landing in front of the player.

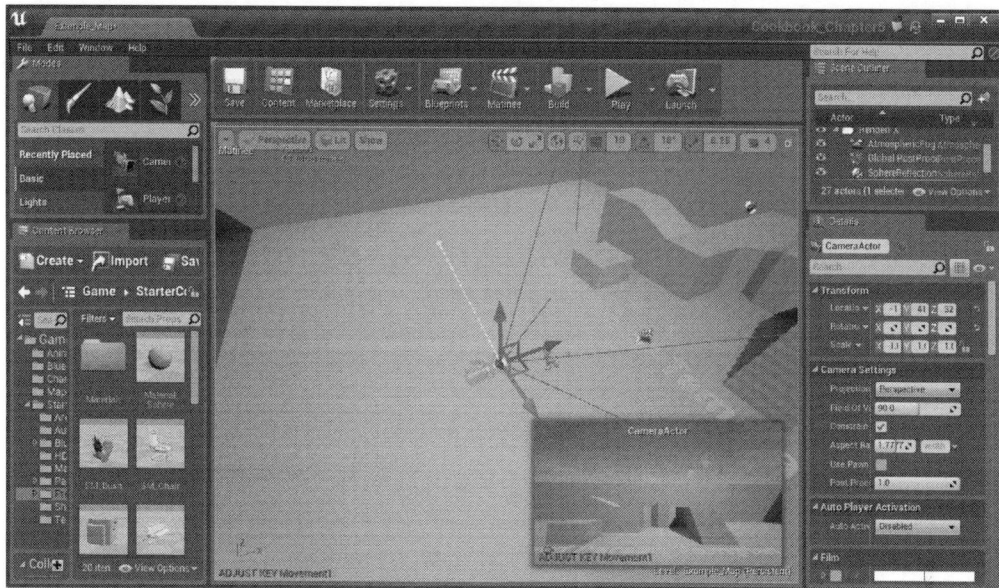

Modifying the rotation of the CameraActor object

If you have both the editors up at the same time, you'll notice that you can move the time bar and see the transition and exactly how it is done. You can also press the **Play** and **Loop** buttons to watch it in real time. For instance, when the editor shows it at this time...

...the editor window will look similar to this:

> You can also click on the camera icon, next to `Camera_01` in the **Tracks** tab in the Matinee Editor so that the entire viewport of the level editor shows the view of the camera during the animation.

6. After creating this first key frame, we want to add another one at the end of the animation to bring the camera forward, so we can create another key by pressing the *Enter* key. After this, right-click on the newly created key and select **Set Time** and under **New Time**, put in 5.

    This can be nice when you know how exactly you want things to change. Play around with the key frames, adding and modifying them, until you get whatever animation you want to have.

Another way to get the exact numbers for your key frames is by using the
Snap option, which you can select from the toolbar or from **View | Snap**.
This will make it so that when you add a key, it will be to the nearest .5
second or when you move, it will snap between the options.

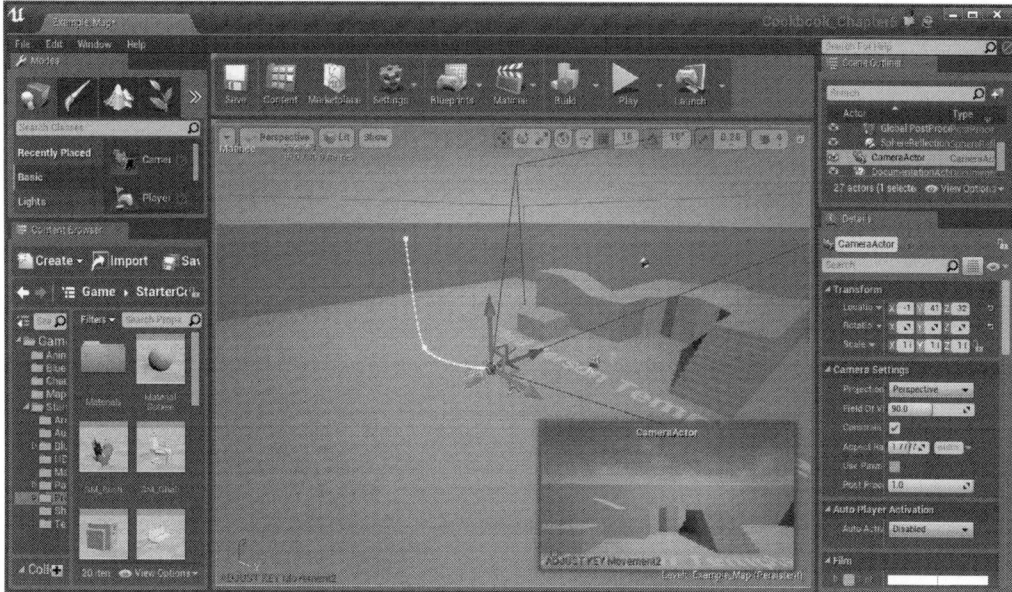

When in the Matinee Editor, you can manually move key frames after
placing them initially into the timeline by holding *Ctrl* and clicking to drag
that key frame in the timeline in both a positive and a negative direction.

7. Lastly, by default, Unreal will use whatever camera is attached to the player. We need to use something called a **director group** in order to dictate which camera we should be using at what time. So with that in mind, right-click underneath the **Camera01** section under the **Tracks** tab and select **Add New Director Group**.

Creating a director group

8. With this in mind, we now have a **DirGroup** control in place with no key frames. Move the time bar to 0, select the **Director** property for modification, and create a new key by clicking on **Add Key** in the top-left of the screen. Once there, it will ask which camera you wish to use. Select Camera01 and press **Ok**.

   You may notice that on the top-left of each group, there is a camera icon on the far right of the different groups with the **DirGroup** currently being selected. This shows which camera you are currently looking at in the **Game** viewport in the main editor. This can be nice for visualizing what you are doing.

9. When the animation is over, we want to return the control of the camera back to the player, so create a new key at the end of the animation and change it to use DirGroup. This will instantly change back to the player's camera, but we can also add in a transition by right-clicking on the key and selecting **Set Transition Time** and putting in 1 for the amount of time in seconds we want the transition for.

Playing a Matinee via Blueprints

After you have your animation ready, we need to play it in the actual game.

Getting ready

Before we start working, you should have a level opened and have a completed Matinee. For assistance with this, check out the *Creating an opening cutscene* recipe.

How to do it...

You need to execute these steps to play a Matinee via Blueprints:

1. Exit out of the Matinee Editor if you are in it and back in the **Game** tab, select the `MatineeActor` object inside the scene (it looks like a clipboard) and then from the top toolbar, navigate to **Blueprints | Open Level Blueprint**.

> Alternatively, you can go to the **Scene Outliner** tab and select the object from there, either by scrolling down until you see it or typing in `Matinee` in the **Search** bar above it.

2. Once inside the **Blueprint Editor**, right-click inside the **Event Graph** tab and navigate to **Call Function On Matinee Actor 0 | Cinematic | Play**.

> For the dropdowns, you need to click on the triangle on the left-hand side to expand it.

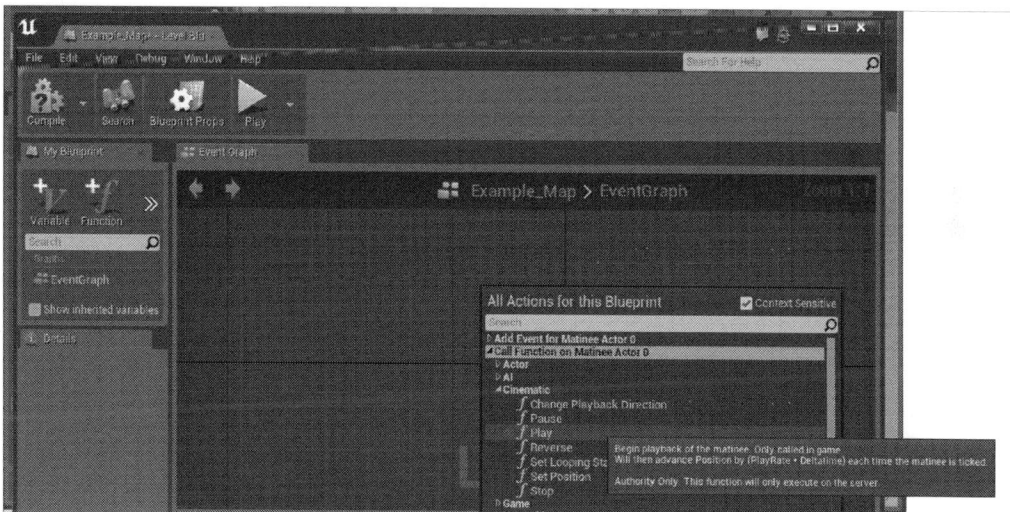

Adding a Play action to call on the MatineeActor

If all goes well, you should see something like this:

If you do not see this, make sure that the `MatineeActor` object is selected from the **Scene Outliner** tab.

3. Now, this is calling a function called `Play`, which will play our Matinee cutscene, but there is no indication as to when this should be triggered (or called, in programmer lingo). So, we need to add an **Event**, saying to play this animation when the game starts. To do this, right-click and go to **Add Event | Event Begin Play**.

4. Lastly, we need to connect the event to the play action. So, click and drag on the right-side's arrow and connect it to the input of the **Play** action on the left-hand side.

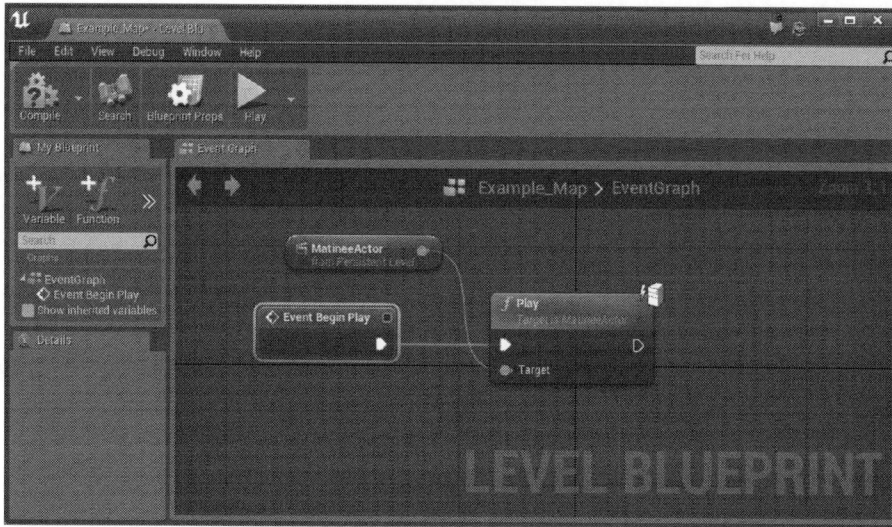

> When working with Blueprints, you may hear actions referred to as actions, nodes, or whatever type they are (event, function, and so on).

5. Lastly, we'll clean up just a bit by clicking and dragging the MatineeActor variable below, near the **Target** connection.

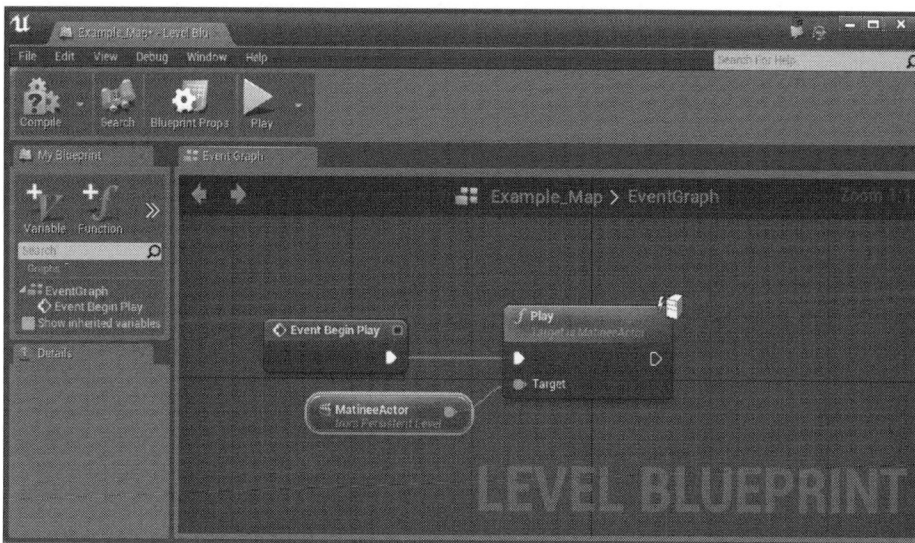

6. Now, jump in and play the game! Just like we were planning, we fall down to the player and move back to the normal player's control.

> For more information on working with Matinee, refer to
> `https://docs.unrealengine.com/latest/`
> `INT/Engine/Matinee/UserGuide/index.html`.

Preventing a player from moving via cinematic mode

Now that we know how to create Matinees, we should be able to create amazing cinematics that make your levels really come alive! However, by default, when you play a cinematic, the player can still move around and turn. This may be the desired behavior depending on whether you're using something like a custom camera system, such as *Resident Evil*, or the Matinee for moving objects such as moving platforms. But, for a cinematic, we don't want it. Thankfully, there is a way to prevent this via Blueprints.

Getting ready

Before we start working, you should have a level opened and have a complete Matinee. You should also have it playing in the actual game. For assistance with this, check out the *Playing a Matinee via Blueprints* recipe.

How to do it...

1. Open up the level blueprint by going from the top tool bar and navigating to **Blueprints | Open Level Blueprint**.

2. From here, we should have the appropriate nodes to play our Matinee.

3. To the right of the **Play** node, right click and type in `Cinematic` in the search bar. At the bottom, you'll see the **Game | Cinematic | Set Cinematic Mode** option. Select it to create its node and drag it so that the arrows are alongside each other.

   The **Set Cinematic Mode** option enables us to remove the game's HUD, hide the player, and prevent movement and turning in the game. Of course, depending on the situation, you may want to use some or none of these options so that they're able to be customized from the node.

4. Connect the output of the **Play** node to the input of the **Set Cinematic Mode** option. Toggle the **Cinematic Mode** option to turn on the cinematic mode. Uncheck **Hide Player** so that we can still see the player. Then, check **Affects Movement** and **Affects Tuning**; this will prevent the player from moving or using the mouse to move around while the cutscene is playing.

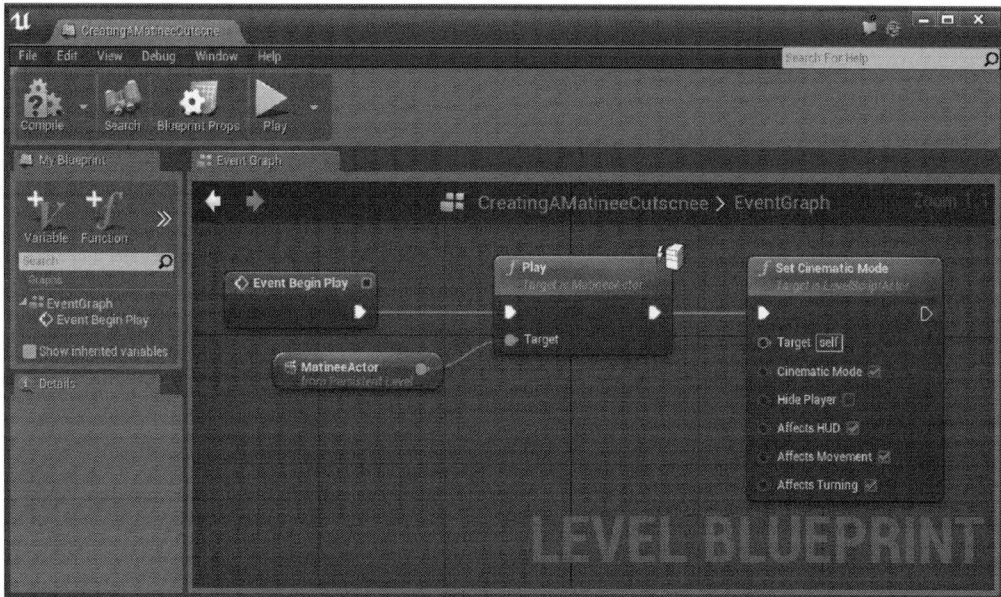

If you were to play the game now, you would notice that it works...maybe a little too well.

That's because after we enabled cinematic mode, we never disabled it. Let's do this next.

1. To fix this, we will need to have an event whenever the Matinee ends. Select your **MatineeActor** in the **Scene Outliner** tab and then go back into your level blueprint.

2. From here, right-click and select **Create a Matinee Controller for MatineeActor**. You'll notice that it gives us a new node that contains a new **Finished** output that will be activated whenever the matinee will end.

3. Next, create another **Set Cinematic Mode** action and uncheck **Cinematic Mode** and **Hide Player** while checking the other three properties below.

4. Finally, connect the **Finished** output to the input of the **Set Cinematic Mode** node.

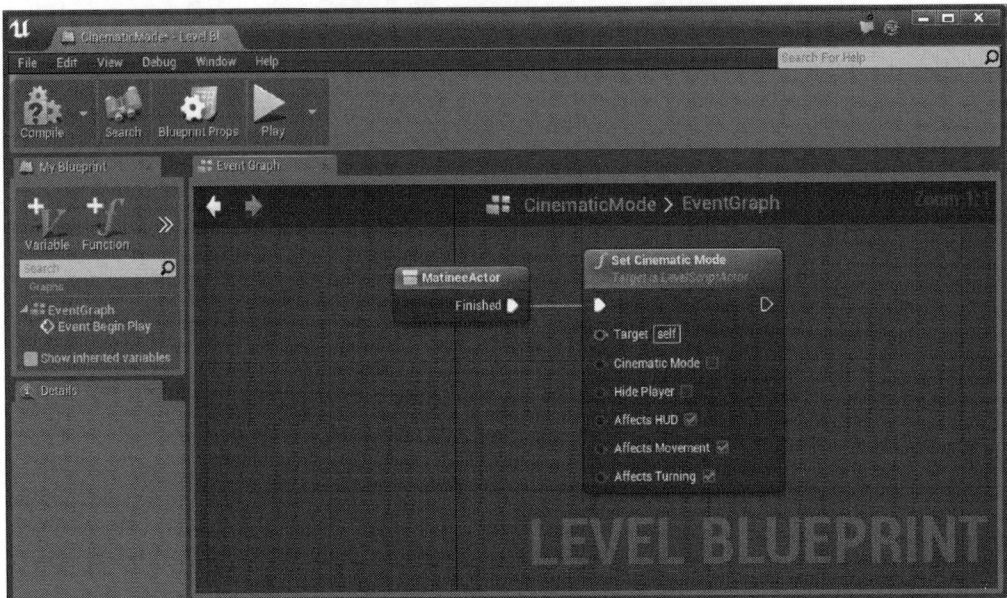

5. At this point, if we go in and play the game, the player will not move during the cinematic, but as soon as it's over, it can!

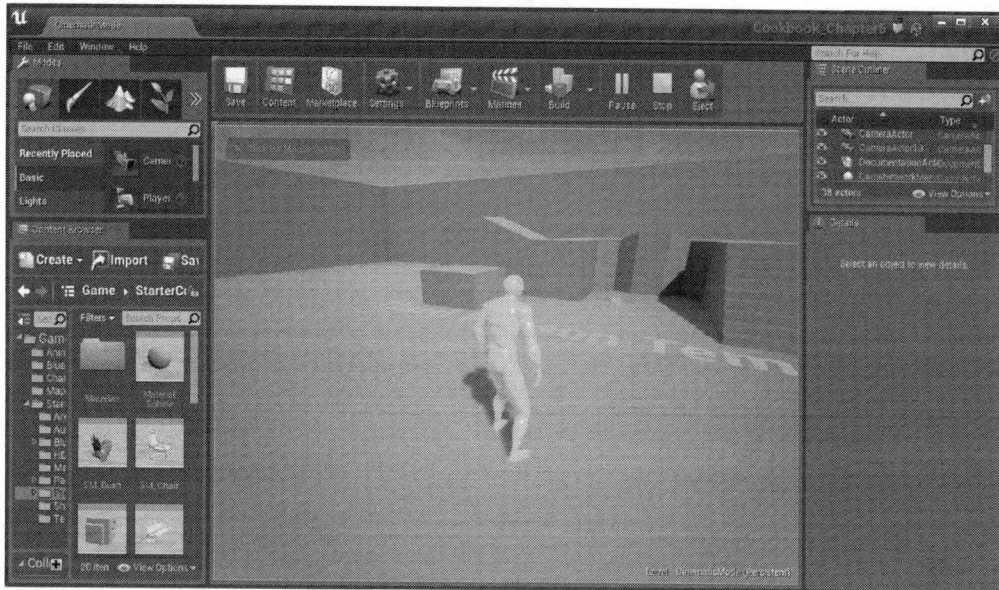

The final view after adding cinematic

> To do this in another way, you can also use a **Delay** action and then set it to another cinematic mode or even use Boolean values, once you've got more experience in scripting to toggle their properties.

See also

There is an amazing amount of things that you can do within the Matinee editor. Sadly, I don't have the space in the book to write about everything, but I do have some links that, if you would like to know more, about some of the many other things you can do:

▶ In addition to cutscenes, you can also use Matinee to create gameplay elements such as moving platforms. A nice text tutorial about doing that is available at `https://wiki.unrealengine.com/Blueprint_Lift_Tutorial`.

▶ Vincent Stimpson has a series of two tutorial videos on Matinee—the first deals with cameras with a fade effect (`https://youtu.be/0tQFrJElkio`), and the second video is on some of the advanced techniques that you can use to work with Matinee with animations and particle effects (`https://www.youtube.com/watch?v=071KTwZtyoo`).

6
Lighting and Shadows

In this chapter, we'll cover the following recipes:

- ▸ Lighting overview – learning the types of lights
- ▸ Adding moveable lights – flashlight, part 1
- ▸ Creating a Day/Night cycle

Introduction

Lighting is one of the most important elements then creating environments. It can communicate the theme, create atmosphere, and give a certain tone to each place that you use it for. However, if done poorly, it can make levels look amateurish. In this chapter, we will look at how to bring life to our game worlds.

Lighting overview – learning the types of lights

Having defined why lighting is so important, let's start creating each of the types and talking about what they do. In this recipe, we will see each of the different kinds of lights available in the engine. We will also discuss how they are different and when and why to use each one.

Getting ready

Before we start working within the Unreal Editor, we will need to have a project to work with:

1. First, open up the Unreal Editor by clicking on the **Launch** button from the Unreal Engine Launcher.

2. Start a new project from the **Project Browser** tab by selecting the **New Project** tab. Select **First person** and make sure that **With Starter Content** is selected. Give the project a Name (`Cookbook_Chapter6`). Once you have finished, click on **Create Project**.

3. You should see a level similar to this:

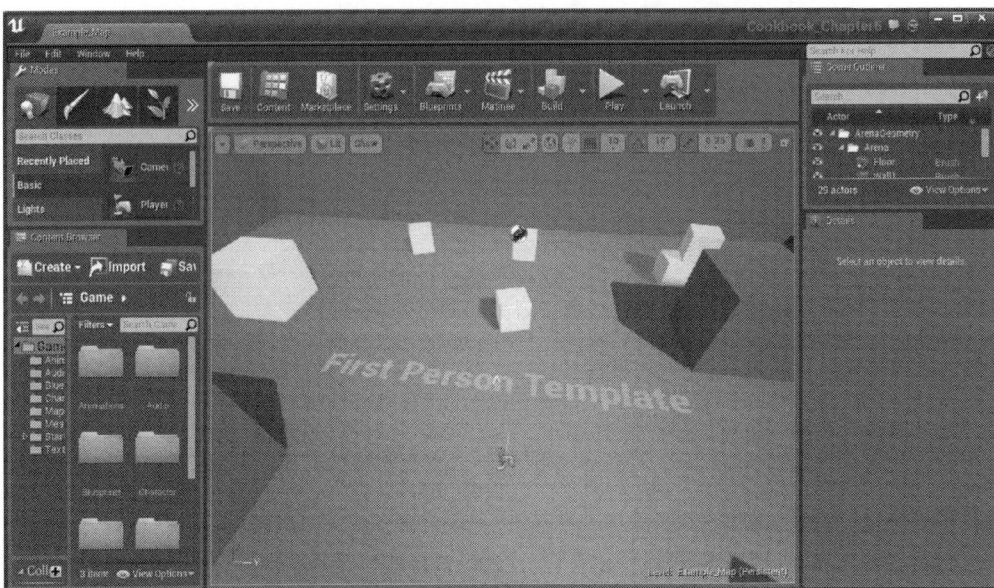

How to do it...

To get started, let's see how we can go about adding lights to our level:

1. Move the camera toward a dark area of our level that we want to light up. Once there, go to **Modes** | **Lights** and click on the **Point** light and drag and drop the light into your level.

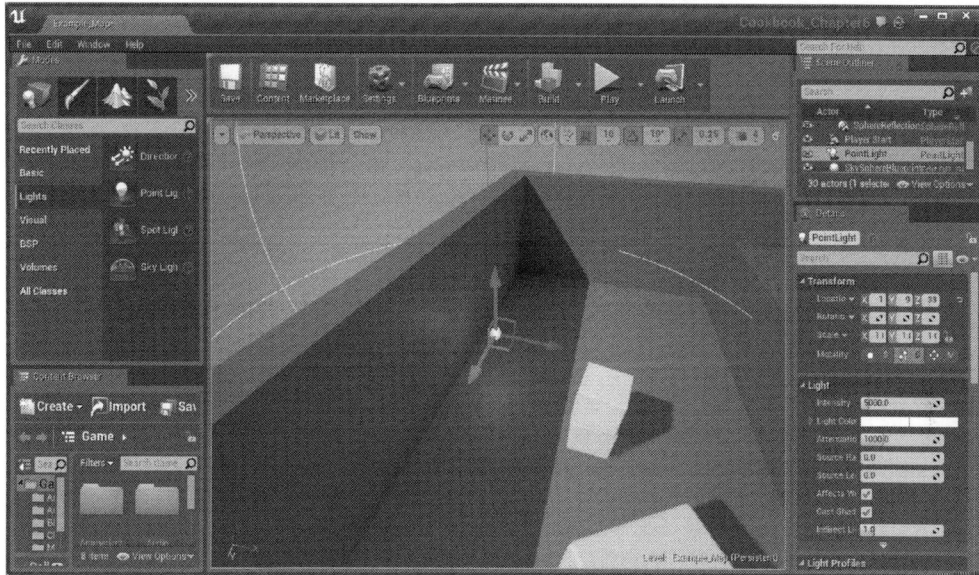

Adding a Point Light to your level

> You can also press and hold the *L* key and then click to create a point light at the location that was clicked.

Point Lights act in a similar manner to a light bulb; they will emit light in all the directions from their center for a certain radius, losing power as the light gets further away.

> For more information on Point Lights, refer to `https://docs.unrealengine.com/latest/INT/Engine/Rendering/LightingAndShadows/LightTypes/Point/index.html`.

2. We can also create lights from our **Level** tab. Let's do this by right-clicking anywhere in the level and navigating to **Place Actor | Spot Light**.

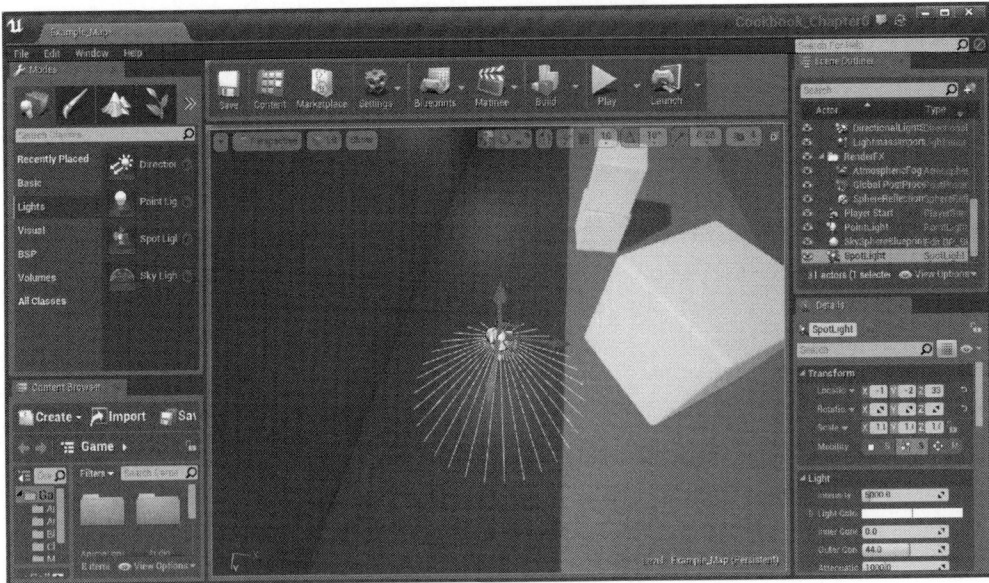

Creating a Spot Light in your level

The object will appear facedown with lights going out in the direction that it is shining. This actually goes much further out, so let's check this out.

3. From Translation mode, switch to Rotation mode by pressing down the spacebar (or *E*) and then rotating the object by -90 degrees along the **Y** axis to face the dark wall.

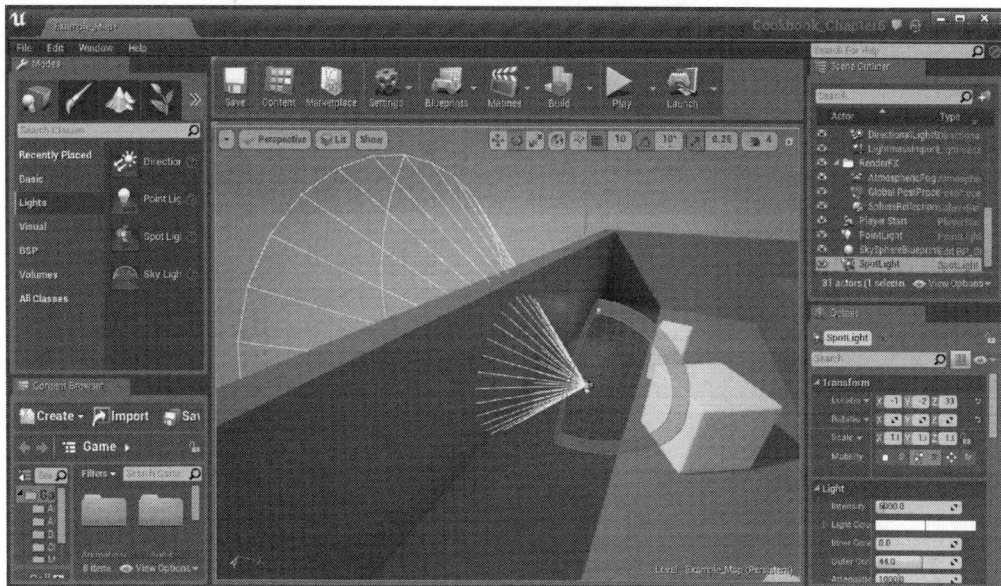

The cone shape effect of a Spot light

Spot lights act much like they do in the real world; specifically, they will emit light from a point out in a cone shape. However, just like real spotlights, there is a center section that is fully bright with the outer edge decreasing in power. We can do this in Unreal as well using the **Inner Cone Angle** and **Outer Cone Angle** properties.

4. From the **Light** section under the **Details** panel, set the **Inner Cone Angle** value to 25 and the **Outer Cone Angle** value to 32. After that, increase the **Intensity** to 50000.0.

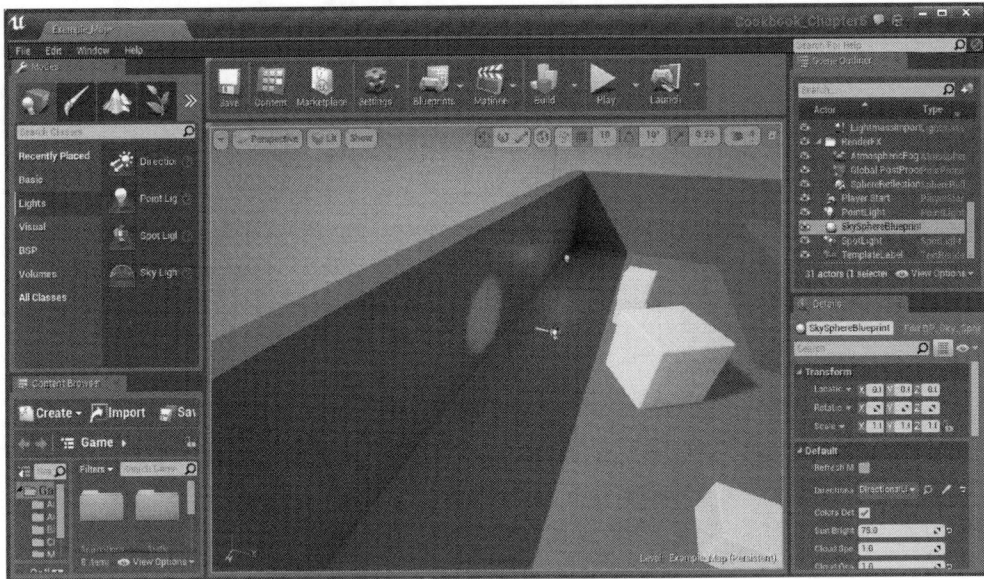

Managing cone angles and intensity

However, spotlights can also lose power as they move away, as shown in the following example:

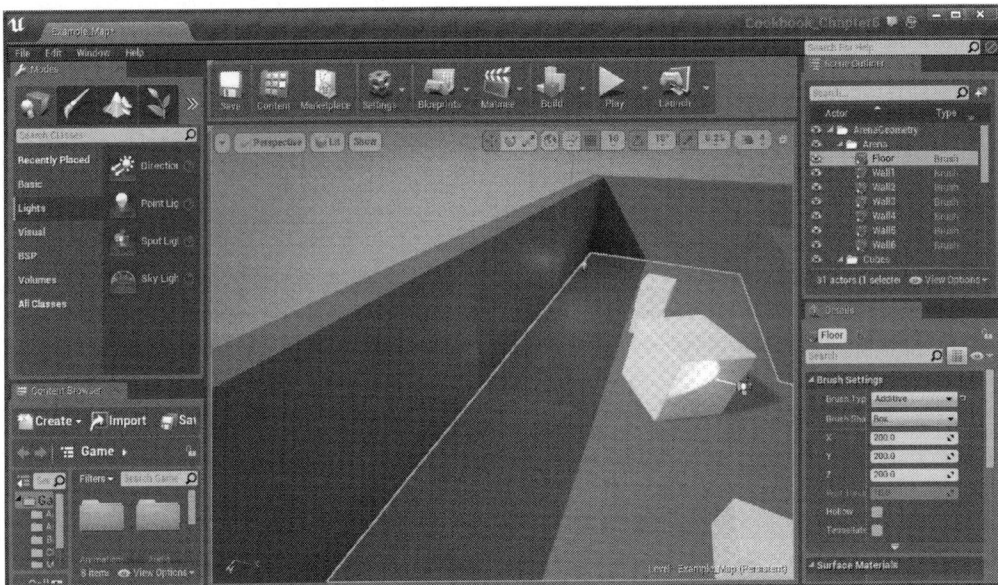

[For more information about Spot Lights, refer to `https://docs.`
`unrealengine.com/latest/INT/Engine/Rendering/`
`LightingAndShadows/LightTypes/Spot/index.html.`]

5. The next light I want to point out is already in the example level by default. Go to the **Scene Outliner** tab and select the **DirectionalLight** object by double-clicking on it.

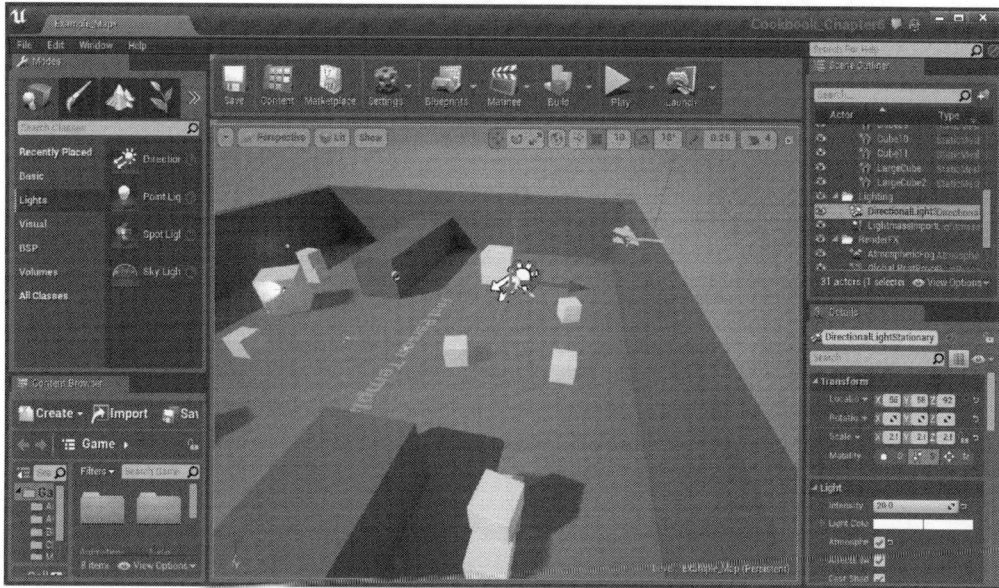

Selecting directional light

Directional lights act much like the sun. Depending on their properties, they affect the entire outer section of the level. You'll notice the arrows pointing in a certain direction which is where the light will be emitting from.

6. Rotate the light by 40 degrees in the **Y** direction.

> For more information on Directional Lights, refer to `https://docs.unrealengine.com/latest/INT/Engine/Rendering/LightingAndShadows/LightTypes/Directional/index.html`.

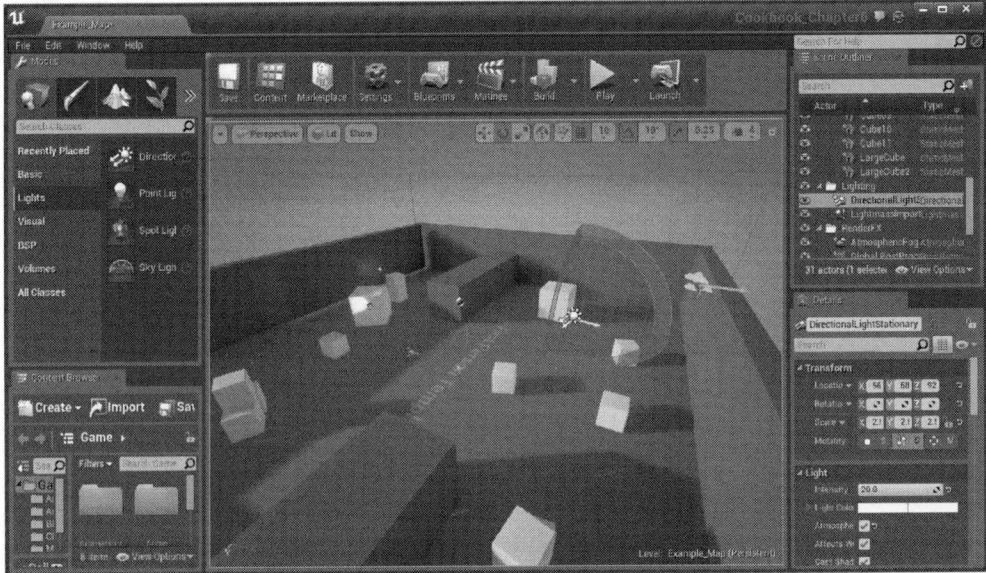

Rotating the directional light

7. Now the last light is the **Sky Light**, which is used to create ambient light from the distant areas in the world. It then applies that light to the world so that the level's lighting will match the rest of the level. To add this, use either method mentioned for the Sky Light and put it into the level.

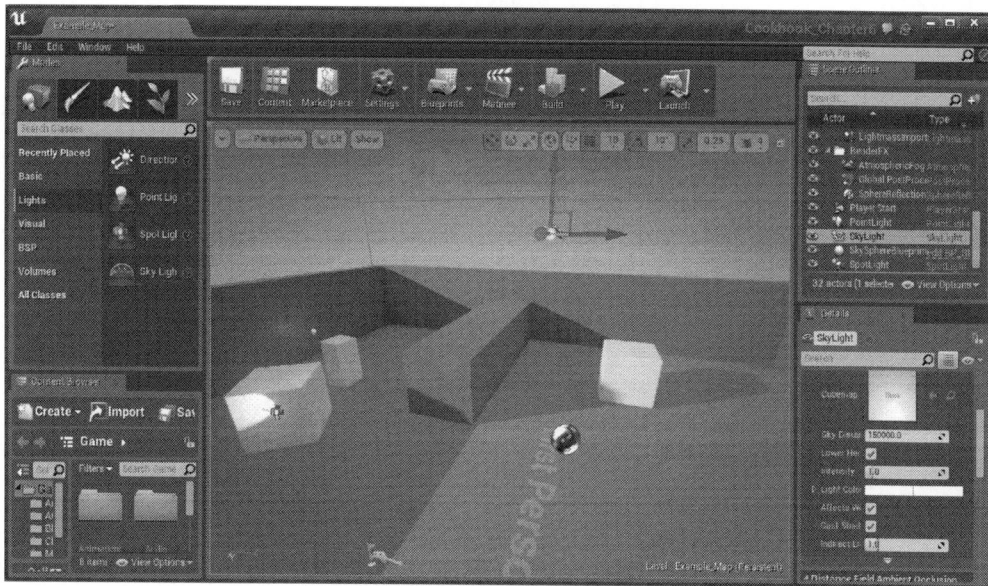

8. The Sky Light will only capture the screen when we rebuild the lighting by selecting **Recapture Scene** or manually going to **Build | Update Reflection Captures**.

> For more information on Sky Lights, refer to `https://docs.unrealengine.com/latest/INT/Engine/Rendering/LightingAndShadows/LightTypes/SkyLight/index.html`.

Adding moveable lights – flashlight, part 1

Now we have an understanding of how these lights work, but so far, they've all been static, non-moving. However, in certain instances, we may want the lighting to change while the game is going on. Let's do that by creating a moving light, in a similar manner to a flashlight!

Getting ready

Before we start working, we should have the `NightScene` level opened. This is provided in the `Example Code` folder for this chapter that you can get off of Packt's website.

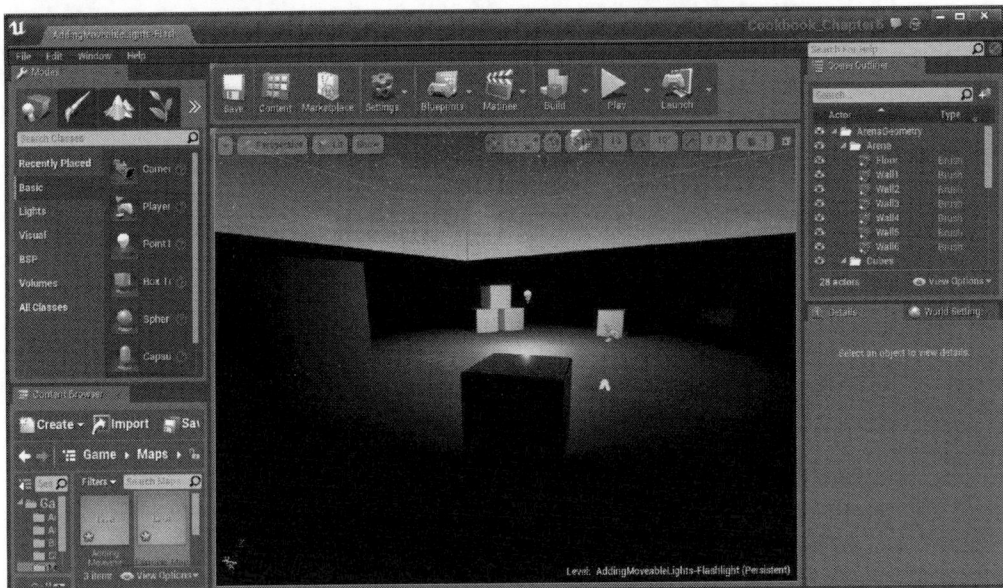

The NightScene level

> This level is a quick example of a night environment with the lighting reduced significantly. For more information on creating a scene using lighting for night time, refer to https://docs.unrealengine.com/latest/INT/Resources/Showcases/RealisticRendering/NightScene/index.html.

How to do it...

To create a flashlight, perform the following steps:

1. The first thing we will want to do is create a `SpotLight` to use as our flashlight. We can do that by right-clicking on the ground near the player and then navigating to **Place Actor | Spot Light**.

2. Rotate the spotlight 90 degrees so that it is facing away from the player's spawn point. Then, change the **Inner Cone Angle** value to 8 and the **Outer Cone Angle** value to 10. Lastly, we want this actor to be movable so that it can move, so in the **Details** tab under **Transform | Mobility**, select the option that is the furthest to the right (**Movable**).

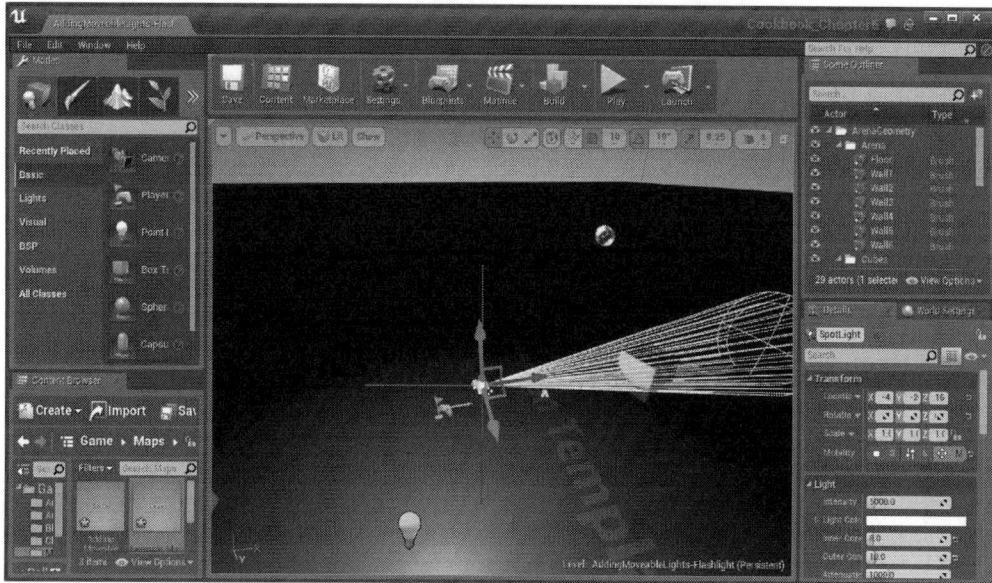

Adjusting the cone angles of the spot light and making the player movable

> For more information on moveable lights, refer to `https://docs.`
> `unrealengine.com/latest/INT/Engine/Rendering/`
> `LightingAndShadows/LightMobility/DynamicLights/`
> `index.html`.

3. Now if you play the game, you will see additional objects in the **Scene Outliner** tab, including an object called `MyCharacter_C4` (or something similar). Select it and scroll down to your `SpotLight`. Drag and drop the `SpotLight` object on top of the `MyCharacter` object (use the mouse wheel to move the object selections up while holding down the mouse).

4. After this, set the **Location** value of the `SpotLight` to `0,0,0` so that it is at the same position of the player. (As we mentioned before, children of an object have a transition relative to the position of their parent.)

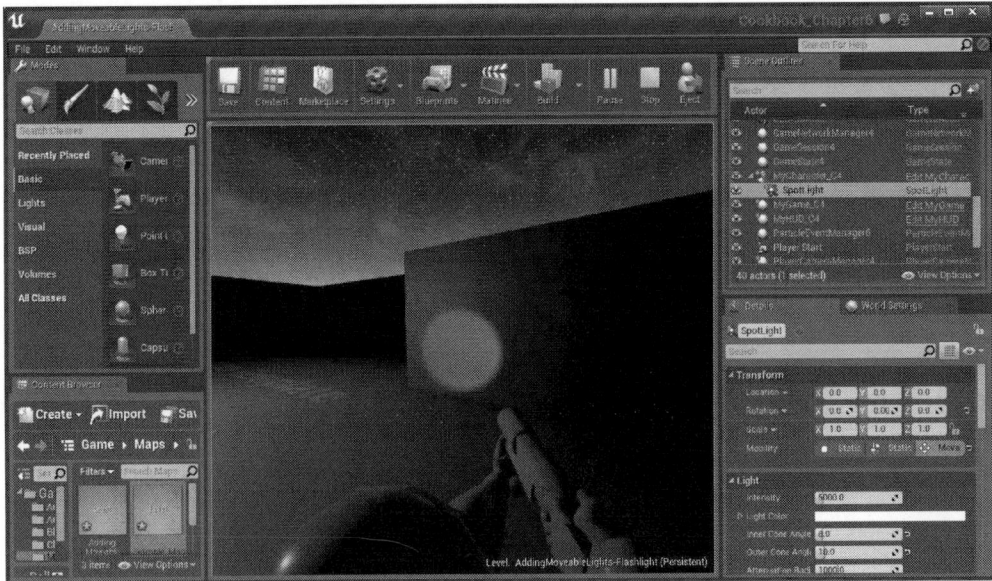

Setting the Location value of the spot light

As you can see, we now have a working flashlight in Unreal. There are a few issues with this, for example, if we look up or down, the light will not go with us because the camera has a different transform than our `Character` class. There's also the issue that since we did this in the game (after the player has been spawned), when we will leave, it'll reset to what it was beforehand. We know that the functionality is possible now, so how can we make this work all the time, and have functionality? Adding it to our Character's Blueprint, we'll dive into how to do this exactly, and the other things to to be considered in our *Adding to an existing Blueprint – flashlight, part 2* recipe, which you can find in *Chapter 8, Blueprint Scripting – Level Effects*.

Creating a Day/Night cycle

If we are creating an open world title or any kind of game where the player is outdoors, one thing that would be nice is the ability to have our world change the time of day at the same rate.

Getting ready

Before we start working, we should have a level created with a `Sky_Sphere` and a directional light (the default map has this). To be sure, you can use the `DayNightCycle-Before` map from the example code folder.

How to do it...

Perform the following steps to create a day/night cycle:

1. As we discussed before, we can use Directional Lights to act like the sun. For our day/night cycle we will want our lighting to change over time, so let's select the `DirectionalLightStationary` object from the **Scene Outliner** tab and then from the **Details** tab, change the **Mobility** property to `Movable`. Finally, change the name of the object to `DirectionalLightMovable`.

> You can either rename the object from the **Details** tab or press *F2* when selected in the **Scene Outliner** tab.

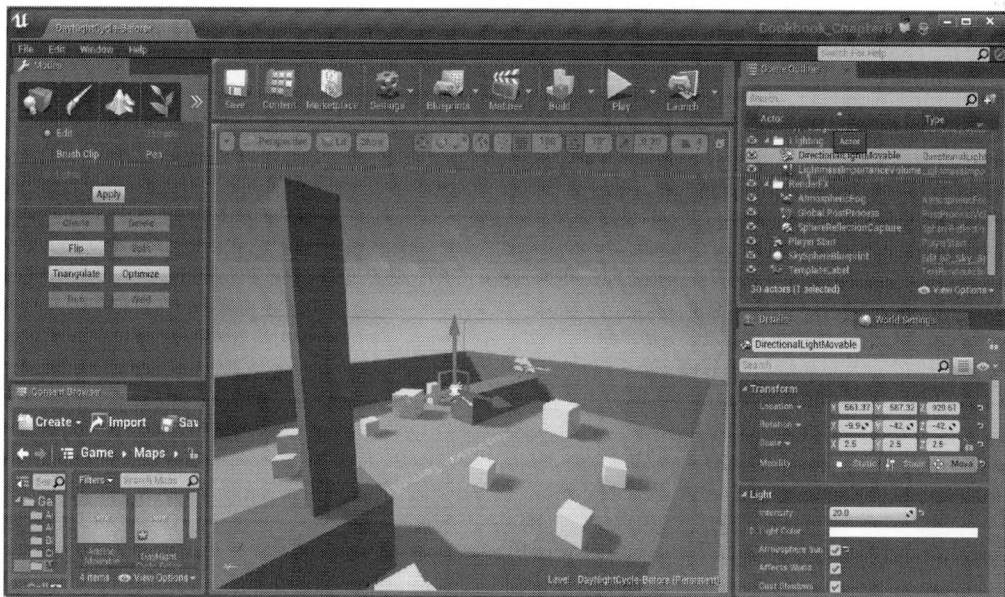

Making our DirectionalLight moveable

2. To have this lighting change reflect correctly, the next thing we should do is build the lighting of our level by going to the toolbar above our level view and navigating to **Build | Build Lighting Only**.

Now, if we were to rotate the light right now, we would see the Sky's color will be modified:

However, the sun that is part of our SunSphere will not be modified by the changes. To fix this, we will need to use Unreal's Blueprints system.

3. Next, from the top-center toolbar, navigate to **Blueprints | Open Level Blueprint**, and you should be brought to the following screen:

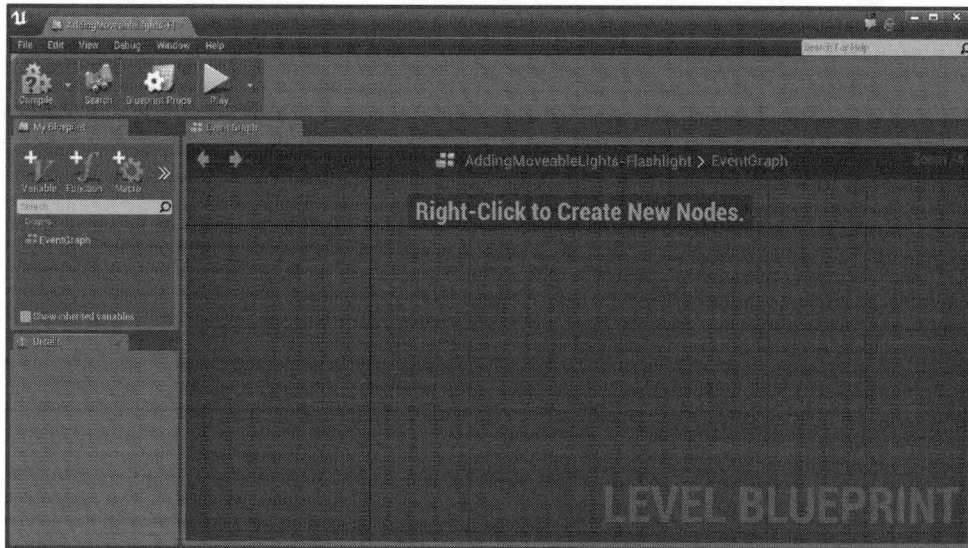

4. From the Blueprints editor, we right-click inside **EventGraph** and then select **Add Event | Event Tick**.

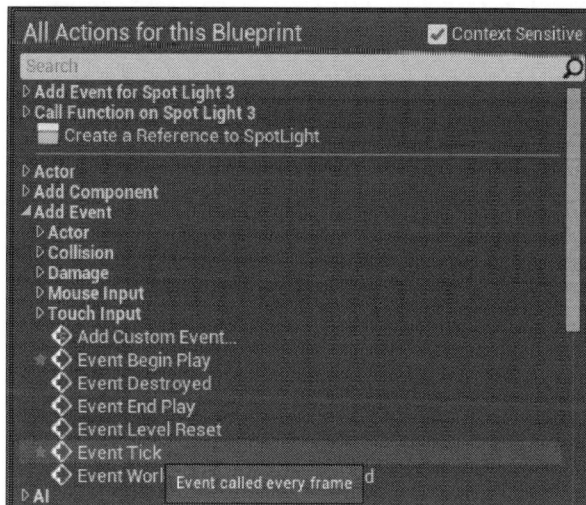

This creates a new event that will get called every frame that it is active and it has a parameter of **Delta Seconds**, which is how much time has elapsed for this particular frame.

5. We want to have the Sky Sphere's sun at the same position as our Directional Light, so let's do that first. Go to the **Scene Outliner** tab and select the `SkySphereBlueprint` object by clicking on it. Once this is done, go back into the Blueprints screen and to the right of the Event Tick event, type in `Sun` to show the properties that contain those letters. From there, select the **Update Sun Direction** option:

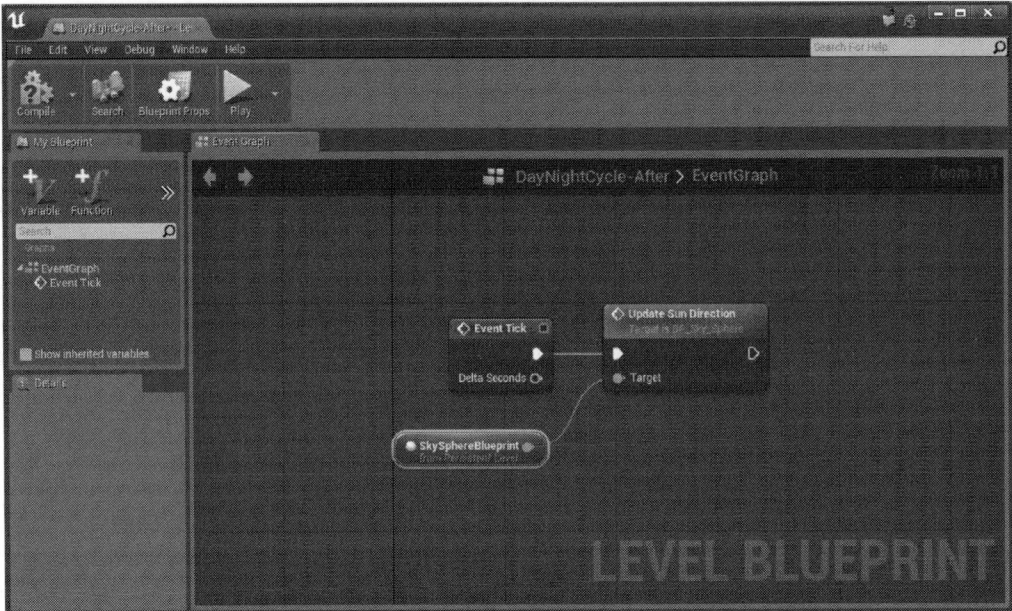

If the object was selected correctly, we should see the **Target** variable already filled in with the `SkySphere`.

To zoom in, use the mouse wheel. This action will find the rotation of the directional light in our level and modify it so that the sun will face the same way.

> If you want to see what **Update Sun Direction** is actually doing, feel free to double-click on the action. We'll talk about what those actions mean later on in *Chapter 8, Blueprint Scripting - Level Effects*.

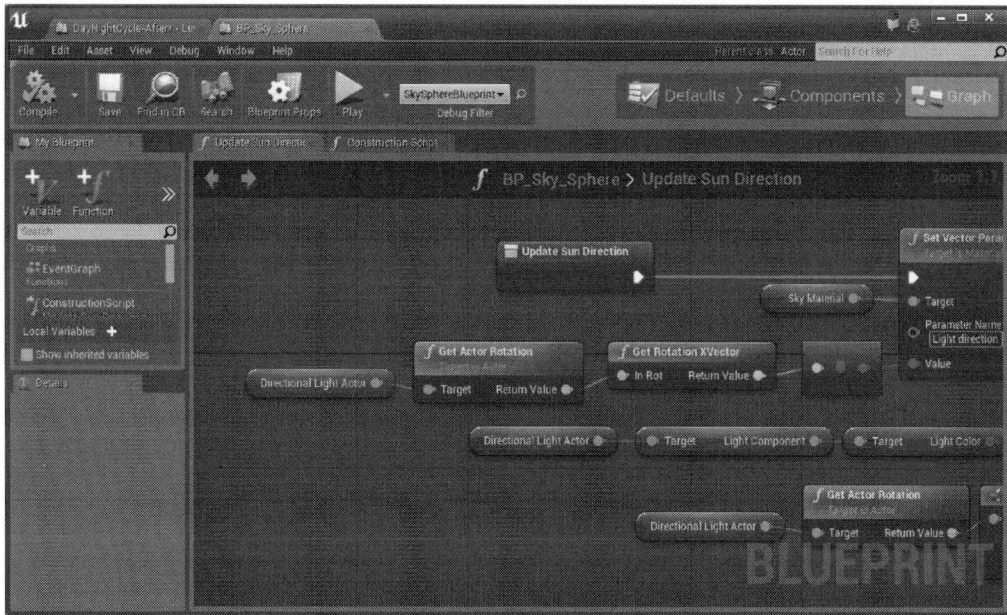

Blueprints are run while the game is played, so at this point, if we play the game, selecting the `DirectionalLightMovable` object, and rotating it from the **Details** tab, we'll notice that the sun in the sky rotates to face it!

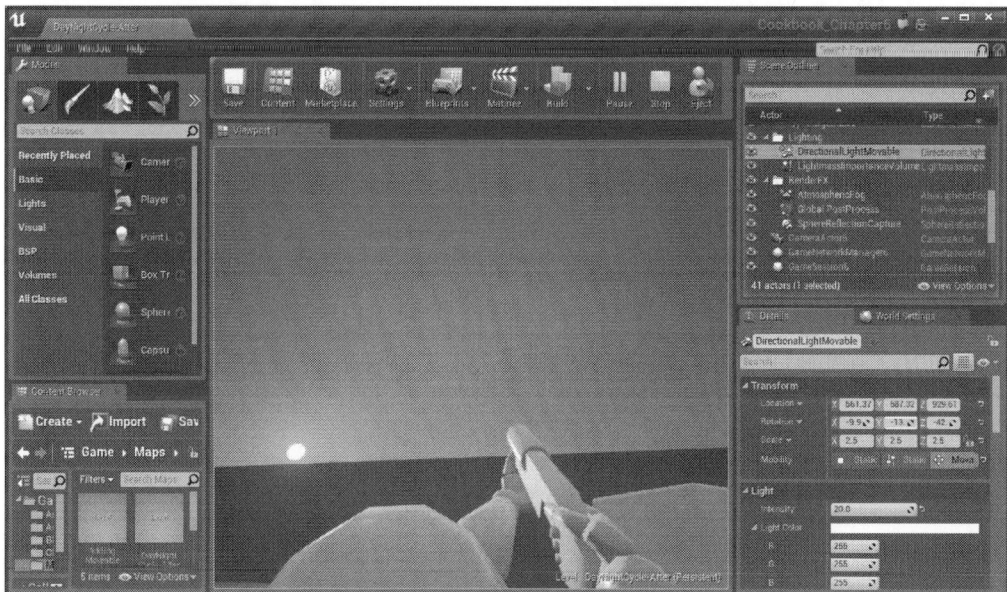

Of course, at this point, we could rotate the light using a matinee for cutscenes and we'd be done, but in this instance, we want it to move automatically, so let's modify the level blueprint to do that.

1. Next, we want to have the directional light continuously rotate along the **Y** axis. To do this, let's first move the **Update Sun Direction** action and the **SkySphere Blueprint** object off to the side so that we can put something in between by selecting both items and then dragging them. Finally, highlight the arrow from the left side of the **Update Sun Direction** action, hold down the *Alt* key and then click in order to break the connector.

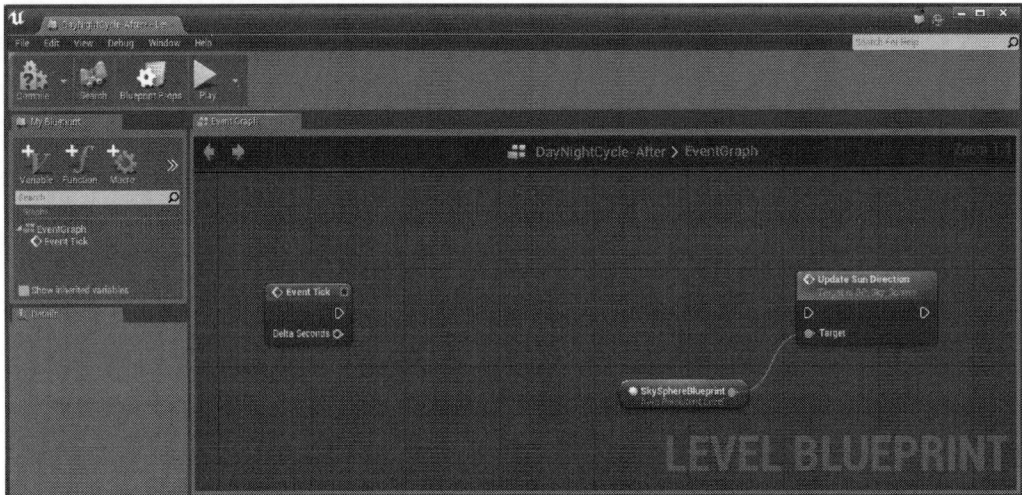

The current state of the Event Graph (note the broken connection)

2. From there, select the `DirectionalLightMoveable` actor from the **Scene Outliner** tab and then right-click on **Event Graph** and select **Add Actor Local Rotation** (searching for `Rotation` from the top search bar). Connect the **Event Tick** event's output arrow to the **Add Actor Local Rotation** node and then connect its output to the **Update Sun Direction** input. Finally, change the **P** (Pitch) value in the **Delta Rotation** property of the **Add Actor Local Rotation** action to `10`.

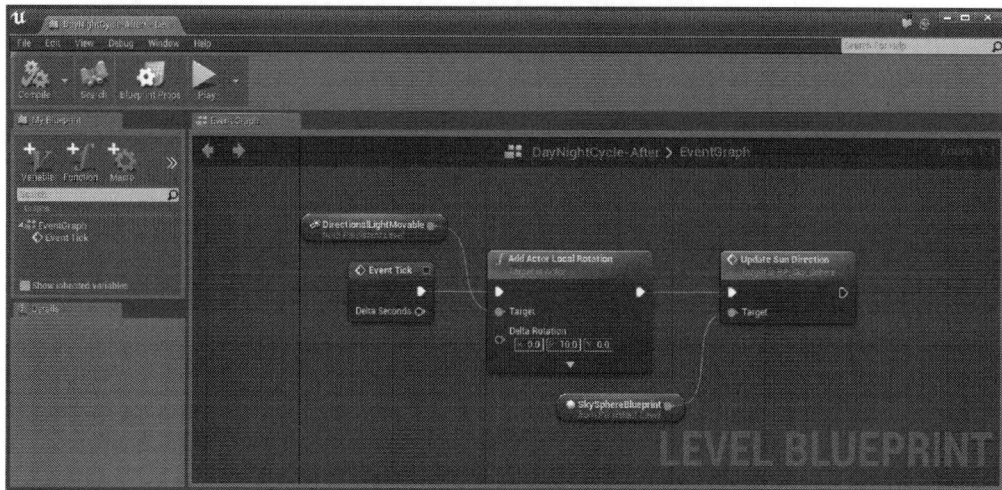

Working with DirectionalLightMoveable actor in the blueprint

The **Add Actor Local Rotation** node takes whatever value the **Target** object (directional light) has as its current Rotation and adds to it by the Delta Rotation vector. We do this before we update the sun's direction because we want the sun and the light to be at the same position (the sun would be a tad off, otherwise). The `10` value acts as the speed at which we want to move in that direction and can be modified to change the speed of our movement.

Now if we play the game, we'll notice that the sun is moving exactly as we wanted, but it is moving extremely fast! We could modify this value to fit whatever speed we'd like, but first, there's something that we need to note as we build even more complex actions—the Delta Seconds property that we talked about earlier.

The **Delta Seconds** value (commonly referred to as the Delta Time or dt in mathematics) is extremely important because in games, even though we often want things to run as quickly as possible (usually 60 times per second), the more complex or graphically intensive things get, the more time it takes the computer to do all of the calculations needed to update and render the completed frame. Using this value as a modifier makes sure that our events are dependent on time, not by frame, ensuring that the same things happen as time goes on. Since the value will also normally be *1/60* (or *~0.016*), being multiplied by 10 will give us a much smaller number, which is what we want.

This value is a **float**, or floating point number; this is a variable or container of information that we can store and use in various areas of code.

Taking that into account, let's use the **Delta Seconds** value in creating our **Delta Rotation**:

1. To the left of the **Delta Rotation** vector, right-click and create a **Make Rot** action (it makes a rotator from a **Pitch**, **Yaw**, and **Roll** value). Connect the **Return Value** from the **Make Rot** action to the **Delta Rotation** vector of the **Add Actor Local Rotation** action.

2. To the left of the **Make Rot** action, right-click and create a **Float * Float** action, which we will use to multiply two floating point numbers together (in coding, the operator for multiplication is *). Connect the **Delta Seconds** value from **Event Tick** into one of the two inputs and connect the output to **Yaw** of the **Make Rot** action. Finally, put in a value of 10 or whatever modifier you want into the other input.

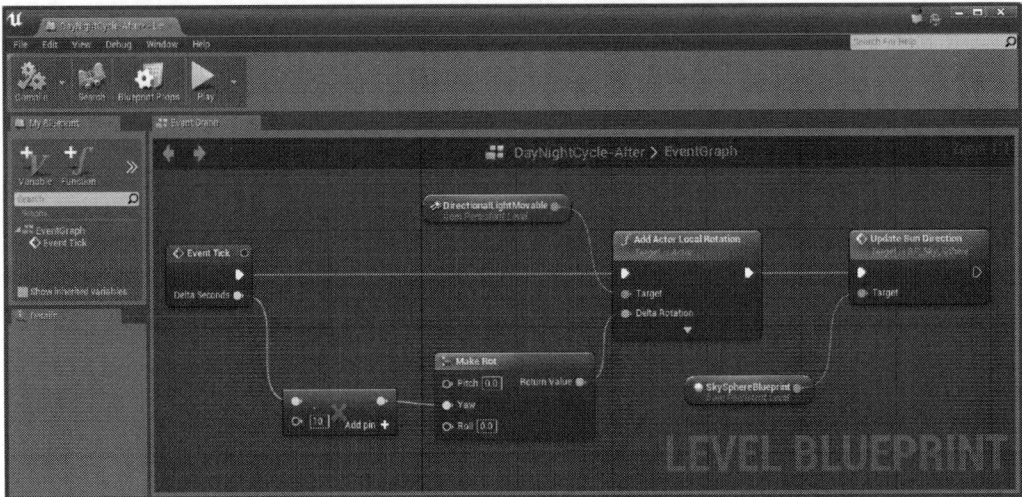

Using delta seconds within our rotation

3. At this point, click on the **Compile** button, exit the level blueprint, and run the game!

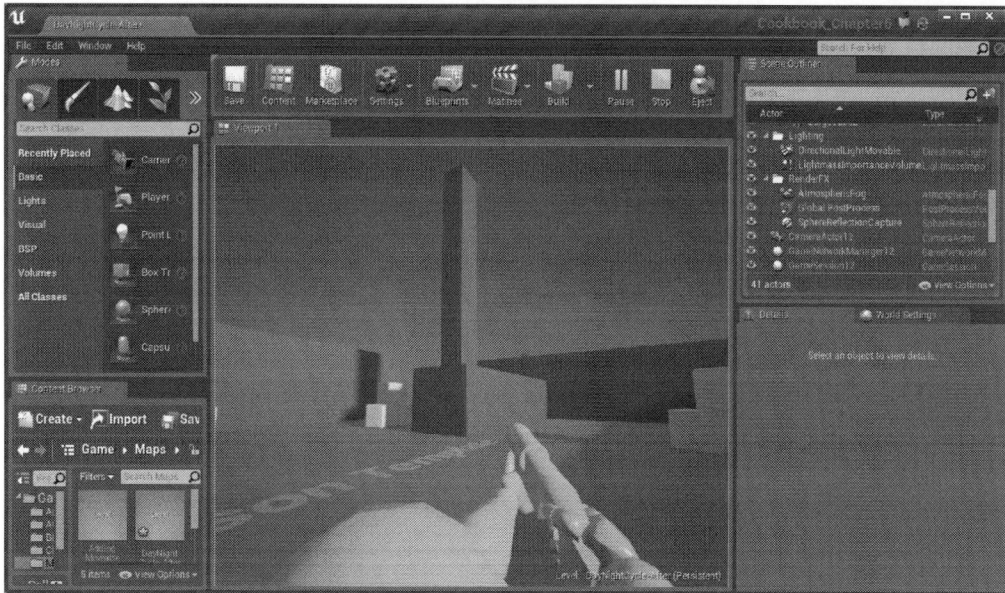

It works perfectly and we can modify this 10 value to make the value go faster (20 for 2x faster) or slower (1 for 10x slower), without having to worry about how complex the game is!

See also

We just touched the tip of the iceberg when it comes to working in lighting! After all, we can't condense what someone's full time job is to 20 pages. However, I do have some external resources that may be useful should you decide to do more with it:

► While creating lighting, for efficiency's sake, it's important to keep in mind what areas need to have the highest quality lighting and what can be reduced. To do that we make use of lightmass. For information on that, refer to `https://docs.unrealengine.com/latest/INT/Engine/Rendering/LightingAndShadows/Lightmass/Basics/index.html`.

- ▶ While it's not needed so much for games, there are a lot of people who want to have realistic lighting for their levels for things such as architectural demos. For more details on that, visit `https://docs.unrealengine.com/latest/INT/Resources/Showcases/RealisticRendering/index.html`.

  - ❑ For this, you can also download the maps shown from the Epic Games Launcher under the **Learn** tab if you select the **Realistic Rendering** option.

- ▶ In case you run into any problems with your lighting, a good guide to look into for troubleshooting can be found at `https://wiki.unrealengine.com/LightingTroubleshootingGuide`.

- ▶ You may also be interested in seeing the lighting of a map. 335Razor has a tutorial that recreates the lighting in one of the Unreal test maps at `https://www.youtube.com/watch?v=KmY7X9cBQZ0`.

7
Art Pipeline – Working with Materials

In this chapter, we'll cover the following recipes:

- Creating a custom material
- Creating a mirror material
- Using Textures and normal maps with Materials
- Creating glowing materials with static emissive lighting
- Seeing through walls

Introduction

Artists are incredibly empowered by working in the Unreal Engine with many features created to make their work come out as aesthetically pleasing as possible. In this chapter, we are going to look at some of the ways that you can work within the art pipeline of Unreal Engine 4, with some additional resources at the end of the chapter with even more content.

Creating a custom material

Materials are the building block of creating environments in Unreal and they are what we use to apply to all of the surfaces of our environment, similar to putting paint onto a wall in the real world.

Specifically, it is a collection of textures and commands that will create a surface with properties such as shininess and color. We've used materials previously when we added them to walls when creating levels, but we've only been using the `Starter Content` folder that has been provided to us.

However, you may want to create a material of your very own. Let's look into that now.

Getting ready

Before we start working within the Unreal Editor, we will need to have a project to work with:

1. First, open up the Unreal Editor by clicking on the **Launch** button from the Unreal Engine Launcher.

2. Start a new project from the **Project Browser** tab by selecting the **New Project** tab. Select **First person** and make sure that **With Starter Content** is selected. Give the project a Name (`Cookbook_Chapter7`). Once you are finished, click on **Create Project**.

3. You should see a level similar to this:

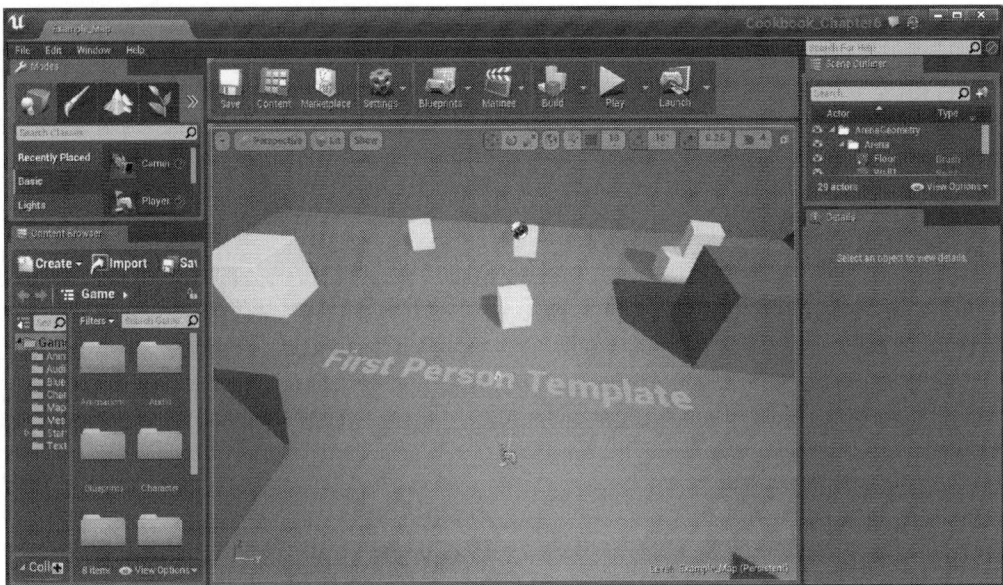

How to do it...

To start off with, we want to have an easy way to see what kind of material we are going to create. To do that, let's open a map that has a lot of examples for us to work with.

1. Go into the **Content Browser** tab and then the `StarterContent/Maps/StarterMap` file and double-click on it to open it. After loading, you should see a level similar to this:

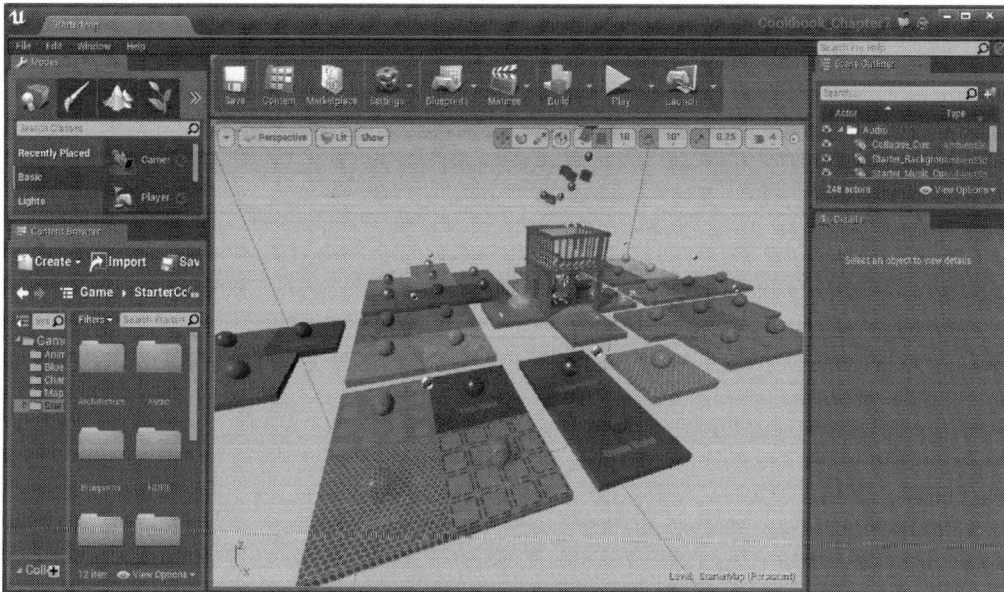

As you can see, all of the materials here are included currently in both a floor title and circle object. This can be quite useful as you may want to create materials that work in all kinds of situations.

2. Let's make a copy of a base here for viewing our own material that we will create. Select the set of items with no material (the checkerboard pattern), hold down the *Alt* key, and drag it forward so that we have a new place to put our objects.

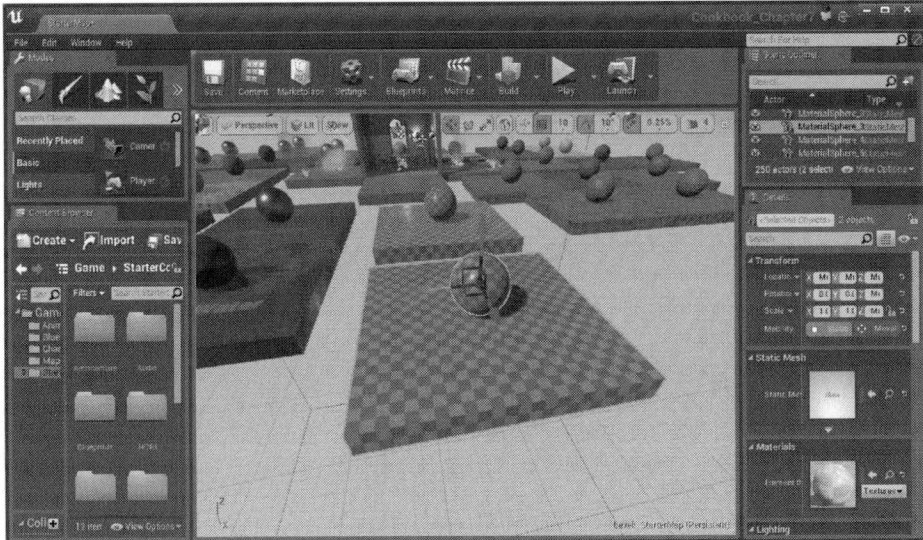

Creating our duplicated base

3. Now I want to differentiate my own content from the Starter Content folder, so from the Game folder in the **Content Browser** tab, right-click and select to create **New Folder** and name it Materials.

4. Select the newly created folder and, from the area, right-click and go to **Create Basic Asset | Material**.

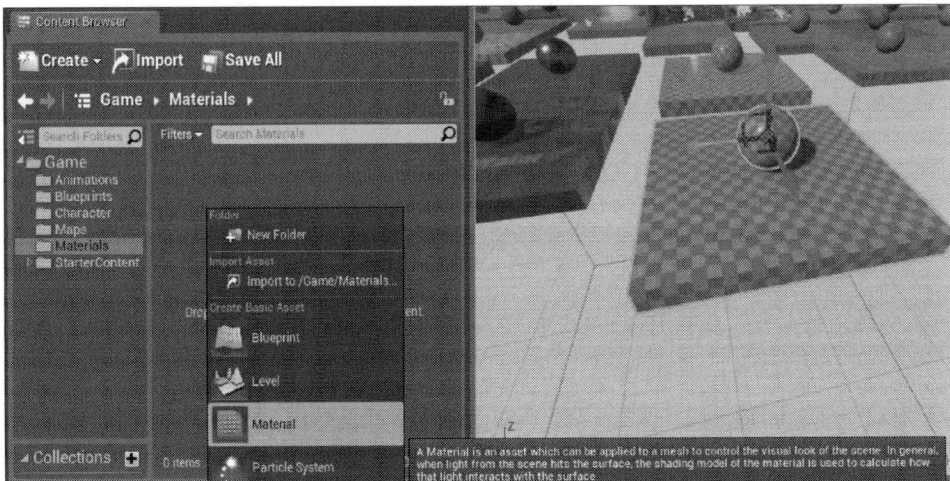

5.   After this, double-click on it to open up **Material Editor**.

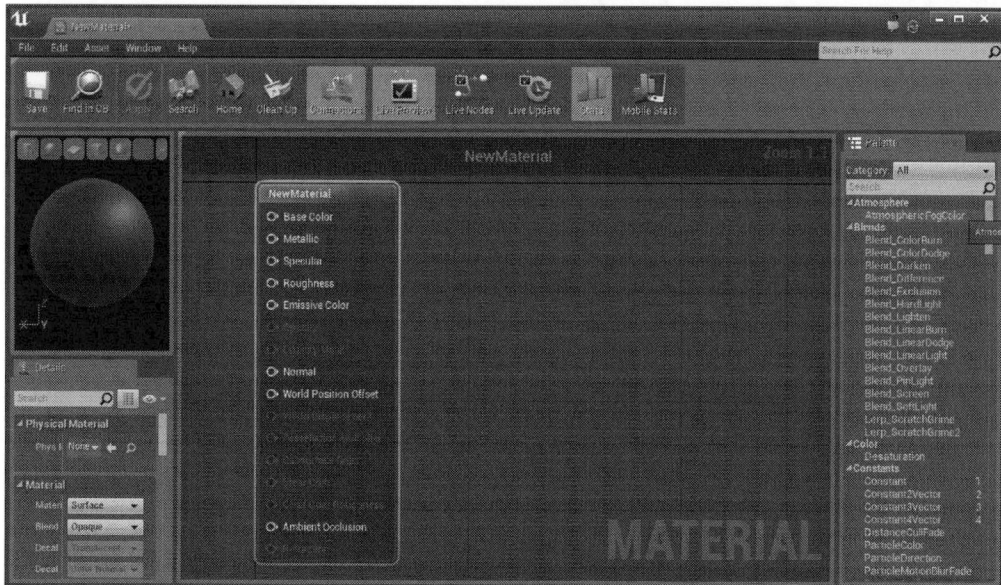

Now just like normal in Unreal, all of the editors have a lot of content in them, so let's break it down.

First, in the center is the actual information that will be used for creating our material, and the entire area is for different operators and variables to modify those properties, much like working in Blueprints. The base material node in the center is included with every material and has a series of inputs associated with a different aspect of the material.

The top-left is a preview window to allow you to see how the material you're creating looks similar to, and you can click on the buttons in the top-right to change the shape used for the preview to help you, depending on what the material will go on. You can use the mouse to move around, just like working with the editor, and you can also toggle the grid as well.

The bottom-left features the **Details** tab or properties for our element. We will use this in order to modify the various properties that each node will have.

To the right, you'll see **Palette** panel, which lists all of the possible nodes you can use to modify your material. However, you can also access this menu by right-clicking inside any empty gray area in the center and typing in the name of the item if you know what it is.

> For more information on the Material Editor UI check out
> https://docs.unrealengine.com/latest/INT/Engine/
> Rendering/Materials/Editor/Interface/index.html

Now that we know what everything is, let's start to modify this material, starting with modifying the color:

1. First, you'll notice **Base Color**, which is similar to a diffuse map in 3D modeling programs. It basically is the color that will be displayed. We can either give it a texture to use, or we can use `Constant3Vector`, which is, to say, a number with three elements to assign the amount of red, green, and blue values that an item has. To do this, right-click in the empty space to the left of the **Base Color** to bring up the object list and type in `Constant3Vector` and then select this new object.

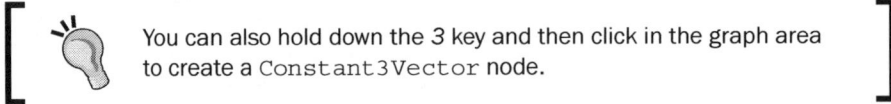

> You can also hold down the 3 key and then click in the graph area to create a `Constant3Vector` node.

2. After this, from the **Details** tab, click on the box in front of the **Constant** section and change the color to something you'd like, making sure to bring up the black bar so that you can actually see something other than black.

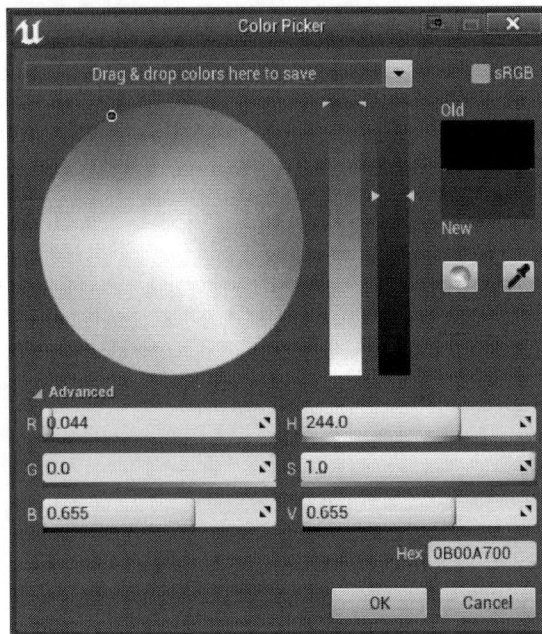

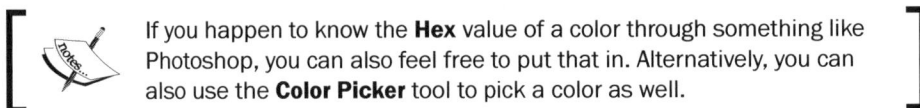

> If you happen to know the **Hex** value of a color through something like Photoshop, you can also feel free to put that in. Alternatively, you can also use the **Color Picker** tool to pick a color as well.

3. When you're done setting the color, press the **OK** button. After this, connect the output pin from the `ConstantVector3` color into the **Base Color** value.

Setting the color

4. Now click on the **Apply** button on the top toolbar to commit those changes into the editor. Then click on **Save** and move back into the editor. From there, drag and drop the new material we have created onto both the objects.

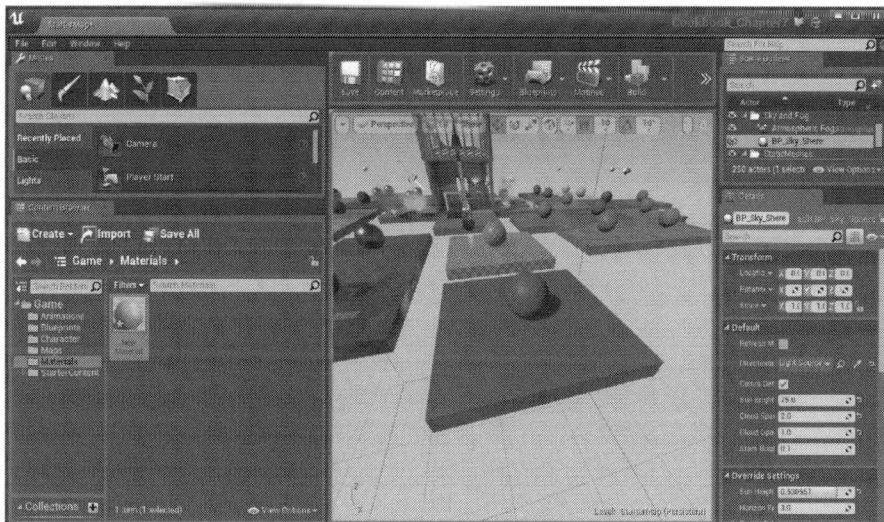

Applying the colored material to our base

And with this, we've created a very simple colored material!

Creating a mirror material

Now that we've created one of the simplest materials, let's get a little more complex by creating a mirror material while learning about some of the other properties the Material Editor has in the process!

Getting ready

Before we start working within the Unreal Editor, we will need to have a project to work with:

1. First, open up the Unreal Editor by clicking on the **Launch** button from the Unreal Engine Launcher.

2. Start a new project from the **Project Browser** window by selecting the **New Project** tab. Select **First person** and make sure that **With Starter Content** is selected and give the project a Name (Cookbook_Chapter7). Once you are done, click on **Create Project**.

3. You should see a level similar to this:

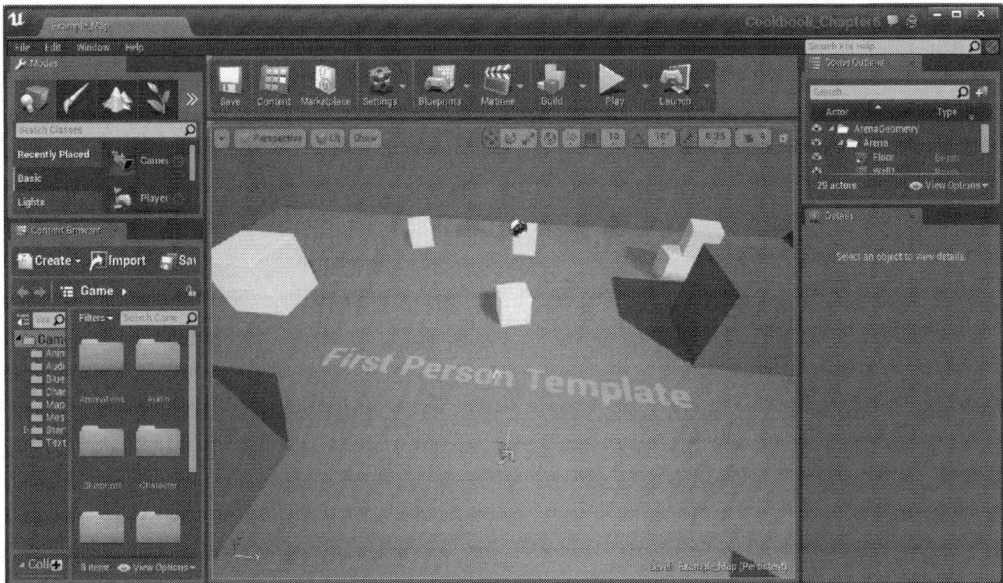

How to do it...

To start creating a mirror material, we will perform similar steps to what we've done before:

1. Go in and create another material in the **Content Browser** tab by going into the `Materials` folder and right-clicking and selecting **Material**.

2. Rename the material to `Mirror Material` and double-click on it to enter into Material Editor.

3. Just like before, we want to give a color to our mirror. To do this, right-click to the left of the **Base Color** value and create `Constant3Vector` and give it a value of `1,1,1` (also known as white).

4. Next, we will want to modify the **Metallic** property, which will modify our material to be more metallic and shiny. Create a **constant** value by right-clicking and searching for **Constant** and set the value to 1.

> Alternatively, you can also press and hold the *1* key and then click on the material graph to create a single scalar constant value.

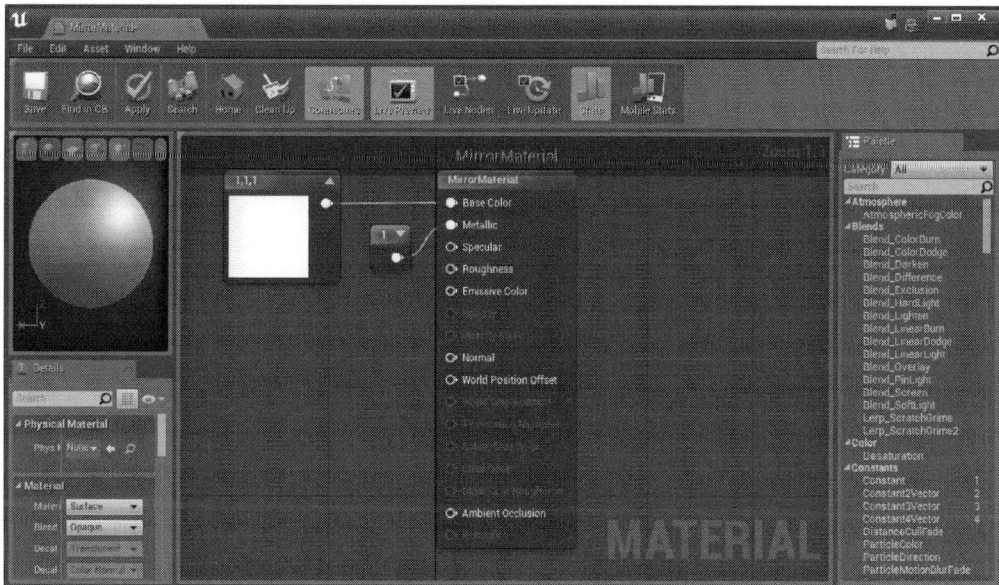

Notice how it makes the item much more shiny just as metals are in real life. When we set this value to 1, it means that it is a full metal object; we use 0 for non-metal objects and increase the number for more metallic things.

> For more information on the Metallic property, visit
> `https://docs.unrealengine.com/latest/INT/Resources/`
> `ContentExamples/MaterialNodes/1_2/index.html`.

5. Next, we will modify **Roughness**; this will modify the material in such a way that it will look more rugged or shiny depending on what we set it to, and it just so happens that when things are shiny, they are reflective, so we will set **Roughness** to 0.

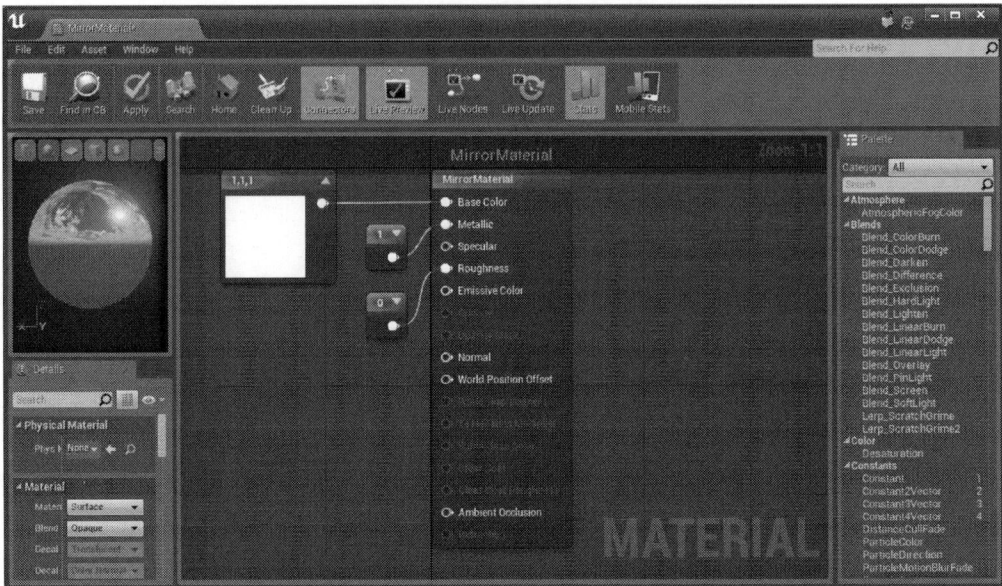

From here, you get to see a skybox being reflected in the background that is representative of what you'd see if you applied this material; everything around it will be reflective like a mirror. The higher the value is for roughness, the less reflective it will become.

> For more information on the Roughness property, visit
> `https://docs.unrealengine.com/latest/INT/Resources/`
> `ContentExamples/MaterialNodes/1_4/index.html`.

6. With this, click on the **Apply** button and close the Editor.

7. Jump into the `Example_Map` level in the `Maps` folder and apply the newly created `Mirror Material` to some of the surfaces by dragging and dropping them onto the scene.

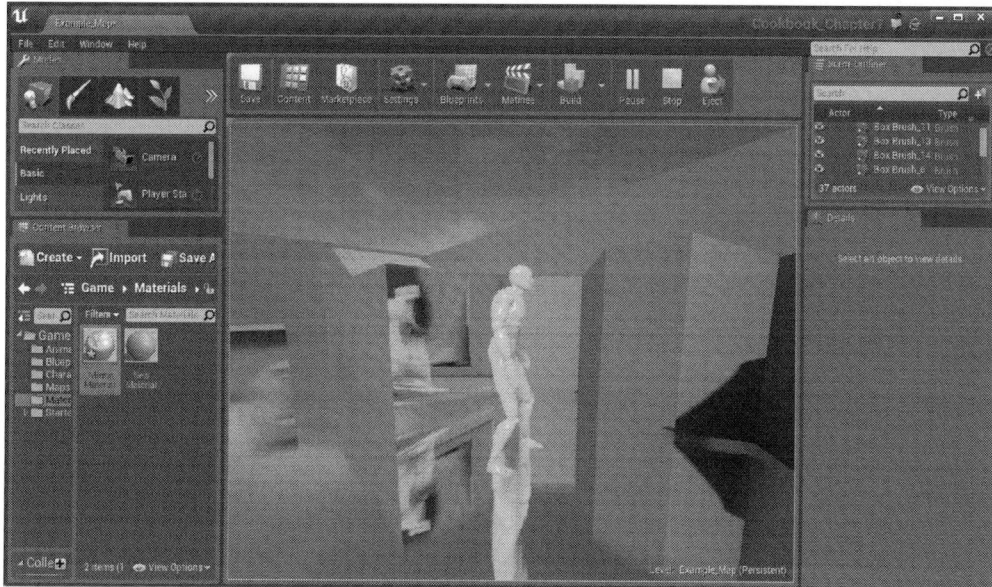

Applying the mirror effect

With this, we now have a new material that we can work with, with a really cool effect while also seeing how the **Roughness** and **Metallic** properties work!

Using Textures and normal maps with Materials

As time goes on, working with just colors isn't enough. You'll want to have more detailed materials that look more like things in the real world, such as wood, water, and walls. To do this, artists will often provide images that we can use for color data for the different parts of materials.

Getting ready

Before we start working within the Unreal Editor, we will need to have a project to work with:

1. First, open up the Unreal Editor by clicking on the **Launch** button from the Unreal Engine Launcher.

2. Start a new project from the **Project Browser** tab by selecting the **New Project** tab. Select **First person** and make sure that **With Starter Content** is selected. Give the project a Name (Cookbook_Chapter7). Once you are done, click on **Create Project**.

3. You should see a level similar to this:

How to do it...

Let's see how we can do this now:

1. The first thing we are going to do is add textures for us to work with. So, from the **Content Browser** tab, right-click on the Game folder and select to create **New Folder**. From there, set the name as Textures.

2. Inside the `Example Code` folder for this chapter, open the `Images` folder and drag and drop the images into this folder.

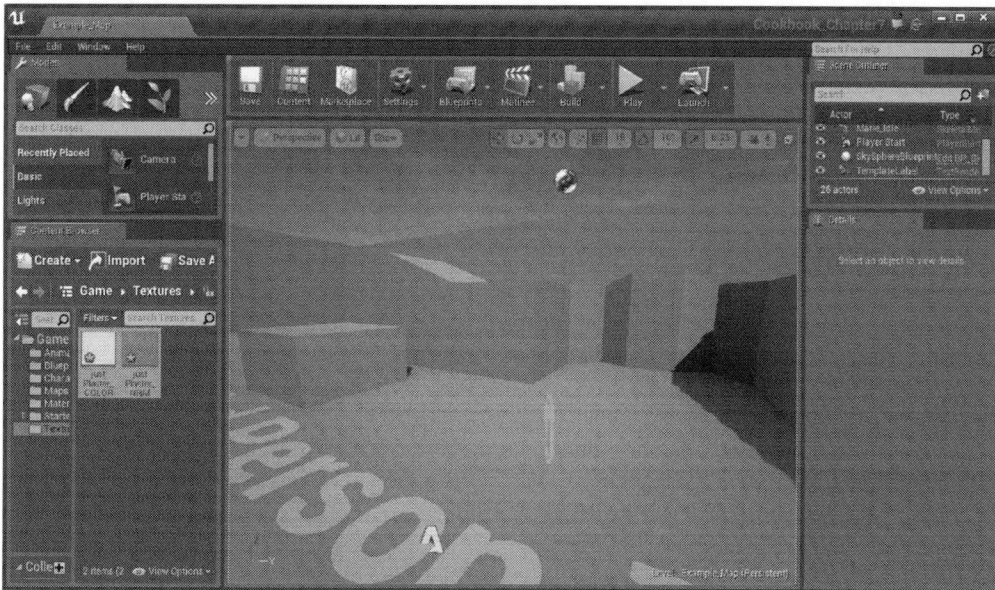

You may get a notification saying that `JustPlaster_NRM` file was imported as a normal map. This is important as we'll be using it later, but first, let's get this information into a material.

3. Go to our `Materials` folder and then right-click and create a new Material which we will call `PlasterWall`. Then double-click to open the Material Editor.

4. To add the texture's data as **Texture Sample**, we can simply drag and drop them into the editor and move them around so the blueish normal map is below the other texture.

Another way to place a texture sample is by selecting the texture maps in the **Content Browser** tab and then in the material editor, pressing and holding the *T* key, and clicking on the **Material Editor** graph to create the texture sample node with a specific texture from the **Content Browser** tab.

5. Next, connect the color material's top white pin into **Base Color**.

You'll notice that it gives us more variation than just a simple color.

6. Next, we set the white pin of the bluish normal texture to **Normal** of the material.

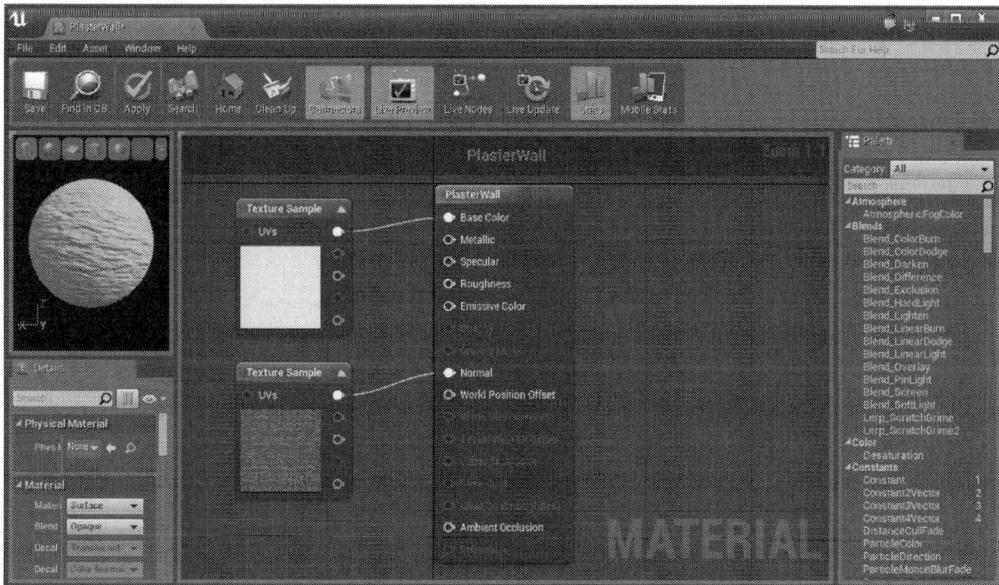

You'll notice immediately that **Normal** has a big effect on how the material works. A normal map is used to give the illusion of lumps and bumps on a surface by simulating the pixels being at different areas.

This effect may be larger than what we are looking for and from the normal map's information, it seems like the green aspect of the map is making it look a lot more pronounced than it should be. A Normal is a vector which points in a particular direction to give each pixel an *angle* that the object is. That angle is defined by assigning the **X**, **Y**, and **Z** direction of the surface normal to the **R** (Red), **G** (Green), and **B** (Blue) channels of the texture, respectively. Thankfully, we can modify this using some additional operators.

[
For more information on normal maps, visit
`http://wiki.polycount.com/wiki/Normal_map`.
]

1. Move the normal map's texture sample over to the left to make room for another node. Next, add a **Multiply** action by right clicking and searching for **Multiply**.

2. Then, below the normal map, right-click and create a `Constant3Vector` and set its value to `0.1, 0.1, 1` in the **Details** tab.

3. Disconnect the normal from the **Normal** section of the material by holding down the *Alt* key and then clicking on it. Then connect it to the **A** part of the Multiply node.

4. Next, connect the white pin from the `Constant3Vector` we created to the **B** slot.

5. Finally, connect the white pin of **Multiply** to the **Normal** section of our material. It should look similar to the following image:

We multiplied each of the channels of the texture sample by a number we provided in our purple-looking item. The green channel is set to `.1`, which means that we are removing the harshness we were seeing previously by removing 90% of what was there previously.

> Note that this is not the same as the dot product or cross product, which are totally different things (but are the two ways that you can *multiply* vectors with vectors which have special mathematical properties that are often used in collision), but are very useful for game development if you're a programmer.

6. After this, click on **Apply** and then exit back into the Editor and apply our material to some walls.

7. Save our newly created content and then click on **Play**!

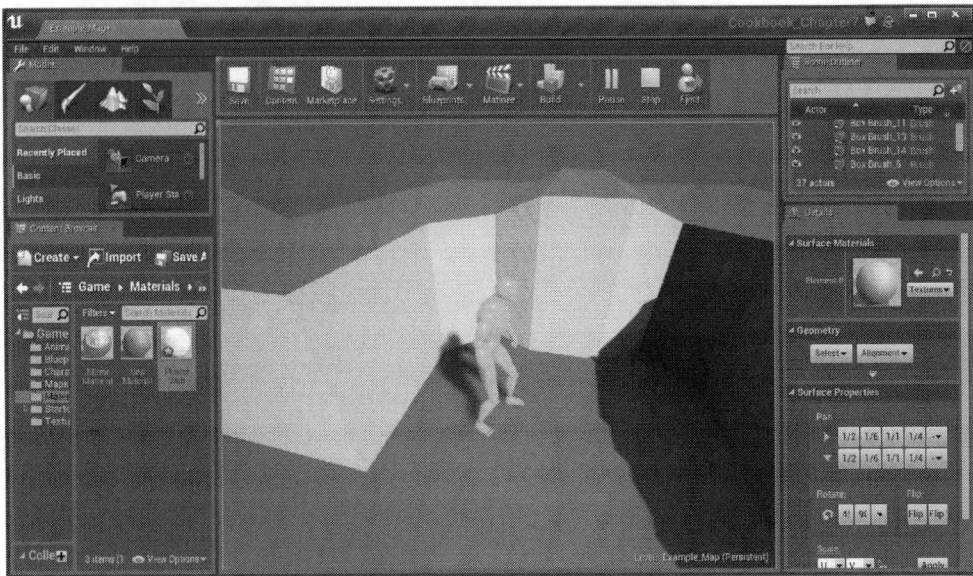

As you can see, there are now some differences between the areas of the walls, making it look much more realistic.

Creating glowing materials with static emissive lighting

If you've ever seen a movie such as *Tron: Legacy* or any game area with neon lights and the like, it may seem very computationally expensive to have that in our levels because of how they have a lot of lighting going on. We can add this efficiently to our materials by using the emissive property.

Getting ready

Before we start working within the Unreal Editor, we will need to have a project to work with:

1. First, open up the Unreal Editor by clicking on the **Launch** button from the Unreal Engine Launcher.

2. Start a new project from the **Project Browser** tab by selecting the **New Project** tab. Select **First person** and make sure that **With Starter Content** is selected. Give the project a Name (Cookbook_Chapter7). Once you are done, click on **Create Project**.

3. You should see a level similar to this:

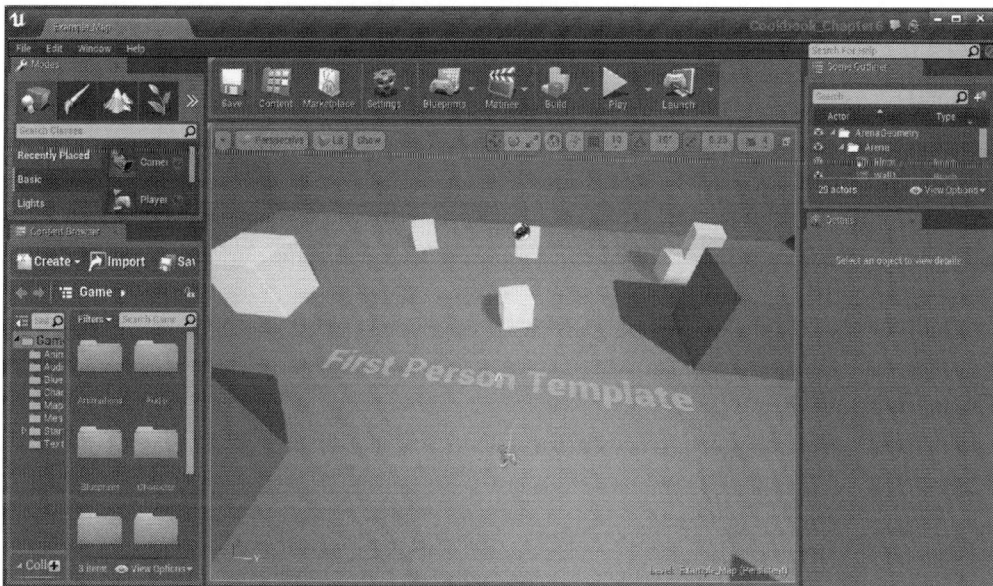

How to do it...

The first thing we are going to want to do is open up a level that is made for this kind of lighting.

1. Open up the `Empty Room` map created in the `Example Code` folder.

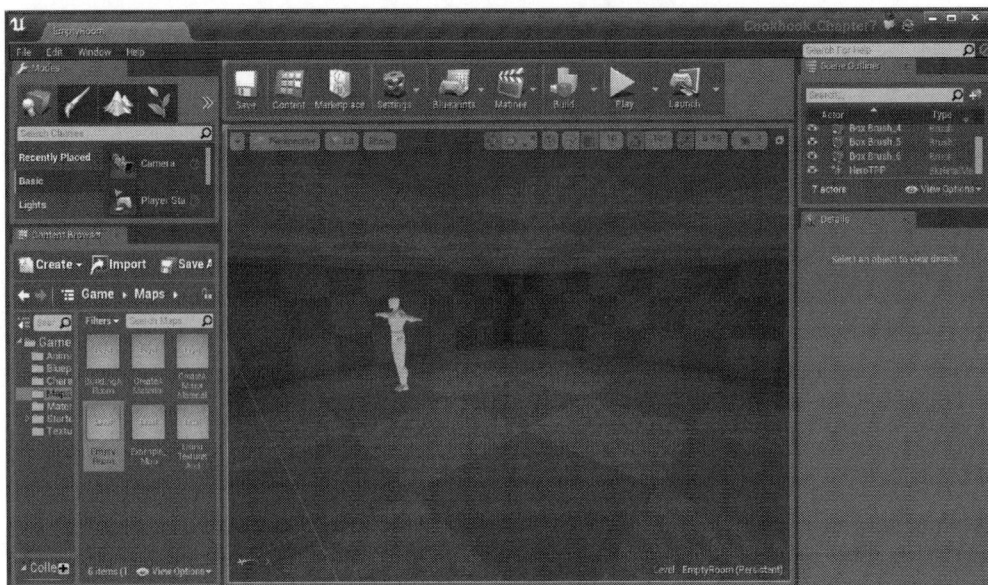

The Empty Room map

This map is the same as the map created in our previous *Building a room* recipe in *Chapter 2, Level Design – Building Out Levels or Greyboxing* aside from removing the directional and point light created in there. Needless to say, if lighting was built and you played the game, it would be in pitch blackness.

2. Let's create a new material which will glow for us. To do that, right click on the `Materials` folder and select to create a new material. Name it `GlowMaterial` and then double-click on it to access the Material Editor.

3. First, let's set **Shading Model** to **Unlit**. This will make it so that it will only output the emissive value for color, which is perfect for this particular application.

For more information on Shading Models, refer to `https://docs.` `unrealengine.com/latest/INT/Engine/Rendering/` `Materials/MaterialProperties/LightingModels/index.html.`

4. Next, let's create a color to represent the color we want to have glowing. To do this, right-click on the left-hand side of the **Emissive Color** section and select `Constant3Vector` and change the color to something you like.

5. After this, in order for **Emissive** to give us a bloom color, we need to make the value larger than 1. We can also modify the color itself using actions. Let's add in a **Multiply** action to the right of the color.

6. Connect the white pin of the color to the **A** value of the **Multiply(,10)** action. Then, connect the white pin at the end of the **Multiply(,10)** action to the **Emissive Color** input.

7. Next, select the Multiply action and rather than creating a new node for the **B** value, just go to the **Details** tab and put in a value in the **Const B** value, such as `10`. If all goes well, you should see a nice glow appear, as shown here:

Creating a glowing material

8. Click on **Apply** to have this applied to our players. Now, set the material to our character in the screen and after a few seconds, it will appear to have a nice glow effect.

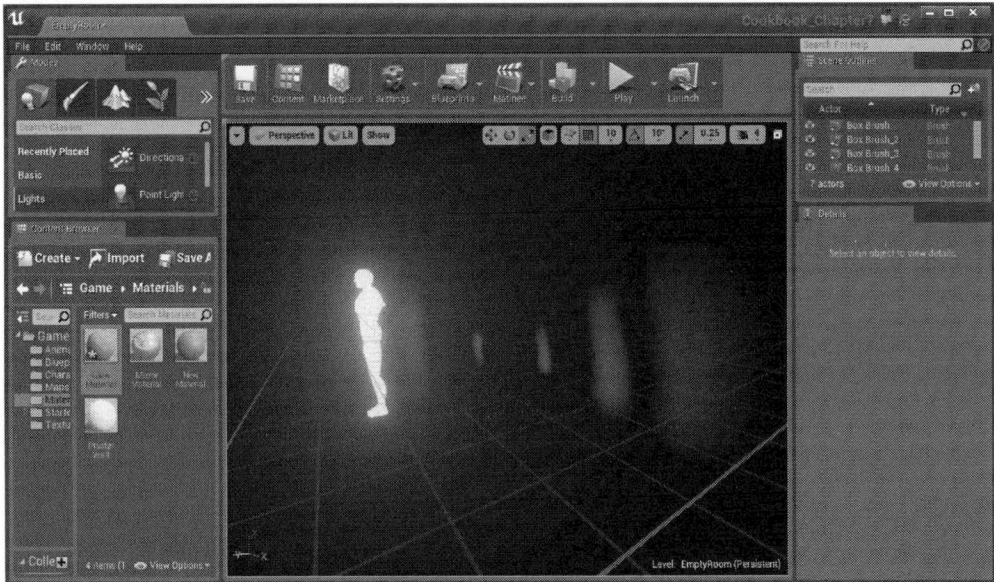

9. Finally, let's play the game and see it in action.

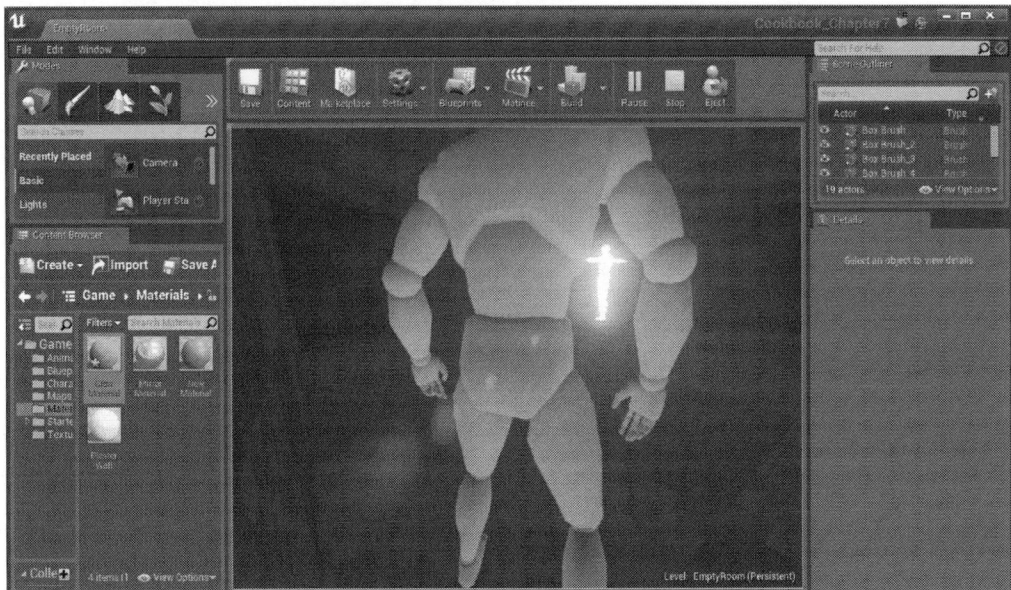

It's important to note that this does not actually cast a light into the scene, but merely provides a glowing effect.

There are some in-progress tools that use a light propagation volume to add lighting. You can check these at `https:// forums.unrealengine.com/showthread.php?6914- Light-Propagation-Volume-now-works-with- Emissive-Material`.

For more information on the **Emissive** property, refer to `https://docs.unrealengine.com/latest/INT/ Resources/ContentExamples/MaterialNodes/1_5/ index.html`.

Seeing through walls

A neat feature of many titles is being able to see enemies or important objects through walls, similar to the detective mode in *Batman: Arkham Knight*, the thermal vision in *Splinter Cell*, or the outlines in *Evolve* and other games. Let's implement similar functionality now.

Getting ready

Before we start working within the Unreal Editor we will need to have a project to work with:

1. First, open up the Unreal Editor by clicking on the **Launch** button from the Unreal Engine Launcher.

2. Start a new project from the **Project Browser** tab by selecting the **New Project** tab. Select **First person** and make sure that **With Starter Content** is selected. Give the project a Name (`Cookbook_Chapter7`). Once you are done, click on **Create Project**.

3. You should see a level similar to this:

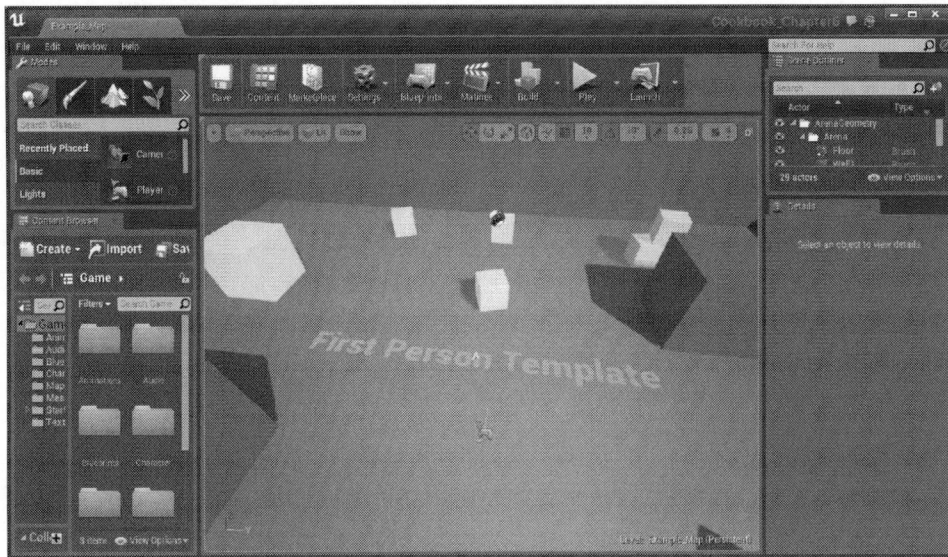

How to do it...

In order to see other objects, let's first add an object that we'd like to see into the level:

1. Open up the `Example_Map` file and from the **Content Browser** tab, go into the `Character` folder and drag a `HeroTPP` skeletal mesh into the level. This will be our enemy that we will want to see no matter where they will be.

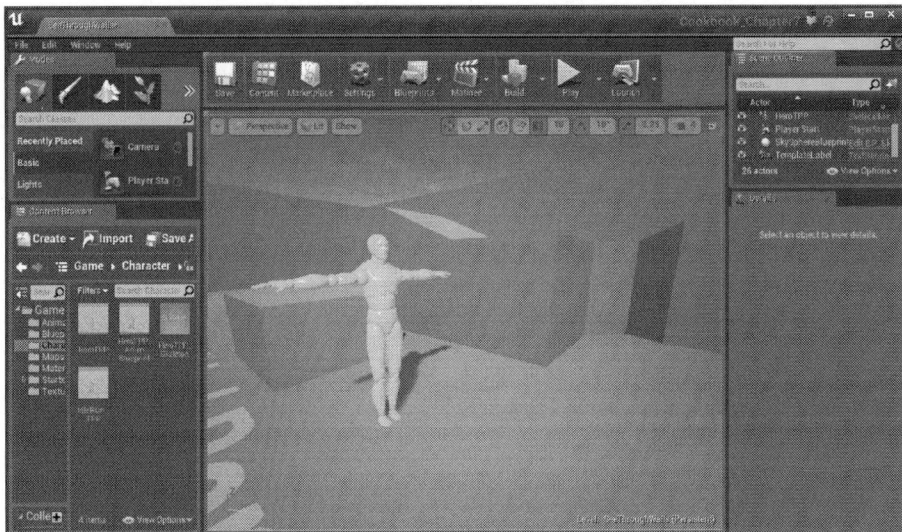

Adding the enemy

2. Let's now create a new material that we can work with and give it a name (SeeThruMaterial). Once it's created, open up the Material Editor.

3. First, create Constant3Vector with a color of your choice and assign it to the **Emissive Color** property.

4. After this, deselect it so that nothing is selected and go to the **Details** tab. From here, change the **Blend Mode** to **Translucent**.

   This blending mode is used for objects that require some form of translucency and is applied onto areas in front of it, but this mode also has another feature that is perfect for what we want to do. We will look into it next.

> For more information on how to use Transparency effectively, refer to https://docs.unrealengine.com/latest/INT/Engine/Rendering/Materials/HowTo/Transparency/index.html.

5. Go into the **Translucency** section and toggle the **Disable Depth Bias** property to be enabled. This will say that we should draw this on the top of the screen even if we're behind something else.

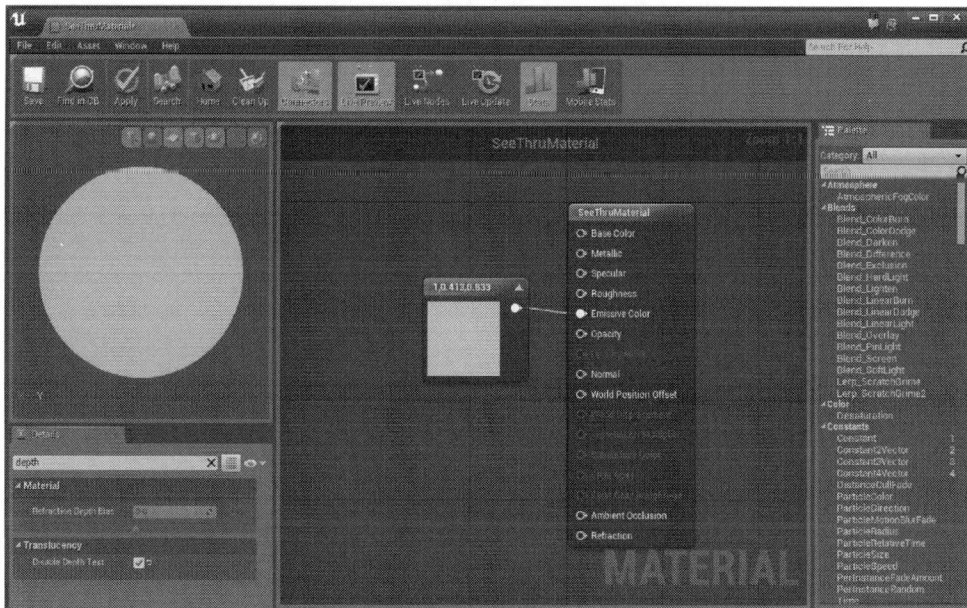

Setting the translucence value

6. Once you're done, hit the **Apply** button and then close the editor. Then, apply the newly created material to the enemy and move around the camera to see the effect that we generated!

Applying translucence to the enemy

7. To see it in action in the game, go to the toolbar and hit the **Play** button to start the project!

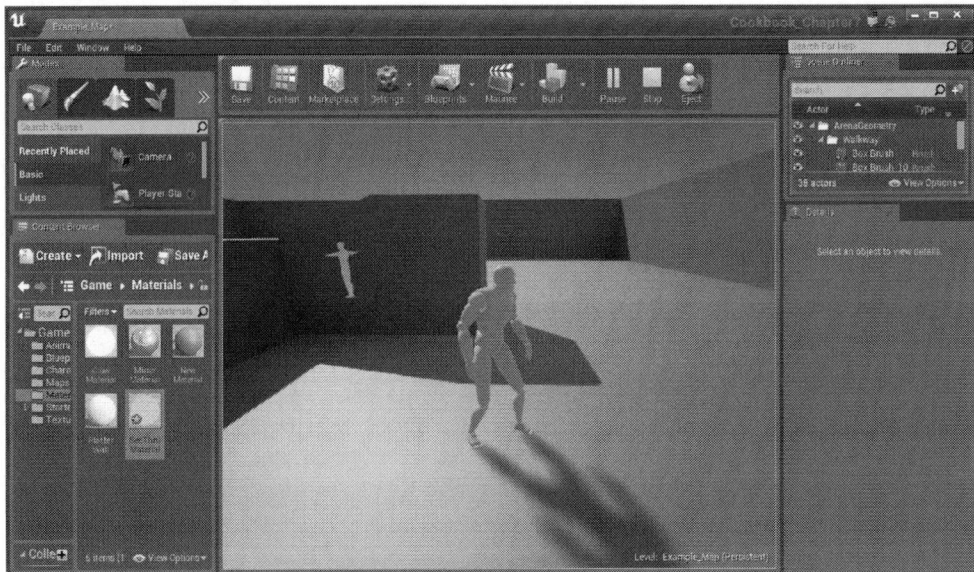

With this, we can see the object no matter what! Later on, you can use this recipe with the knowledge of blueprints to toggle the effect.

> Tom Looman also came up with another implementation using the Render Custom Depth flag that looks similar to the game *Evolve* with outlines. It can be found at `http://www.tomlooman.com/ue4-evolves-outline-post-effect/`.

See also

Now, there is much more that exists in the Material editor, especially when you add more complex interactions and/or apply them to meshes to create some interesting effects. Here are some additional tutorials that may be useful to you going further:

- Much like working with brushes, you can also modify the UVs of the materials. Learn how to do this at `https://www.youtube.com/watch?v=YcoHWSxFEko`.

- You can use a process called instancing using parameters to change the material as the game continues. There's a good tutorial on this at `https://www.youtube.com/watch?v=NX-NNyGV3oQ`.

- Sjoerd De Jong (also known as Hourences) also has some amazing resources for you to look at, with an Example Project of his with materials and meshes that you can take apart, some videos of the project. I originally started learning Unreal Engine 3 8 years ago from his tutorials, and I'm really glad to hear that he's still creating awesome stuff. Check it out at `http://www.hourences.com/thesolusproject/`.

- While this book is focused on using Unreal Engine 4, it may be useful to see a brief tutorial talking about building a level from scratch using a 3D modeling program and bringing it into the engine. A fairly good example tutorial series by The 3D Tutor on the subject can be found at `https://www.youtube.com/watch?v=eJ0zu6GIqxQ&list=PLK3nRt7ToxJ0kxAocxw1KvpM1tF3X5JB2`.

- Once you feel comfortable creating levels, you may also want to build out a character with animations. An introduction to UE4's animation tools can be found at `https://www.youtube.com/watch?v=knbZ_g8Hgvk&list=PLZlv_N0_01gb2ZoKzTApbv3LvhaXJ9elg`.

8
Blueprint Scripting – Level Effects

In this chapter, we'll cover the following recipes:

- ▶ Building a flickering light
- ▶ Converting from Level to Class Blueprints
- ▶ Using Trigger Volumes – opening a door using Matinee
- ▶ Adding to an existing Blueprint – flashlight, part 2
- ▶ Creating a Health/Damage system, part 1 – taking damage

Introduction

Introduced in Unreal Engine 4, **Blueprints** is a visual scripting language that is built into the engine. By using visual scripting, instead of writing code from scratch inside Visual Studio or some other IDE (which we will cover in the next chapter), we can use predefined actions and connect them together, similar to drawing a graph. This is often a great starting point for artists and game designers as it is much more visually oriented and easier to grasp than just plain code.

There are two types of blueprints you can create:

- ▶ **Level Blueprint**: This works similarly to how UE3's Kismet system worked as events and actions that will occur in just this particular level. This is good for things such as triggering enemies to spawn or moving platforms.
- ▶ **Class Blueprints**: Introduced in UE4, this can be put into any level. They just work using their predefined behavior that we create beforehand, similar to prefabs in Unity.

It may take some time to get used to it, but we will dive into some simple systems first.

Building a flickering light

For our first Blueprint, let's make use of the Level Blueprint system to create a simple action of a flickering light. Often a staple of horror games, lights that flicker can cause fear in players of not being able to see certain things for a random period of time.

Getting ready

Before we start working within the Unreal Editor, we will need to have a project to work with:

1. Open up the Unreal Editor by clicking on the **Launch** button from the Unreal Engine Launcher.

2. Start a new project from the **Project Browser** tab by selecting the **New Project** tab. Select **First person** and make sure that **With Starter Content** is selected and give the project a Name (Cookbook_Chapter8). Once you are finished, click on **Create Project**.

3. After the project is opened, go to the Example Code folder, drag and drop the **NightScene** map provided into your project folder and open it:

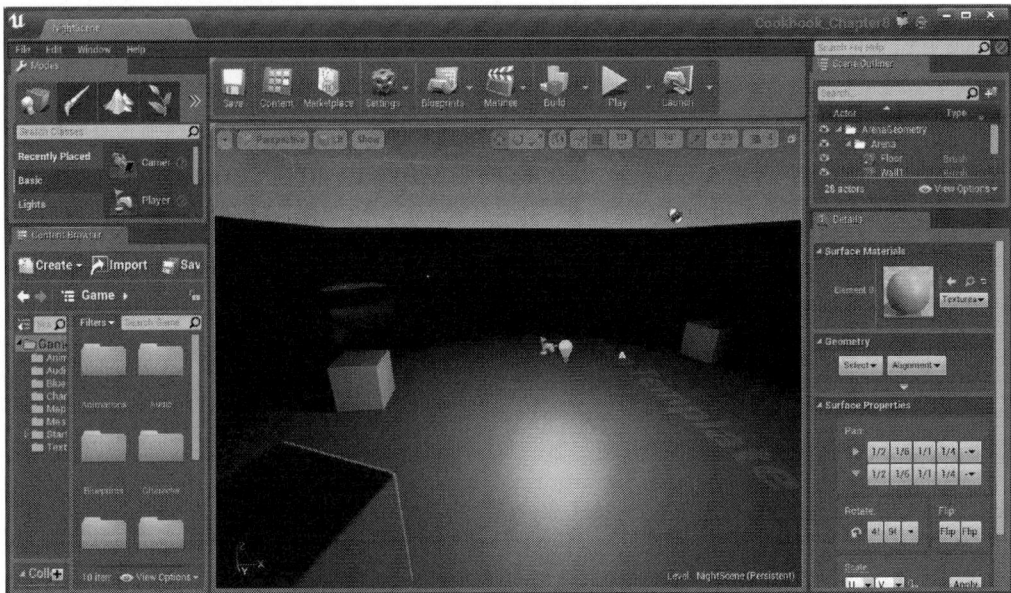

How to do it...

In the middle of the map, you'll notice that there is a light. We're going to make this randomly start to flicker for a time:

1. For a light to change and work correctly with lighting, the first thing we will need to do is change its **Mobility** to **Movable** on the far right. While this may imply the object will move, this is also a way of saying we want the ability to make properties (such as the Light's Intensity) modifiable while the game is running.

2. After this, move down and under **Light**, notice the value of the **Intensity** property. Note that when modified, it makes the light brighter or darker.

3. Click on **PointLight** to select it and then from the top panel, go to **Blueprints | Open Level Blueprint**.

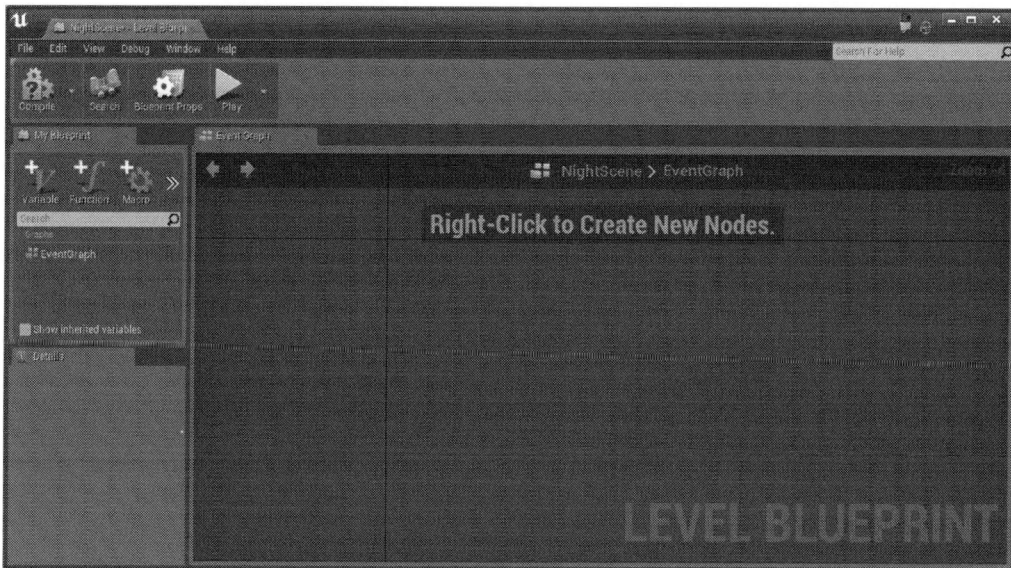

This panel consists of a number of parts that will look familiar to those who have worked with UE3's Kismet system. The **EventGraph** on the right-hand side will contain the **events** and **functions** (which I'll sometimes also refer to as **actions**), which are called inside the game. Think of this in terms of when something happens (the events), we will do something (the functions).

4. From here, when we right-click within the main graph area in the center of the **Event Graph** tab, we will see a context menu pop up. In the search bar, search for `Begin Play` and select the **Event Begin Play** event. This event occurs whenever the game starts, so as soon as the player is spawned, whatever functions are called from it, will happen.

Adding the Event Begin Play event to the level blueprint

5. Next, we want to modify the light. To do this, we will right-click and select **Create a Reference to PointLight**.

This will create a variable that is a reference to the object in the scene. We can use this variable in the function's parameters.

6. Click and drag the blue wire from the right-side of the point light and drag out to place a new node. The menu that pops up will only show the actions, which can use the point light. From here, type in `Intensity` and select the **Set Intensity (Light Component)** function.

7. After this, connect the output (white arrow on the right-hand side) of the **Event Begin Play** node to the input of the **Set Intensity** function.

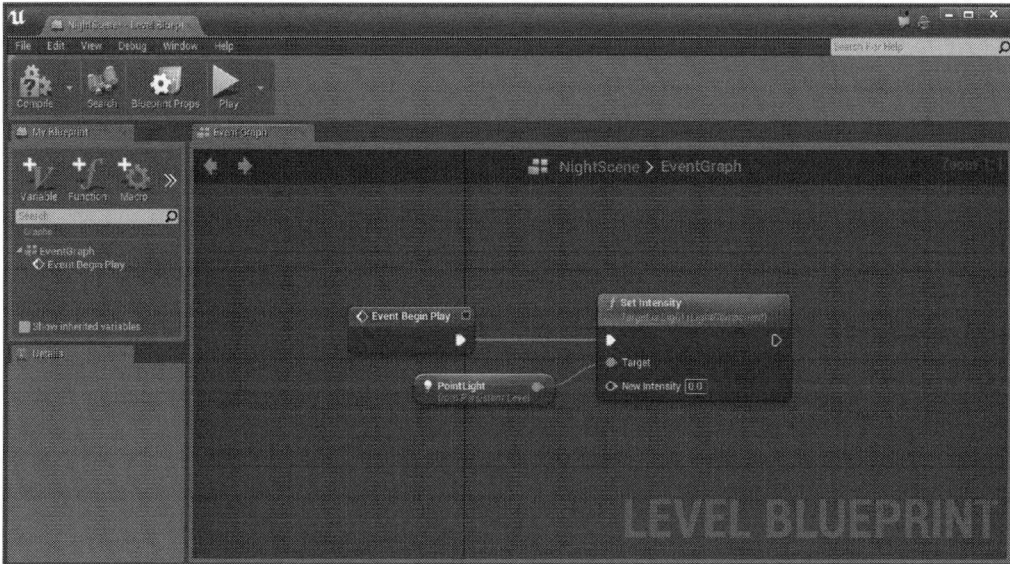

Connecting the output of the Event Begin Play node to the input of the Set Intensity function

You'll notice that the function (note the fancy **f** icon on the left-hand side) has two properties, the **Target** and the New Intensity. This will change the **PointLight** (**Target**) to whatever the value on **New Intensity** is.

8. Click on the **Compile** button to commit our changes and then, back in the editor, hit the **Play** button.

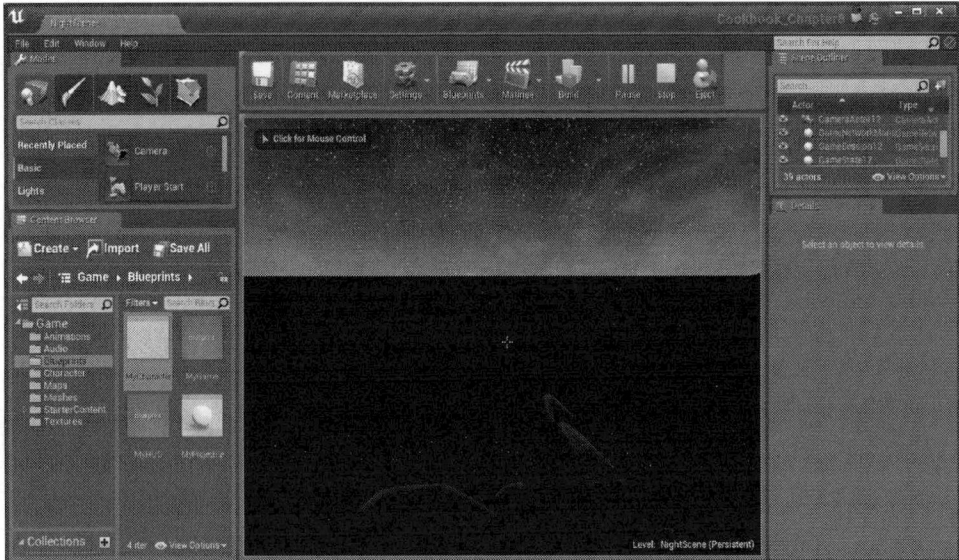

Starting the game after compiling

You'll notice that now the world is pitch black. This is because the value of **Set Intensity** is now set to 0. If you have the **Level Blueprint** window open and then hit the **Play** button again, you'll actually see the action being executed:

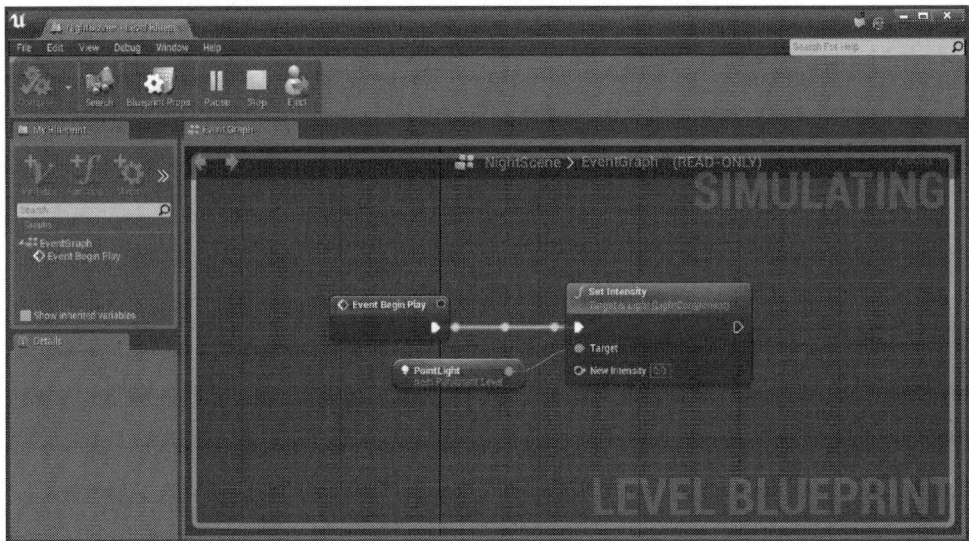

Execution in the level blueprint

9. Of course, we don't want it to be set to **0**. We want it to flicker with random values, so let's create a new variable to be our new intensity. Drag out from the **New Intensity** arrow toward the left, and you'll see a number of different functions that return a float value. In the search bar, look for Random and from the list, select **Random Float in Range**. Under **Max**, put in **2000**.

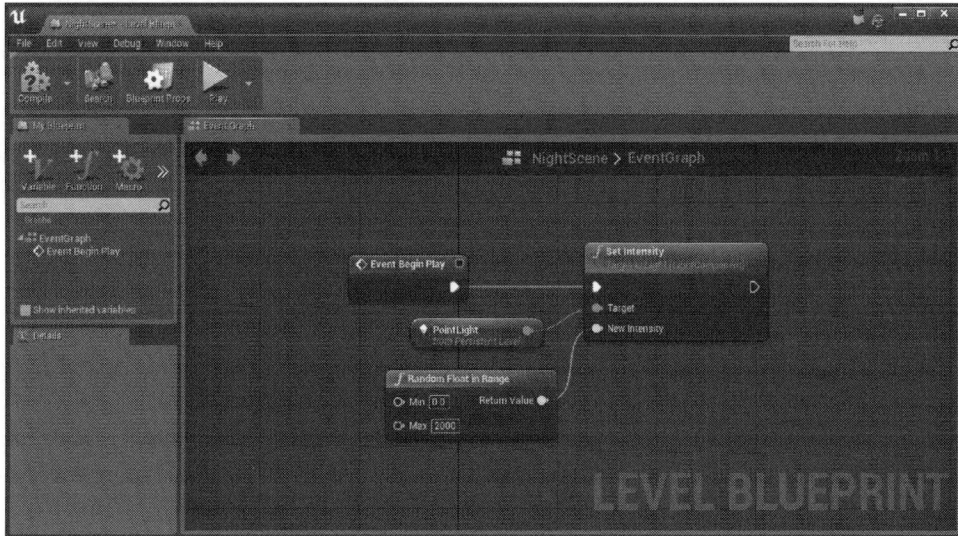

Setting a random intensity in the level blueprint

> To move around the **Level Blueprint's Event Graph** window, right-click and hold, then drag. To zoom in and out, use the mouse wheel. To drag individual elements around left-click and drag them. For more hotkeys and information on moving around Blueprints, refer to https://docs.unrealengine.com/latest/INT/Engine/Blueprints/UserGuide/CheatSheet/index.html.

Now if you were to play the game, you should notice that the light has a different brightness every time we play it. However, if we want the light to flicker, we should change the intensity value a lot of times as long as the game is running.

10. To the right of the **Set Intensity** function, right-click and create a **Delay** function node. Then, connect the exec output of **Set Intensity** to the input (left-hand side) of the **Delay** action. Then connect the **Completed** output to the input of the **Set Intensity** function.

> You can also hold the *D* key and then click to create a **Delay** function within the Blueprints Editor.

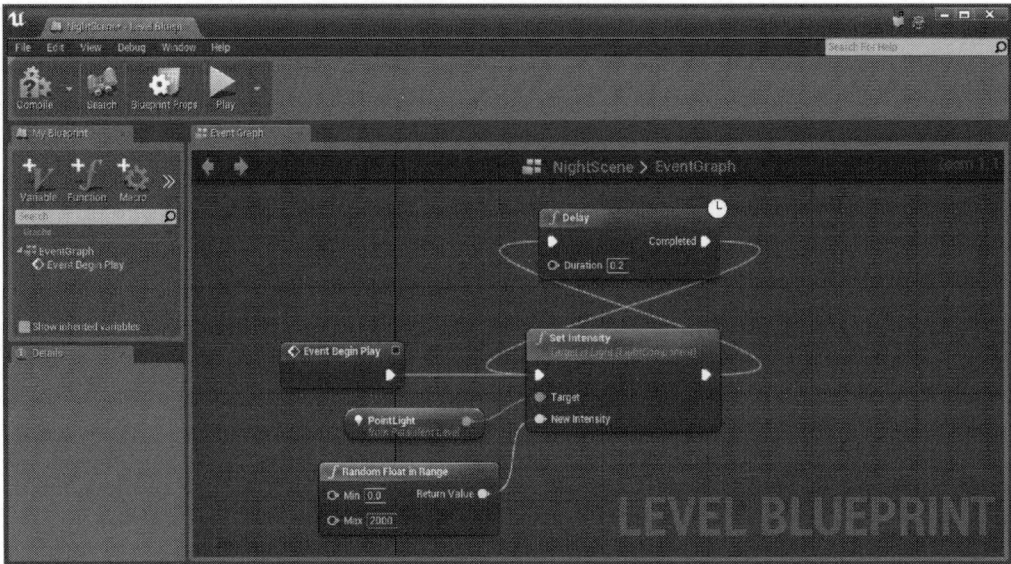

Creating a loop for the Set Intensity function to be called every 0.2 seconds

This is effectively creating a loop, causing the **Set Intensity** function to be called after every .2 seconds. If you hit the play button to see the actions executed, you'll notice that the actions are continuously happening, and in the game, you'll see that the values are indeed changing, but we notice that it will always change at a fixed rate which is predictable. A flickering light would be nicer to not be as static in terms of when the value changes so players are unsure as to when it will happen.

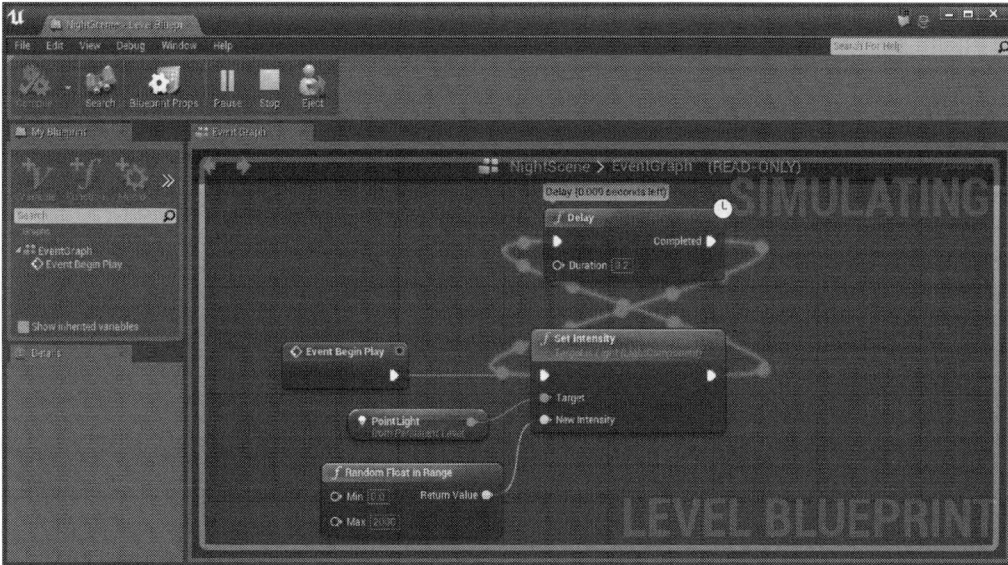

Executing the flickering effect

11. For the sake of readability, move the **Delay** action to the right of the **Set Intensity** function. Doing the same steps as before, create another **Random Float in Range** for the **Delay** action's **Duration** variable with a value between 0 and 0.2.

12. When working on scripting like this, it is also a good idea to comment your code. This will help people looking at your code (including your future self) to find things more easily.

13. To do this, do a marquee selection around the entire blueprint by clicking slightly on the top-left of the **Event Begin Play** action. Then, drag to the right and down until all of the actions are selected and right-click on one of the functions. From here, select **Create Comment from Selection**. Name the box that was created, `Flashing Light`, and press *Enter*.

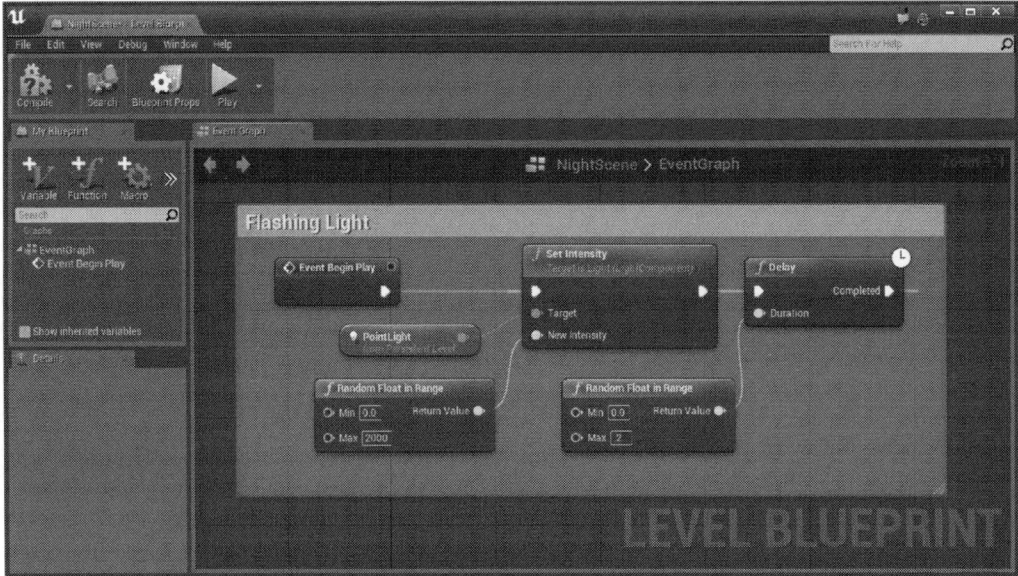

Adding comments to the script

> You can also press the *C* key to create a comment around whatever you have currently selected.

14. Save your level and hit the **Play** button!

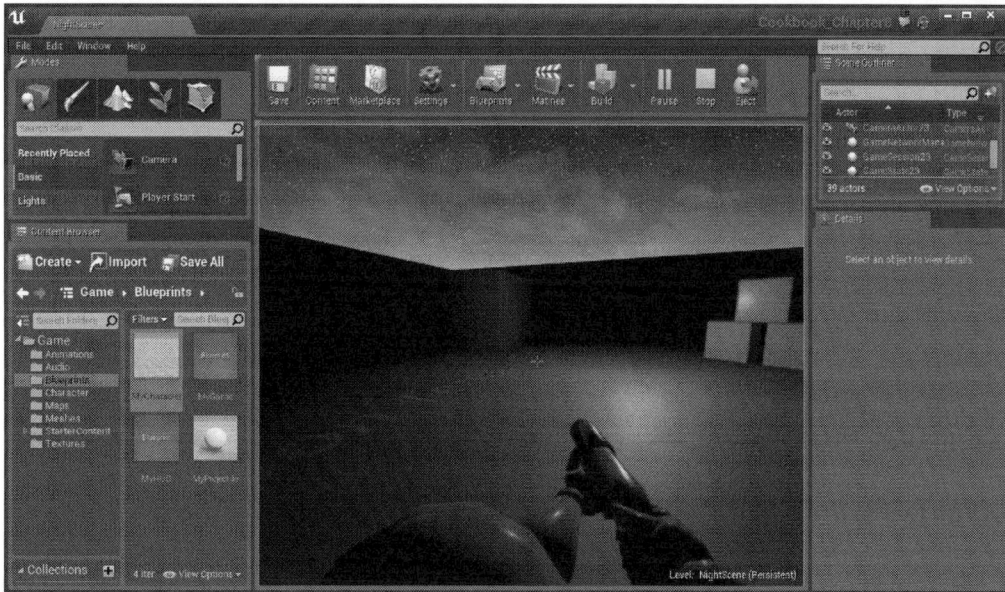

With that, our flickering light is working correctly and it's looking good!

Converting from Level to Class Blueprints

In the previous recipe, we used the **Level Blueprint** system in order to create a prototype of a feature we may want to have. In this recipe, we will see how we can convert this prototyped feature into a **Class Blueprint** which can be reused in every level.

Getting ready

Before we start working on this, we need to have a level blueprint to convert. Follow the previous recipe or open up the `FlashingLight` level provided in the example code.

How to do it...

The **Level Blueprint** is great, but it's limited in the fact that everything created is stuck within that level, and we'll generally have to copy/paste a lot to move things between levels (this was a problem back in the UE3 days with Kismet). To solve this issue, we have **Class Blueprint**, which we will create now:

1. With our `Point Light` selected, go to the **Details** tab and scroll down to the **Blueprint** section. Then, click on the **Replace With Composited Blueprint** option. When the **Select Path** dialog comes up, select the `Blueprints` folder and enter the name `FlashingLight_Blueprint`, then press **Create Blueprint**.

You'll then be brought to the **Class Blueprint** for our newly created action and it has the Point Light, which we created earlier, added. We are currently on the **Components** tab, which is where all of the pieces that make this blueprint reside. We'll look over this in another recipe, but for now, let's move over to the **Event Graph** tab.

2. Click on the **Event Graph** tab. Just like before, we are given an empty blueprint to work with. However, this time you'll notice that the **My Blueprint** tab now has the `PointLight_0` object as well as any other objects that may be part of the **Components** tab.

3. Move over to our **Level Blueprint** and select all of the nodes we created. Hit *Ctrl* + *C* to copy the nodes.

4. After this, move back to the Graph of FlashingLight_Blueprint again, select the **Event Graph** tab and then paste (*Ctrl* + *V*).

   You'll note that all of our previous content moved over nicely, except for the Point Light. This is because we were previously using a reference to something in the level. When working with blueprints, you are only able to access things inside the blueprint itself (unless you can get a reference to it).

5. Delete the **Unknown** element by selecting it and then hitting the *Del* key.

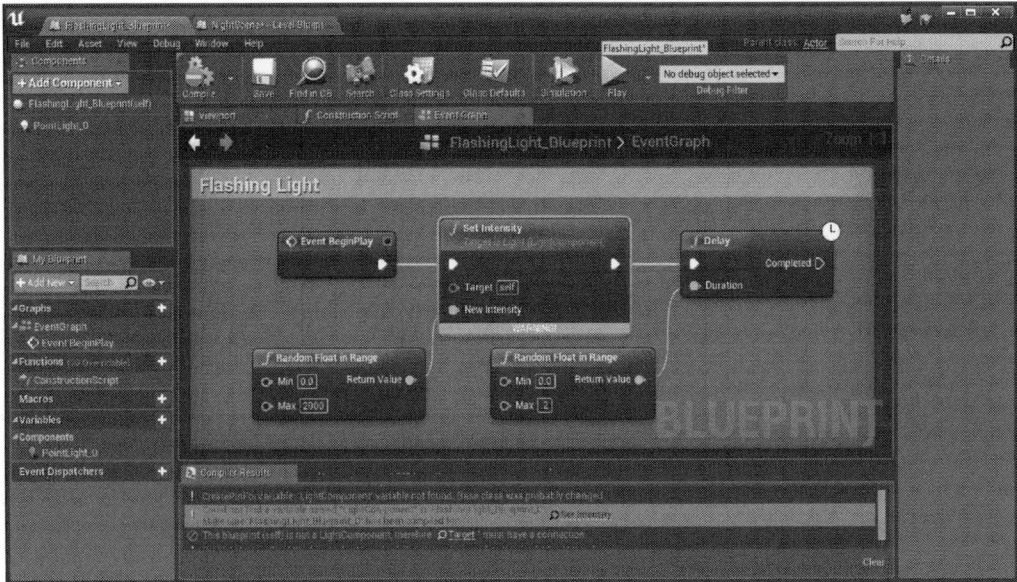

Deleting the Unknown element causes an error

This causes an error because we do not have something set for **Target**, but we will use our Blueprint's component to work with it.

6. From the **My Blueprint** tab, drag and drop the `PointLight_0` object into the Event Graph. You'll then have the two options of whether we want to modify the value of it (**Set**) or obtain the value to use (**Get**). In this instance, we will use **Get**.

However, at this point, if we try to drag and drop the point light into the **Target**, you'll notice that there is a conflict due to the types not being the same.

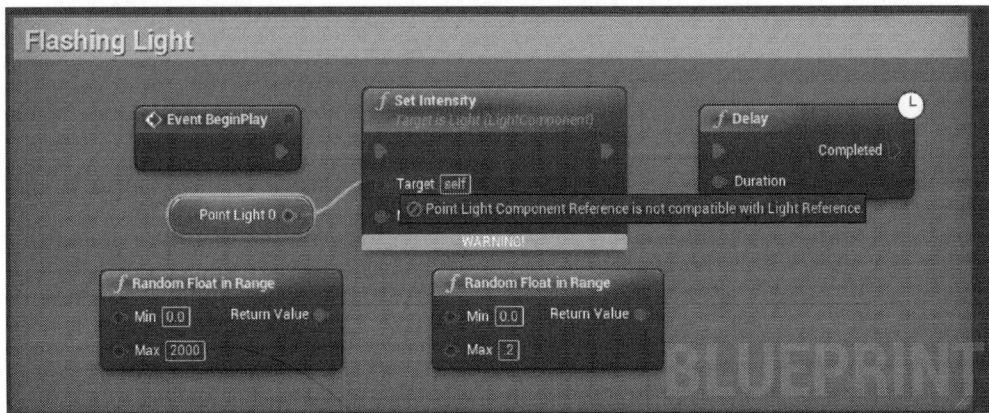

This is easily solved, but I wanted to point out the similar problems like this may happen on occasion, so let's fix it.

7. Delete the **Set Intensity** action and drag from `Point Light 0` and create a new **Set Intensity** function using the correct component. Then, connect everything back the way it was in the previous version and then press the **Compile** button to make sure everything is working correctly.

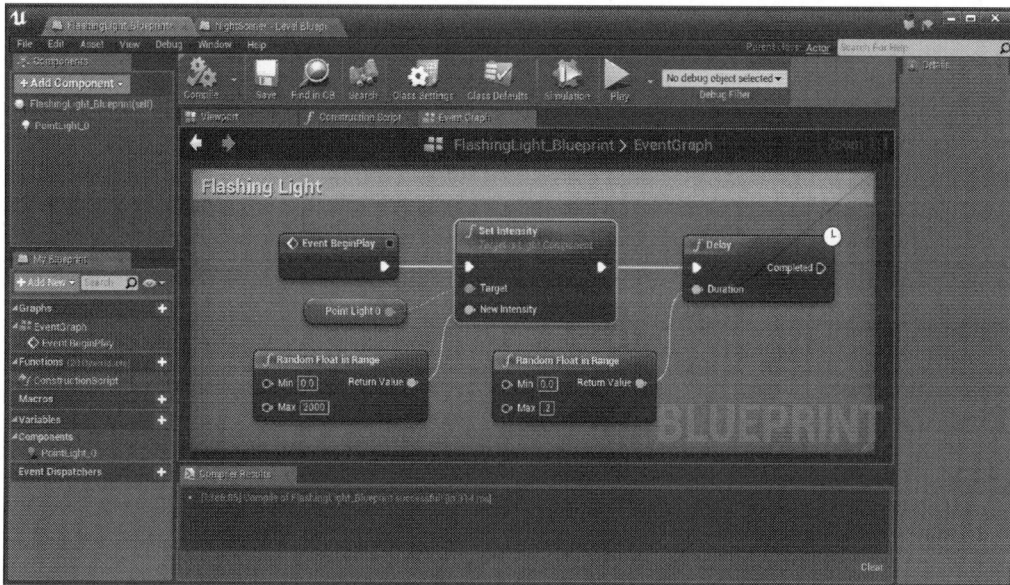

Creating new Set Intensity function

8. Lastly, move into the **Level Blueprint** window and delete our previously created actions. We won't need them anymore (note the warning that exists now because the object is now a blueprint).

9. Save your blueprint and the level and then hit the **Play** button.

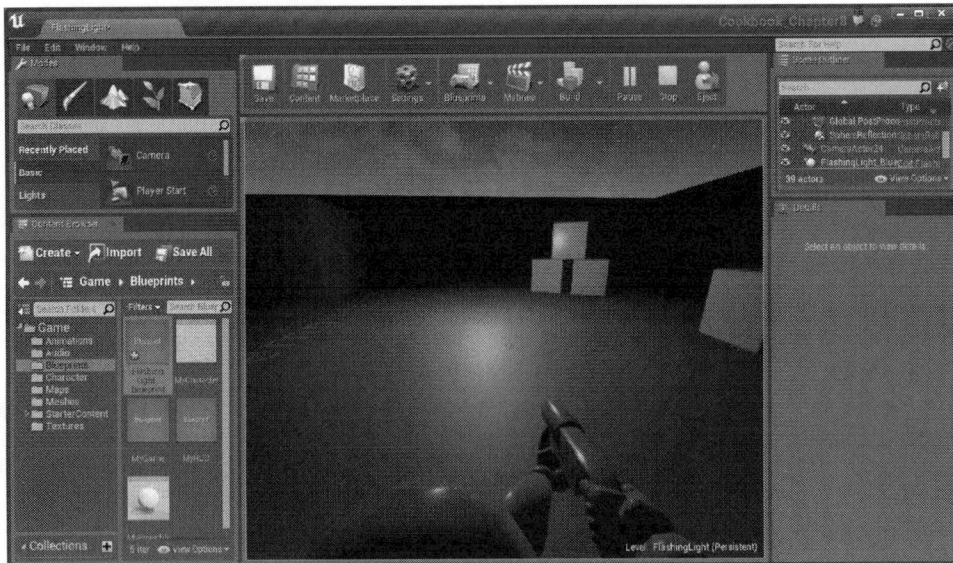

Everything is the same as before! However, now that our light is a blueprint, we can use it as many times as we want without having to copy/paste any actions.

10. Drag and drop two copies of the blueprint into the level and position them wherever you'd like to and play the game again.

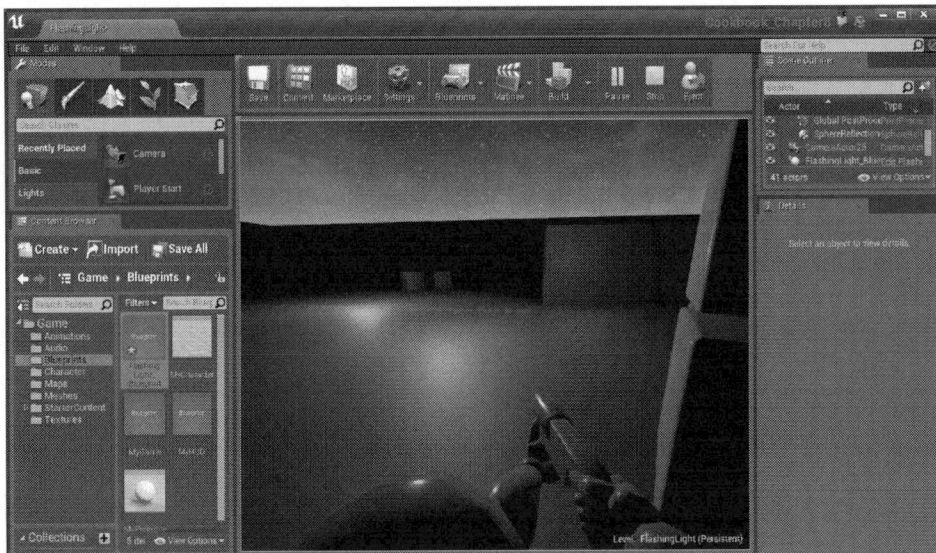

Playing the game with two copies of the blueprint

Now we have multiple lights, reacting in their own independent ways while learning about class blueprints! Also, since you have learned how to modify a property, you can also modify any of the other properties of the light, such as its color, position, and so on!

Using Trigger Volumes – opening a door using Matinee

Of course, there are many other things that we can do inside Blueprints instead of flickering a light. Another example would be to open a door when we get near it making use of Matinee.

Getting ready

Before we start working within the Unreal Editor, we will need to have a project to work with which contains the Starter Content that Epic provides. After the project is opened, go to the `Example Code` folder and drag and drop the `HouseExample` map provided into your project folder and open it.

How to do it...

In order to have our doors open, we will want them to be animated. To do this, we will use Unreal's Matinee system:

1. Select both doors and ensure that the **Mobility** section is set to **Movable**. If this is not done, you may have errors in Matinee when we say we want to move them.

    Currently, our doors do not have collision. Let's fix this by looking at the common reasons for why things cannot be working correctly.

2. Back in the **Details** tab, go into **Collision** and note that **Collision Presets** is set to **BlockAll**. This means that if the object has collision data, anything will collide with it.

3. The key thing to note is that the object will only collide *if* there is collision data. Let's check this now. Scroll up to the **Static Mesh** component and double-click on the door to open up the **Static Mesh Editor**.

> Alternatively, you can also press *Ctrl + B* when the doors are selected in the scene to automatically find the asset in the **Content Browser** tab and then double-click from there.

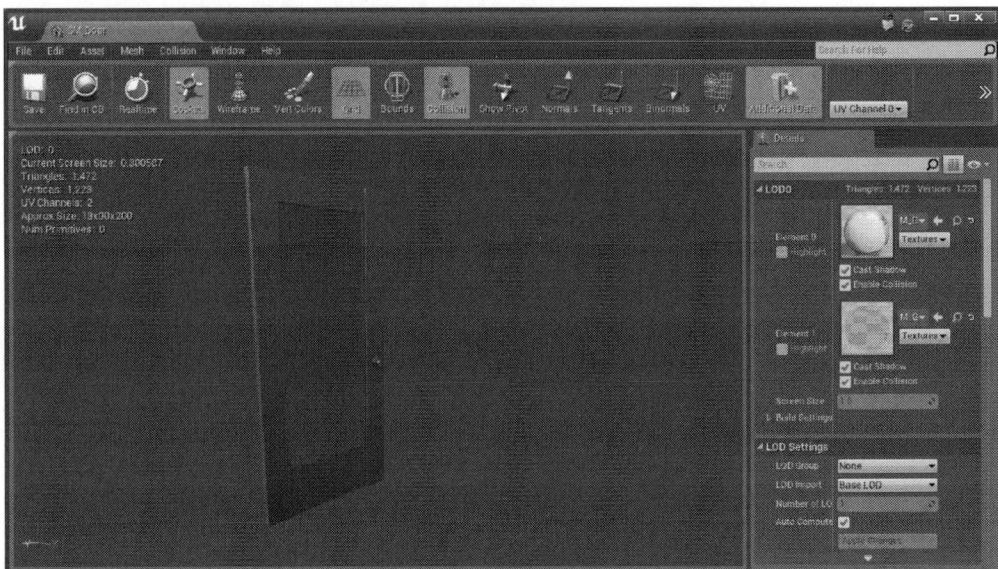

Opening the Static Mesh Editor

Inside this editor, you can modify any properties that are part of this mesh, including the materials used and the way it reacts to shadows.

> For more information on the Static Mesh Editor, refer to `https://docs.`
> `unrealengine.com/latest/INT/Engine/Content/Types/`
> `StaticMeshes/Editor/index.html`.

4. There's currently no collision on this object, so let's add it. Go to **Collision** and select **Add Box Simplified Collision**, and with that, you'll notice that there are green lines over the edge, which is correct enough for a simple model like this.

5. Click on the **Save** button and exit the Static Mesh Editor.

   Now, if we play the game, you'll notice that we can no longer walk through it!

Playing the game after adding collision to it

6. Now that the doors are ready, let's learn how to animate them. From the main toolbar, navigate to **Matinee | Add Matinee**.

Opening up the Matinee Editor

Once this is created, there is a new Actor added to our **SceneOutliner** called `MatineeActor1`, and the Matinee Editor opens up.

> For information on the Matinee Editor and what each section is for, refer to `https://docs.unrealengine.com/latest/INT/Engine/Matinee/UI/index.html`.

7. Back in the main editor, click on the left door and then open up the Matinee Window again. From the **Tracks** tab, right-click and select **Add New Empty Group** and give it a name—`Door1`. Once this is created, right-click on **Door1** and select **Add New Movement Track**.

This is letting Matinee know that we want to modify the movement (position, rotation, and scale) of the door object during our animation. It's also worthwhile to note that if the door is not a moveable object, Unreal will automatically change it to one at this point.

8. Next, we want to do the same thing with the right door. Select it in the main editor and then back in the Matinee Editor, right-click and create a new group with a movement track.

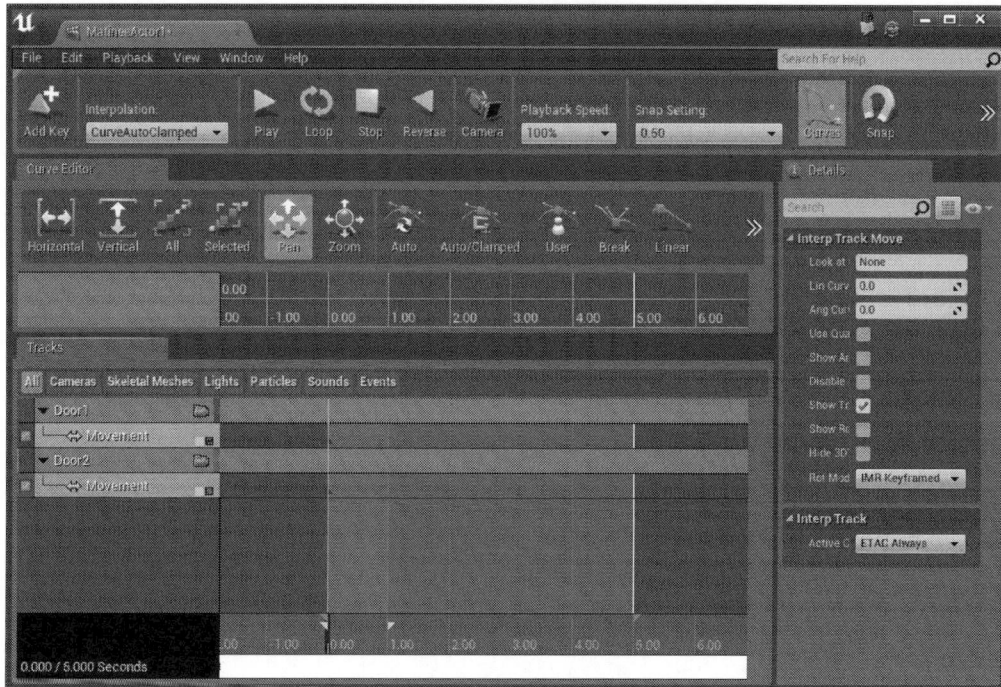

Adding the movement track

Animations are done in terms of keyframes. You can already see one created on each Movement track with those red triangles. This current animation lasts for 5 seconds (which you can see with the **5.00** value where the edges are). Use the mouse wheel to zoom in and out).

9. Click on the gray area where the time is to show a spot on the timeline. Move it to around 1.5 seconds. Then, select each **Movement** track individually and click on **Add Key** on the top-left (or press *Enter*). To see the animation with the playback system, also move the green highlighted timeline to 1.5 seconds.

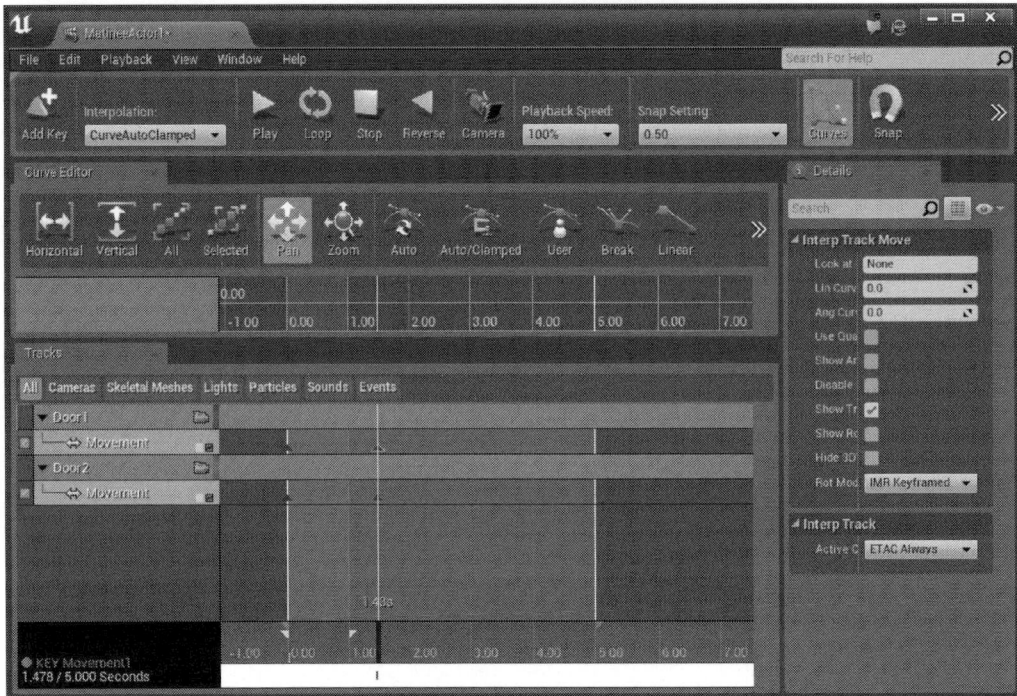

Setting a new keyframe at 1.5 seconds

This is stating that in 1.5 seconds, I want these objects to be somewhere else and I want the computer to intelligently move between the two values (also known as a **tween**).

10. Now, select the key on the **Door1 Movement** and move back into the game. Switch to the **Rotation** tool (*E*) and then rotate the door to open 120 degrees.

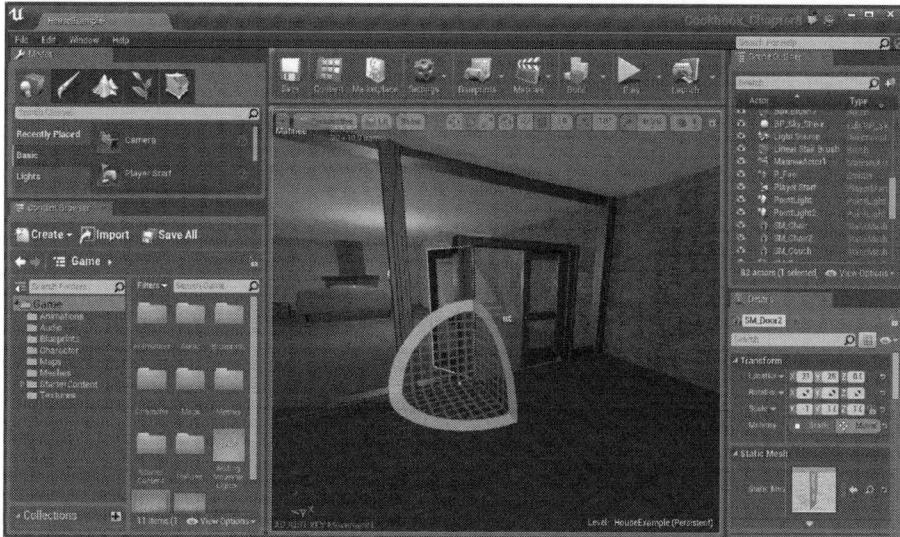

Rotating a door

11. Next, select the key on **Door2** and do the same in the other direction. If you move the timebar between the two keys, you should notice that it parts way between opening the door.

Rotating the other door

12. When our Matinee is completed, close the editor.

We now want this animation to play whenever we get near the door, so with that in mind, we can use **Box Trigger** to detect when we are near.

A **trigger** is something that detects collision, but unlike other things, with collider, it does not attempt to block the player from entering it. This is used often in games for the events that happen when something enters an area. If you've played a first person shooter, you may notice a trigger being used whenever you see a group of enemies spawning to attack the player because you entered an area.

13. Go to the **Modes** tab and then select **Basic** and drag and drop **Box Trigger** into the scene where the door is. Scale and translate it until it covers the door and the space ahead and behind it.

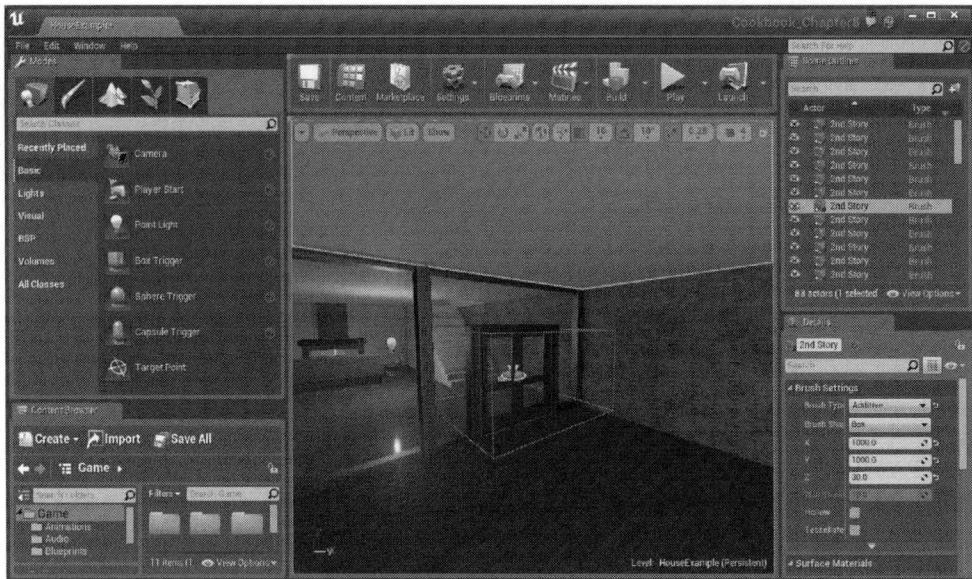

Setting a box trigger at the doors

14. In the **Scene Outliner** tab, select our `TriggerBox` actor and scroll down to Blueprint. From here, select **Add Level Events for TriggerBox** and from the popup, select **Add OnActorBeginOverlap**. This will be called whenever our **TriggerBox** has been overlapped by another object.

15. While we are here, also add an event for **OnActorEndOverlap**.

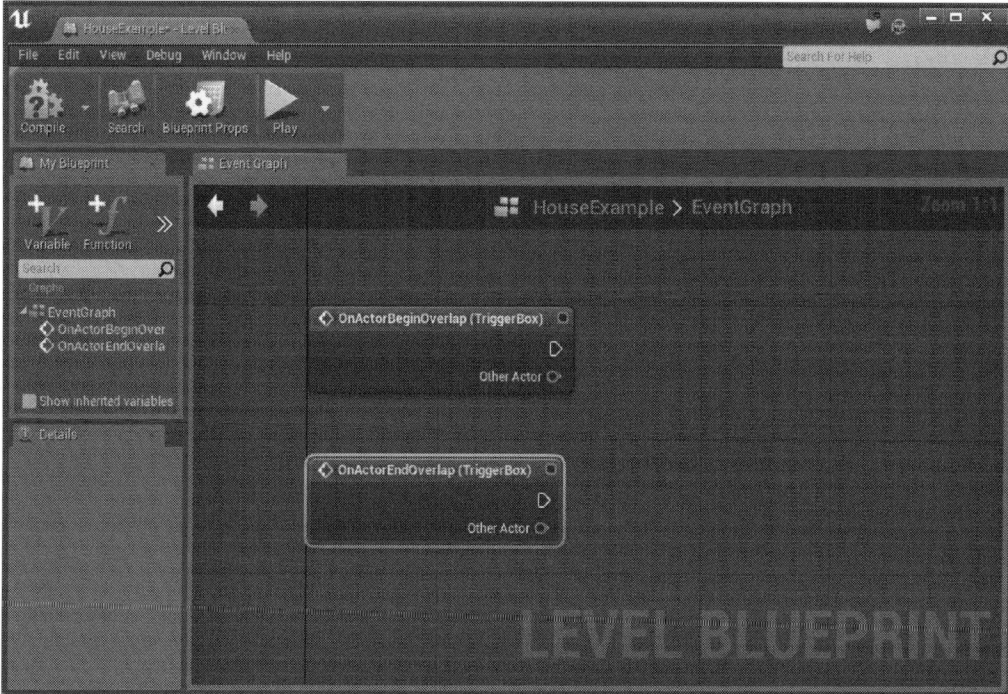

16. We want to play our Matinee when we collide with the trigger, so from the **Scene Outliner** tab, go to `MatineeActor` and drag and drop it into the **Blueprints** window. Then, drag from its blue line to bring up the possible functions that use it and search for **Play**. Connect the output from **BeginOverlap** to the input of **Play**.

17. With that in mind, extend from the Matinee actor once again and search for **Reverse**. Connect the output from **EndOverlap** to the input of **Reverse**.

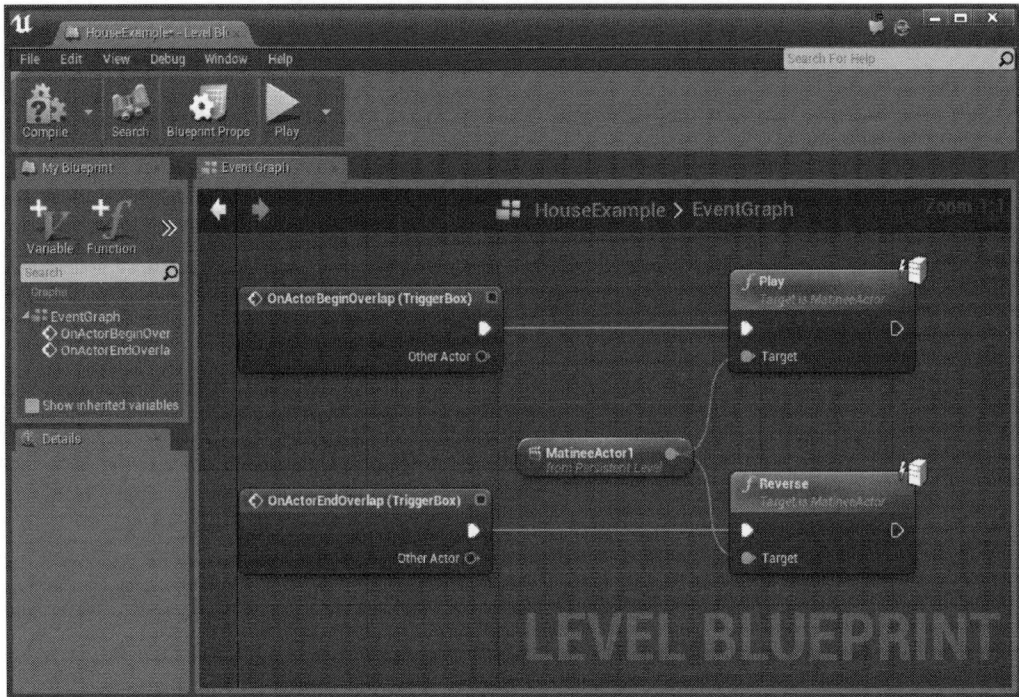

18. Hit the **Compile** button and play the game.

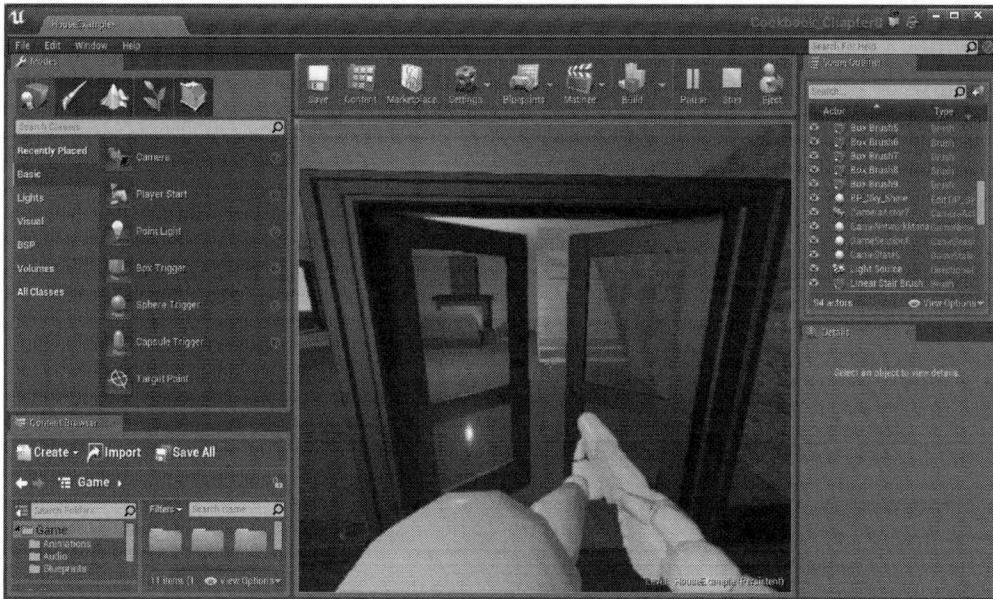

With this, you have learned to use Triggers to modify things that happen in the game!

> For simple animations, such as the one done here, it's also possible to make use of UE4's Timelines. For a tutorial on that, visit `https://docs.unrealengine.com/latest/INT/Engine/Blueprints/UserGuide/Timelines/Examples/OpeningDoors/index.html`.
>
> For additional examples on how to use Matinee to do different things, refer to `https://docs.unrealengine.com/latest/INT/Engine/Matinee/HowTo/index.html`.

Adding to an existing Blueprint – flashlight, part 2

Now that we have some experience working with Blueprints, let's modify one that's already been created for us. In this section, we will cover how to add a flashlight to our game's character.

Getting ready

Before we start working within the Unreal Editor, we will need to have a project to work with. Follow these steps:

1. First, open up the Unreal Editor by clicking on the **Launch** button from the Unreal Engine Launcher.

2. Start a new project from the **Project Browser** tab by selecting the **New Project** tab. Select **First person** and make sure that **With Starter Content** is selected. Give the project a Name (Cookbook_Chapter8). Once you are done, click on **Create Project**.

3. After the project is opened, go to the Example Code folder and drag and drop the NightScene map provided in your project folder and open it:

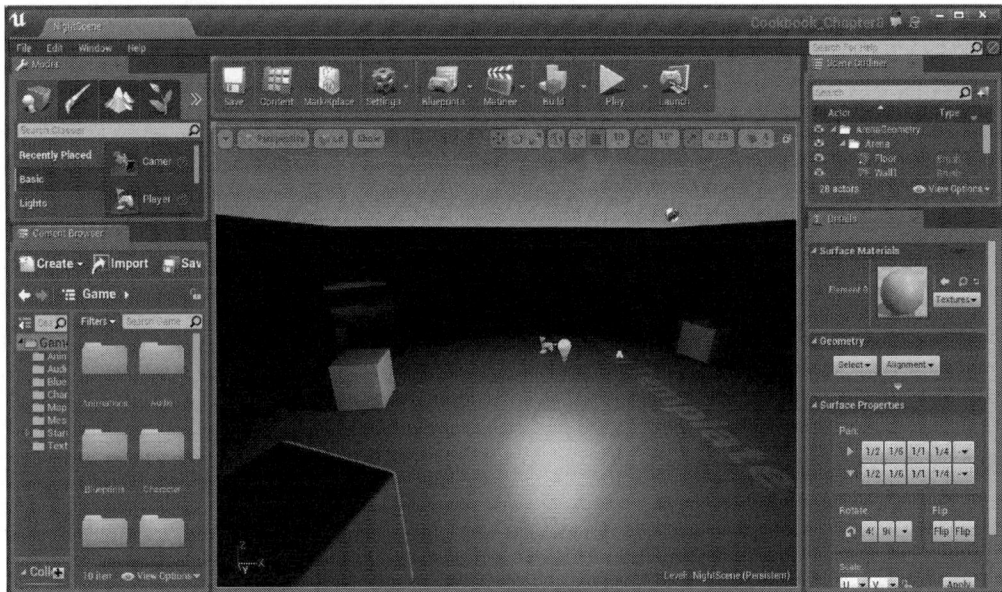

At this point, if you were to play the game, it would be incredibly dark, as shown in the following screenshot:

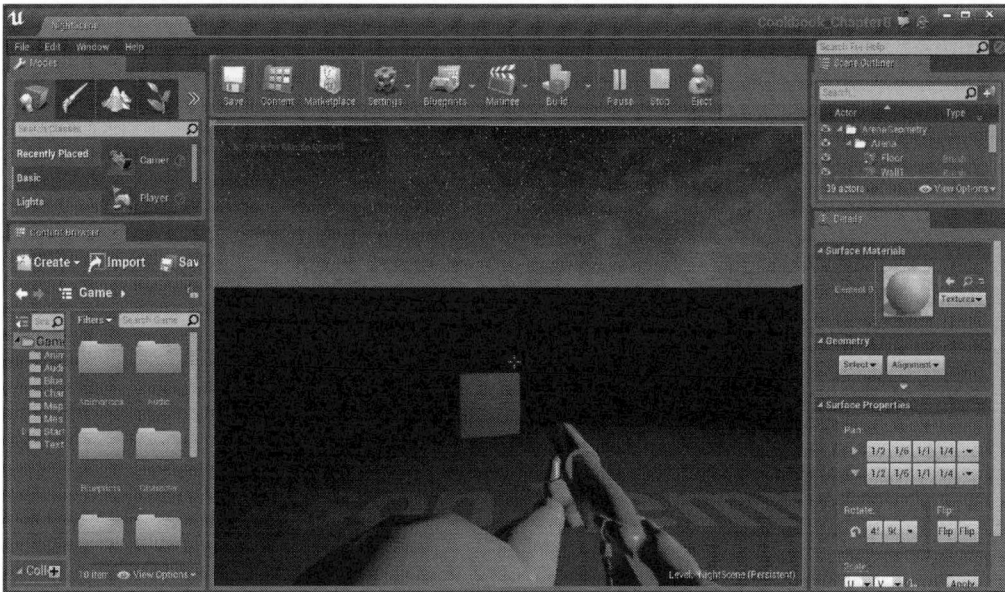

How to do it...

For those who have gone through *Chapter 6*, *Lighting and Shadows*, this should look quite familiar. In that chapter, we actually created a flashlight and then attached it to our player at runtime.

However, we can modify the character's blueprint to make it so that our player will always have a flashlight on. Follow these steps:

1. Go to the **Content Browser** tab and then to the Blueprints folder. Find the MyCharacter file.

Selecting the My Character blueprint

This blueprint is what's spawned when the game is started. It contains all of the logic for movement, the camera, and the shooting behaviour.

2. Next, double-click on the file to open up the **Blueprints** for it. Initially, it will be on the **Event Graph** tab, which will have a lot of scripts on it, very similar to a level blueprint. But for now, click on the **Viewport** tab and zoom the camera out if needed.

The Viewport tab view in the blueprint editor

This section is similar to our level in that it has objects and they're placed in the *world* of our object, but it's apart from the level. You can move around the viewport on the right-hand side in exactly the same way as the main game. Zoom out so that you can see everything.

3. To the left, you'll see a tab marked **Components**. Under this, it has the mesh, camera, and everything else that is to do with the physical presence of the class. We can add to this using the **Add Component** option. With this in mind, click on **Add Component** and select **Spot Light** (if you can't see it, use the search bar at the top).

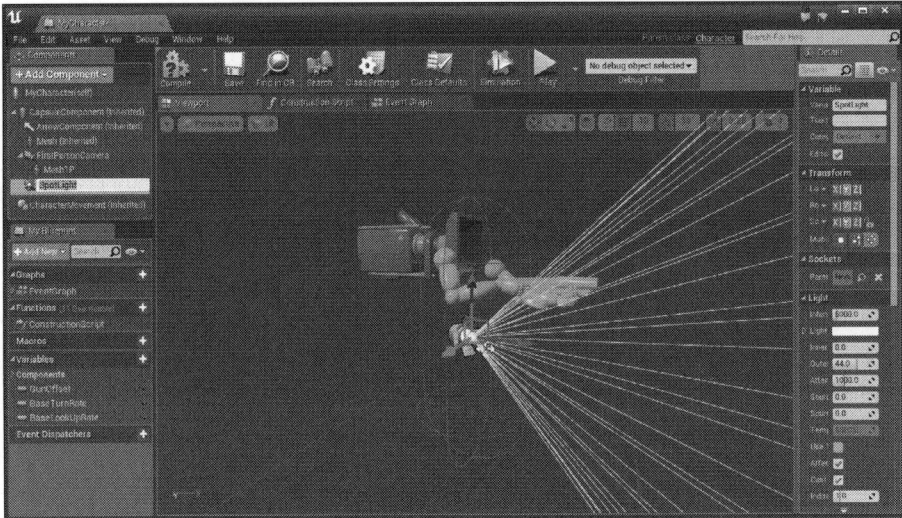

Adding a Spot Light to our character

You can see that the spotlight is already added for us.

4. Go back into the main editor and play the game again.

You'll notice a couple of issues. First of all, the light is lighting the player in addition to what's in front of it. Also, if we look up and down, it does not move with us.

5. With the game still playing, go back to the `MyCharacter` blueprint and select our **SpotLight** object and move it (if the **Move** tool isn't there, press *W*). Notice that when we move it in the blueprint, it modifies what is done in the game. Move the light until it is in front of the barrel of the gun.

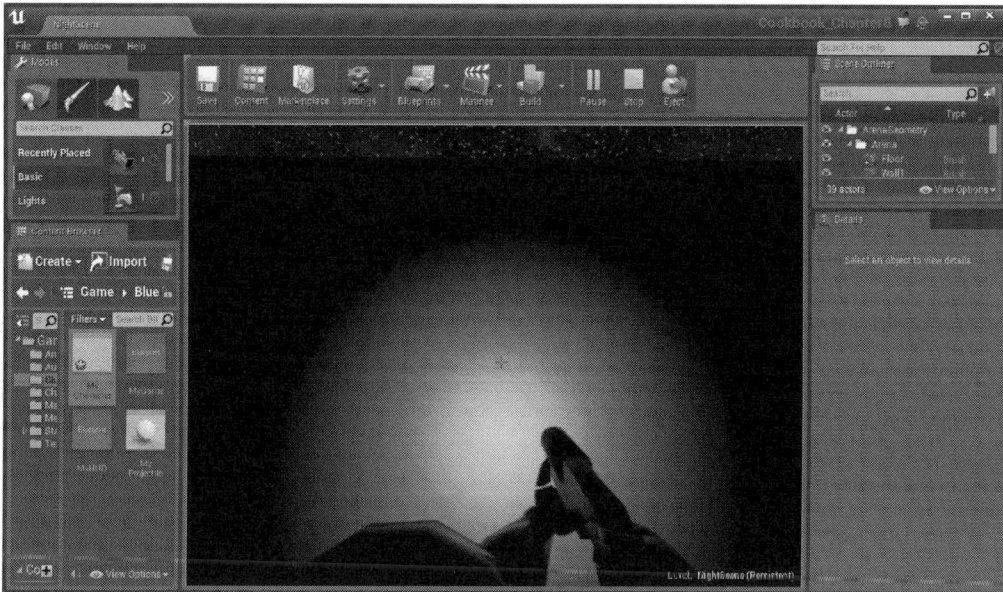

Moving the spot light in game

This solves the issue of lighting the player, but moving up and down is not working. To do this, we can make the **SpotLight** object a child of the camera. That way, whenever it moves, the light will move as well. Sadly, we cannot change this while the game is running.

6. Stop the game and then drag and drop the `SpotLight` object on top of the `FirstPersonCamera` object. You should see a green checkmark, saying that we can attach it.

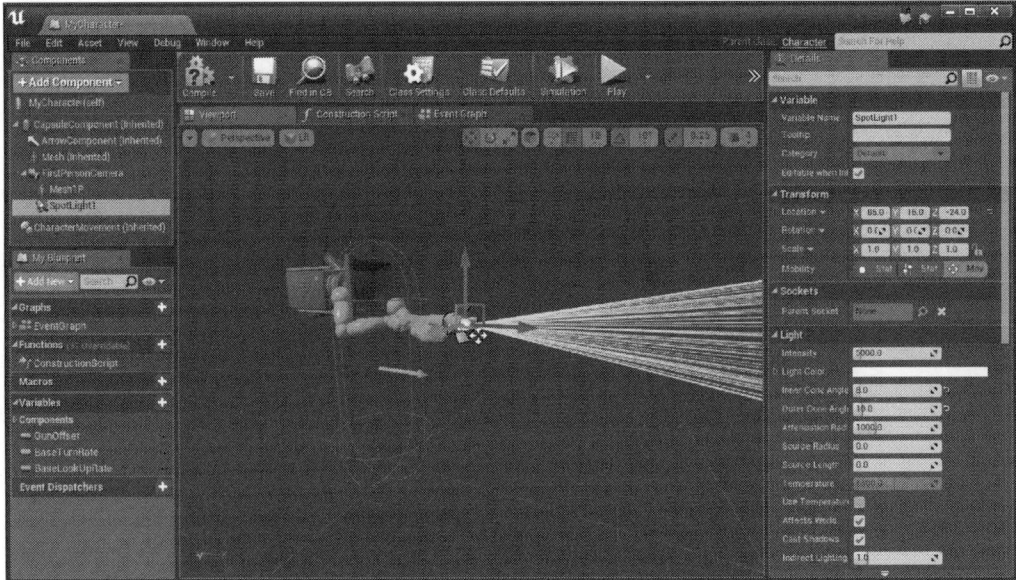

Attaching spotlight to the FirstPersonCamera object

7. After this, go into the `SpotLight` objects and set the same parameters that we did in the *Adding moveable lights – flashlight, part 1* recipe of *Chapter 6, Lighting and Shadows* or translate the object so that it is in front of the camera with **Inner Cone Angle** of 8 and **Outer Cone Angle** of 10.

8. Click on the **Compile** button to save all the changes we've made before and confirm that it all works correctly with our project.

9. Lastly, let's add in the ability to turn the flashlight on and off using an input event. Click on **Event Graph** and move it over until you have some empty space.

> While in **Event Graph**, it may be beneficial to take a look at the actions that are actually part of the player class, giving you an idea of what can be done with blueprints and other actions that you can use!

10. Right-click on the empty space and type in `keyboard events`. This will display all of the keyboard keys and allow us to trigger events based on when they are pressed or released.

11. Select **F**, and you'll see an event is created. To the right of it, right-click and create a **Toggle Visibility (SpotLight1)** action. Toggle means that it will turn it off if it's on and on if it's off.

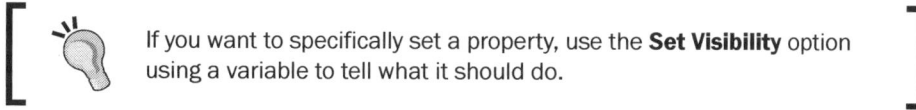

> If you want to specifically set a property, use the **Set Visibility** option using a variable to tell what it should do.

12. Next, connect the **Pressed** output of the **F** event to the input of the **Toggle Visibility** action.

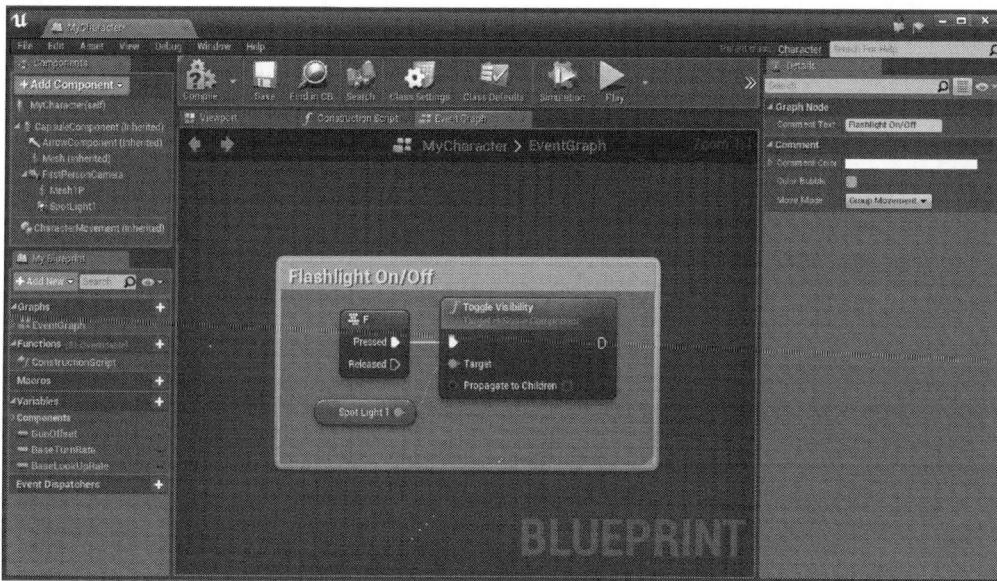

Connecting the Pressed output to the input of the Toggle Visibility action

13. Compile, go to the **Content Browser** tab, save the `MyCharacter` blueprint, and **Play** the game!

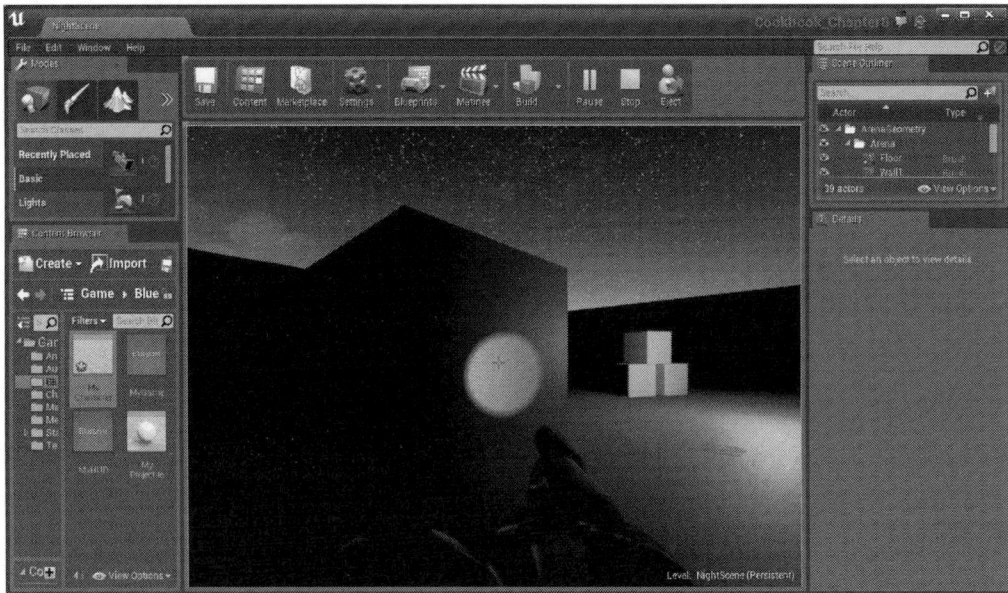

With this, we now have a flashlight that will follow our player's camera in all directions and exist in every single level we have in the game! Here, you learned how to modify the already existing blueprints and added in some simple player input using the *F* key to toggle visibility.

Creating a Health/Damage system, part 1 – taking damage

Games will often need the ability to give health to players and/or enemies and players need to have the ability to gain and/or lose the health. In this recipe, it being the first of a two-part recipe, we will create the ability to take and heal damage, whereas later on in *Chapter 10, User Interface*, we will use the UI tools in Unreal to display this information.

Getting ready

Before we start working on this, we need to have a project created and set up for our character to actually have health and a way to damage it. Follow these steps:

1. First, open up the Unreal Editor by clicking on the **Launch** button from the Unreal Engine Launcher.

2. Start a new project from the **Project Browser** tab by selecting the **New Project** tab. Select **Third person** and make sure that **With Starter Content** is selected. Give the project a Name (Cookbook_Chapter8). Once you are done, click on **Create Project**.

How to do it...

Now, once the project is created, the first step here will be to create some action to damage the player. In this instance, I'm going to create a trigger. When the player touches the trigger, it will get damaged. To make it easier to see, I'm going to add a fire particle system. Follow these steps:

1. From the **Content Browser** tab, open up the StarterContent/Particles folder and drag and drop the P_Fire particles onto the floor of the starting level.

2. Next, from the **Modes** tab, go to the **Place** mode (if you weren't there already) and select the **Volumes** section. From the options, scroll all the way down until you see **Trigger Volume** and then drag and drop that into the level so that the fire overlaps it.

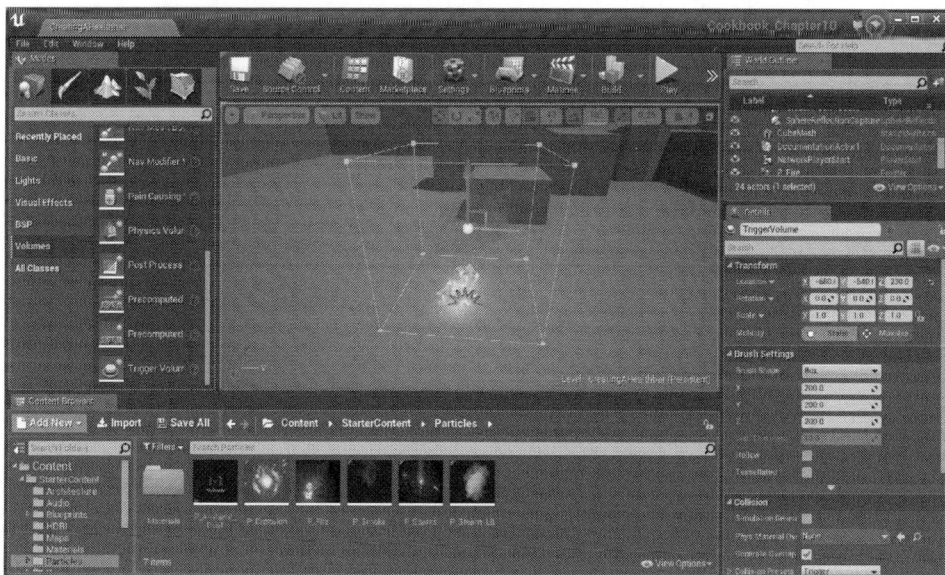

Creating a trigger to damage the player

Now that we have the trigger in place, we need to create a blueprint to do the damage for us.

3. With the **Trigger Volume** object selected, go to **Blueprints | Open Level Blueprint**.

4. From the **Event Graph** tab, right-click somewhere on the grid and then navigate to **Add Event for Trigger Volume 1 | Collision | Add On Actor Begin Overlap**.

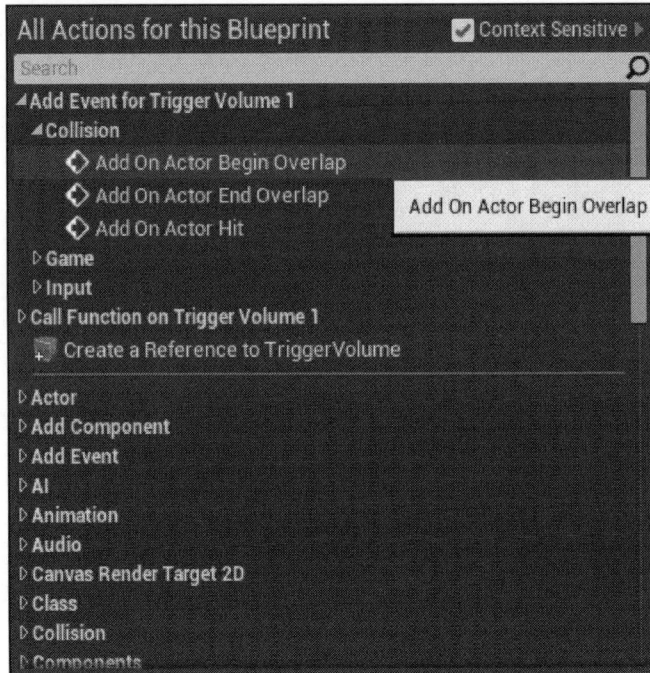

This event will be called whenever any other actor begins to overlap this actor.

> For more information on **OnActorBeginOverlap** and all of the other Collision Responses in UE4, refer to `https://docs.unrealengine.com/latest/INT/Engine/Physics/Collision/index.html`.

5. Next, when we collide with the trigger, we want to damage the player. Thankfully, Unreal comes with an **Apply Damage** action that we can use. To the right of the **OnActorBeginOverlap** action, right-click and start typing `Apply` and when **Apply Damage** is selected, press the `Enter` key.

6. Connect the output from the **OnActorBeginOverlap** action to the input of the **Apply Damage** action. Then, connect **Other Actor** of **OnActorBeginOverlap (TriggerVolume)** to **Damaged Actor** of **Apply Damage**. Finally, under **Base Damage**, type in `10`.

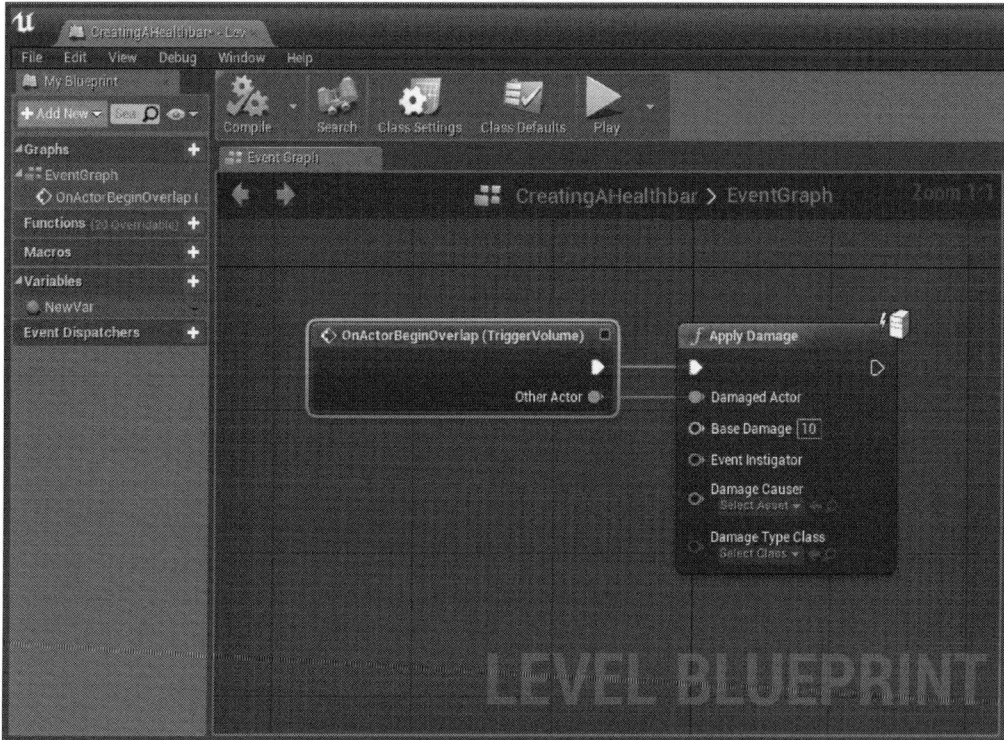

Blueprint to cause damage event when an object touches the trigger volume

What this will do is whenever an object touches the trigger volume, it will call a generic damage event on that object with a damage parameter of `10`. Note that this will only do something if someone has created an `AnyDamage` event, which we will learn how to do later on in this recipe.

Now that we have something that can damage the character, we need to actually give our character a way to take damage:

1. Exit out of the level blueprint and from the **Content Browser** tab, open up the `ThirdPersonBP/Blueprints` folder and double-click on the `ThirdPerson Character` object to open it up.

2. From the **MyBlueprint** tab, you'll see a section called **Variables**; extend it out (if it's not already extended) and press the **+** button to create a new variable. When it's created, give it a name (`CurrentHealth`) and then from the **Details** tab, change **Variable Type** value to `Float`.

3. After this, create another float variable called `MaxHealth`.

4. Next, click on the **Compile** button to verify everything is working correctly; then, we can assign a **Default Value** of `100` to each of the two numbers.

Assigning Default Value to the numbers

5. Now that we have the health variables, we can use them. Move down the **Event Graph** until you reach some empty space and right-click to create a new **Event AnyDamage** event (**Add Event | Game | Damage**).

   This event is called if the `ApplyDamage` function is called on an object. The default character controllers do not have it, so we need to put it in.

   First, we will subtract the damage from the current player's health and then, set the current health to this new value.

6. Drag and drop the `CurrentHealth` variable from the **Variables** section of the **MyBlueprints** tab into **Event Graph**. From the options, select **Get**.

7. Next, create a **float – float** action (which will subtract a float from another float). On the top, connect the **Current Health** variable. For the bottom, connect the **Damage** value from the **Event AnyDamage** action.

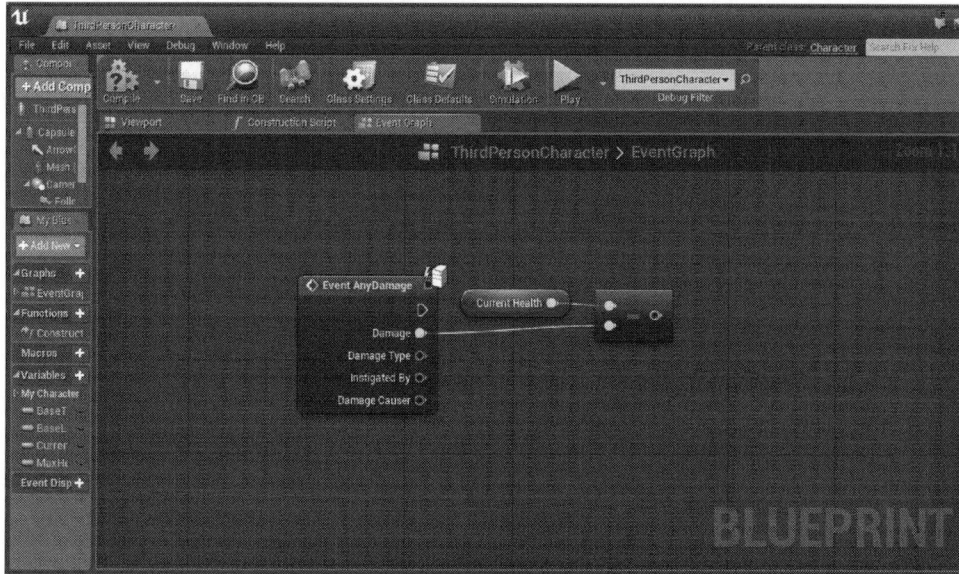

Setting up the final behavior for the damage event

Next, we want to ensure that the value that we get from this, will always be between 0 and our **Max Health** value (we can have someone later on create a trigger with a negative **Damage** value for **Apply Damage**, which will then heal our player). To do this, we can use a **Clamp** action that will make it so that when the number is less than 0, it will set it to 0 or if it is larger than **Max Health**, it'll come down to **Max Health**.

8. Right-click and create a **Clamp(float)** action. Connect **Value** to the output of our subtraction action. Leave the **Min** value at its default of 0, but then for **Max**, connect our **MaxHealth** variable (drag and drop and select **Get**).

9. Now that we have the valid value, we need to actually set this value. To the right of the **Clamp** action, drag and drop a **Current Health** variable, but this time, select the **Set** action. Connect the Clamp action's **Return Value** to the **Current Health** variable of the **Set** action. Then, connect the output from **Event Any Damage** to the input of the **Set** action.

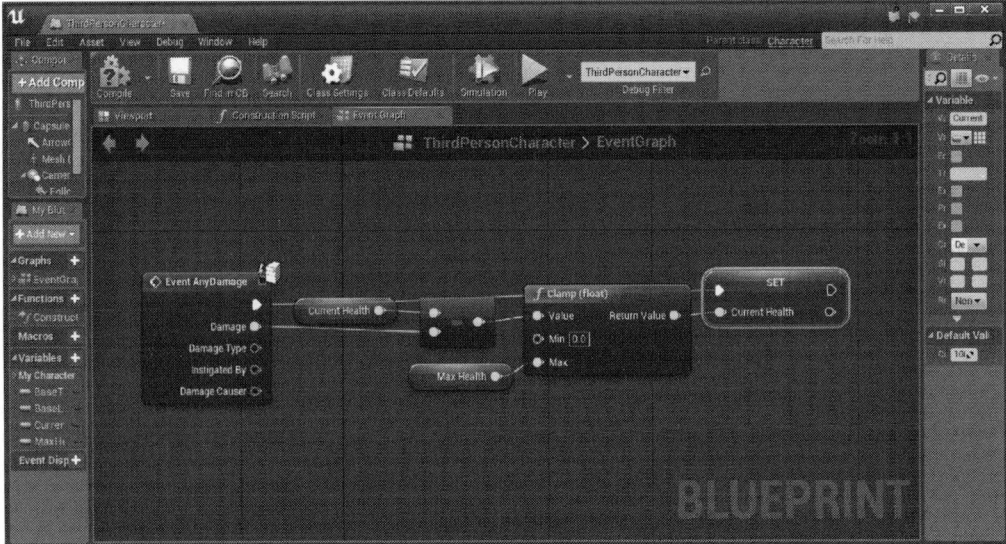

Now we have the ability to take or heal damage to our player. Later on in *Chapter 10, User Interface*, we have the second part of this recipe in which we use this recipe and then create a healthbar to show the player exactly where their health is!

See also

We've covered quite a lot, but we have only touched the tip of the iceberg, that is, scripting. To give yourself a little exposure to what else can be done with blueprints, take a look at the following tutorials:

▶ If you're working in teams, having a set of practices will make it much easier for you to work together and perform well. Some recommended best practices for blueprints can be found at `https://docs.unrealengine.com/latest/INT/Engine/Blueprints/BestPractices/index.html`.

▶ Scott McCutchen has created a tutorial for having a character swap their mesh and animations during gameplay, making it seem like one character poofs out of existence with another taking its place. Check it out at `https://www.youtube.com/watch?v=5R1z3rytu7Y`.

- ▶ Another more advanced use of blueprints is in the creation of an inventory system. Tom Looman has come up with a tutorial on one that you can check out at `http://www.tomlooman.com/tutorial-basic-inventory-system-in-blueprint/`.

- ▶ This tutorial is a bit dated, but Joel Shapiro's blueprints tutorial does go through the creation of a 2D platformer from scratch, so I think it's worth checking it out at `http://www.raywenderlich.com/97058/unreal-engine-tutorial-for-beginners-part-1`.

- ▶ Finally, we also have a tutorial from Peter Newton where they build an AI, making use of NavMeshes. While it is a long tutorial, it does go into a number of different aspects of building an AI Bot. Check this out at `https://wiki.unrealengine.com/AI_Bot:_Blueprint_Scripting_Playlist`.

9

C++ Programming – Gameplay

In this chapter, we'll cover the following recipes:

- ▸ Setting up your development environment
- ▸ Displaying text during runtime
- ▸ Networking 101 – creating collectables with networking
- ▸ Saving or loading games and keyboard input with C++
- ▸ Creating custom blueprint nodes

Introduction

So far, we've been using blueprints in order to generate gameplay. This has been great and has worked well, but one of the main advantages that Unreal has over its competition, such as Unity and Cry Engine, is the fact that you can get access to the full source code of the engine and rework it to fit exactly what you're looking for.

It would be quite easy for me to write an entire book just about programming, and within these few pages, I can't possibly cover everything you need to know to write code. Rather, in this chapter, we are going to cover how to set up your development environment and some of the possibilities of programming in C++ for UE4.

> If you are interested in taking this further and learning how to program C++ using UE4, read *Learning C++ by Creating Games with UE4* by Packt Publishing.

When to use C++/Blueprints

One of the things that I often hear people asking is whether to use C++ or Blueprints within their projects, or which one is *better*. As it currently stands, there's not really a straightforward answer to it. If you aren't a programmer at all or feel that you're more of a designer, then blueprints may be better for you due to the fact that it's more visually oriented. However, if you've been coding for years, you may be frustrated with having to use so many nodes to do some actions that you could write in a line of code. Factors such as the number of teammates and the project itself can also be taken under consideration.

It's often a lot easier to transition into C++ after you've been using blueprints and Unreal for a while as you'll be used to how Unreal names certain things, but we'll get some exposure in this chapter as well. That being said, you'll often switch between the two within the same project, with level-specific stuff being done in blueprint and content that will be reused in C++.

In previous versions of the Unreal Engine, runtime performance was something you also needed to consider, but it's less of a problem now. Don't worry about it unless something done in blueprint in your game is going to happen lots of times or is causing your game to slow down a lot. If this does happen, check out the guide on improving performance at `https://www.unrealengine.com/blog/how-to-improve-game-thread-cpu-performance`.

Often in game studios, designers will prototype a game mechanic so that it feels right and if it's decided to be used in the game, it's revisited and if it needs to be revised, a programmer can then reimplement it knowing exactly what the designer had in mind while making it as efficient as possible. Lionhead Studios is currently doing this during the development of their new game *Fable Legends*. For more information on that, refer to `https://www.unrealengine.com/showcase/fable-legends`.

Setting up your development environment

One of the first things that we'll need to do when working in Unreal Engine 4 using C++ is having our **Integrated Developers Environment** (**IDE**) set up and making it in such a way so that we can run our new code. Let's see how we can do this now.

Getting ready

You'll need to install Visual Studio 2013 (at the time of writing, the 2015 RC version is not supported, so you'll need to install 2013) on Windows or Xcode on Mac to work with this chapter.

How to do it...

Since I'm working in Windows, I'll be using Visual Studio in which there is a Community edition that is free for students, open source projects, and teams of less than five people. Follow these steps:

1. Open up your web browser and go to the Visual Studio Community's page at `https://www.visualstudio.com/en-us/downloads/download-visual-studio-vs.aspx`. Once the page is loaded, scroll down to the **Visual Studio downloads** section and from Visual Studio 2013, select the Community 2013 edition and then click on **Download**.

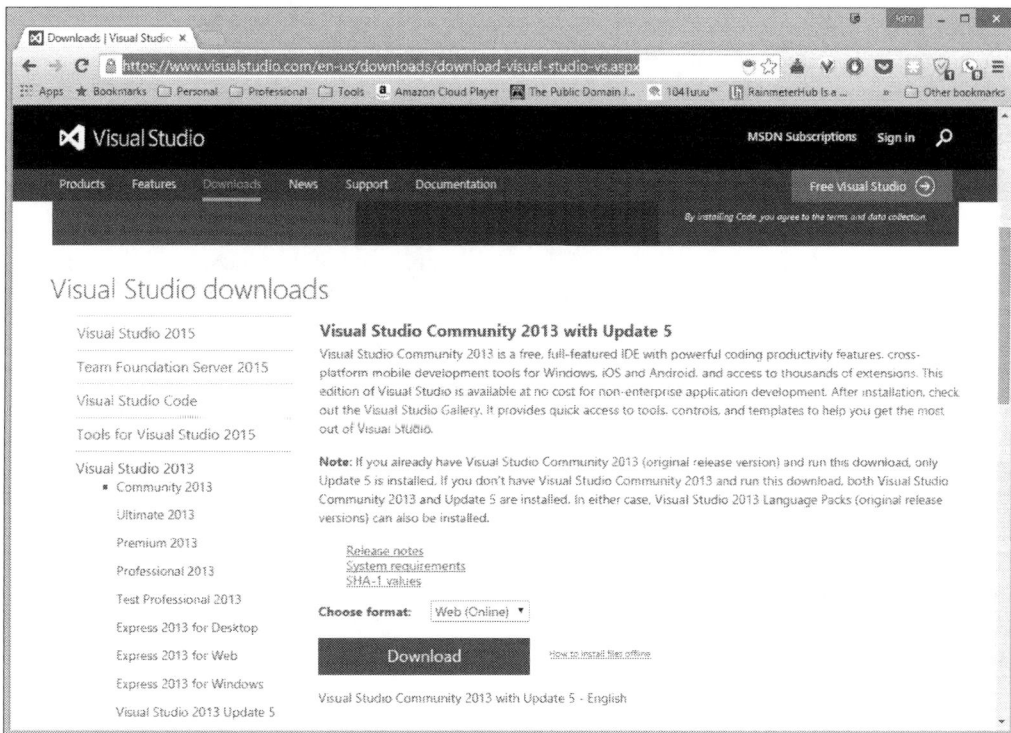

<table>
<tr>
<td>

Visual Studio downloads

Visual Studio 2015

Team Foundation Server 2015

Visual Studio Code

Tools for Visual Studio 2015

Visual Studio 2013
- Community 2013

Ultimate 2013

Premium 2013

Professional 2013

Test Professional 2013

Express 2013 for Desktop

Express 2013 for Web

Express 2013 for Windows

Visual Studio 2013 Update 5

</td>
<td>

Visual Studio Community 2013 with Update 5

Visual Studio Community 2013 is a free, full-featured IDE with powerful coding productivity features, cross-platform mobile development tools for Windows, iOS and Android, and access to thousands of extensions. This edition of Visual Studio is available at no cost for non-enterprise application development. After installation, check out the Visual Studio Gallery. It provides quick access to tools, controls, and templates to help you get the most out of Visual Studio.

Note: If you already have Visual Studio Community 2013 (original release version) and run this download, only Update 5 is installed. If you don't have Visual Studio Community 2013 and run this download, both Visual Studio Community 2013 and Update 5 are installed. In either case, Visual Studio 2013 Language Packs (original release versions) can also be installed.

Release notes
System requirements
SHA-1 values

Choose format: Web (Online) ▼

[Download]   How to install files offline

Visual Studio Community 2013 with Update 5 - English

</td>
</tr>
</table>

> Xcode can be downloaded from the Mac App Store for free at `https://itunes.apple.com/us/app/xcode/id497799835`.

2. Once you've got the installer installed, check the agree checkbox and then click on the newly-appeared **Next** button.

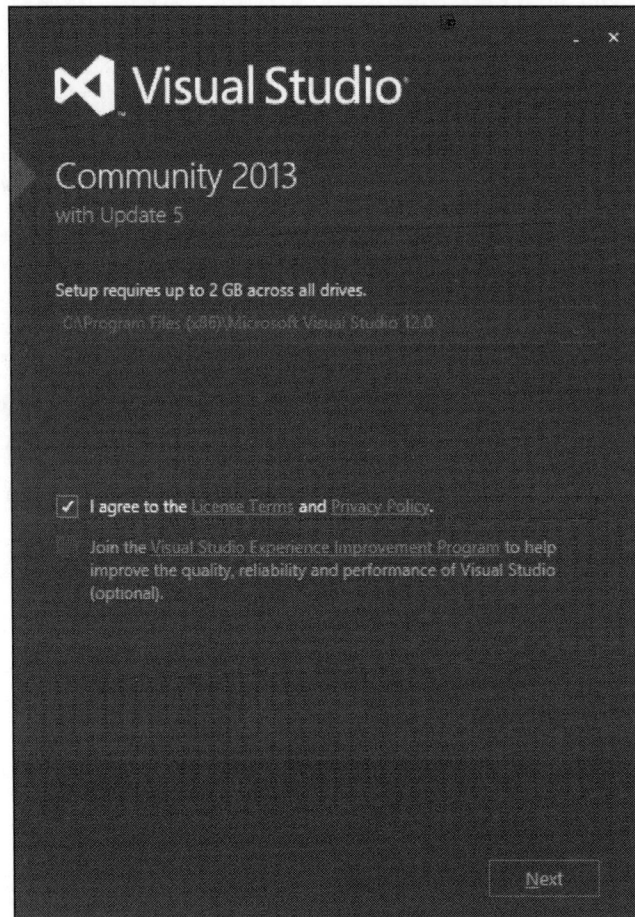

3. Just keep the initial default settings to install and then click on the **Install** button and wait for it to download the software. This may take a while, so feel free to take a rest and come back later (I had it go overnight, but depending on your Internet connection, it may be completed sooner).

> For more instructions on setting up Visual Studio to build a project from scratch, visit `https://docs.unrealengine.com/latest/INT/ Programming/Development/VisualStudioSetup/index.html`.

4. Once Visual Studio is installed, we can then open up the Unreal Editor by clicking on the **Launch** button from the Unreal Engine Launcher.

5. Start a new project from the **Project Browser** tab by selecting the **New Project** tab. Click on the **C++** tab and then select **Third person** and make sure that **With Starter Content** is selected. Give the project a Name (`Cookbook_Chapter9`). Once you are done, click on **Create Project** and wait for it to finish compiling the project.

> If, on the bottom of your screen, you see a red box saying there was no compiler found, you'll need to install Visual Studio 2013. If that's the case, just follow the same instructions I mentioned earlier.

6. Now once we create the project, we'll see that unlike before when the editor opened up by itself, this time Visual Studio or XCode has opened up for us as well.

7. If it is your first time opening Visual Studio, you may be asked to sign in. Do so if you'd like to, or click on the **Not now, maybe later** button. Afterward, you may be asked to choose a color theme (I picked **Dark**). Then, click on **Start Visual Studio** and wait for it to finish preparing the program for use.

8. Now that we know what's in here, let's set up our project to actually compile correctly. There are two steps that we'll need to look into. Firstly, at the top bar, you should set the **Solution Configurations** property (if you hover your mouse over a part of the toolbar for a short time it will display what property it is) and secondly, under **Solution Configurations**, select `DebugGame Editor`. To see where the property and dropdown are, take a look at the following screenshot:

> If you do not see the **Solutions Configurations** property, on the far right,
> click on the dropdown button and make sure that the property is checked.

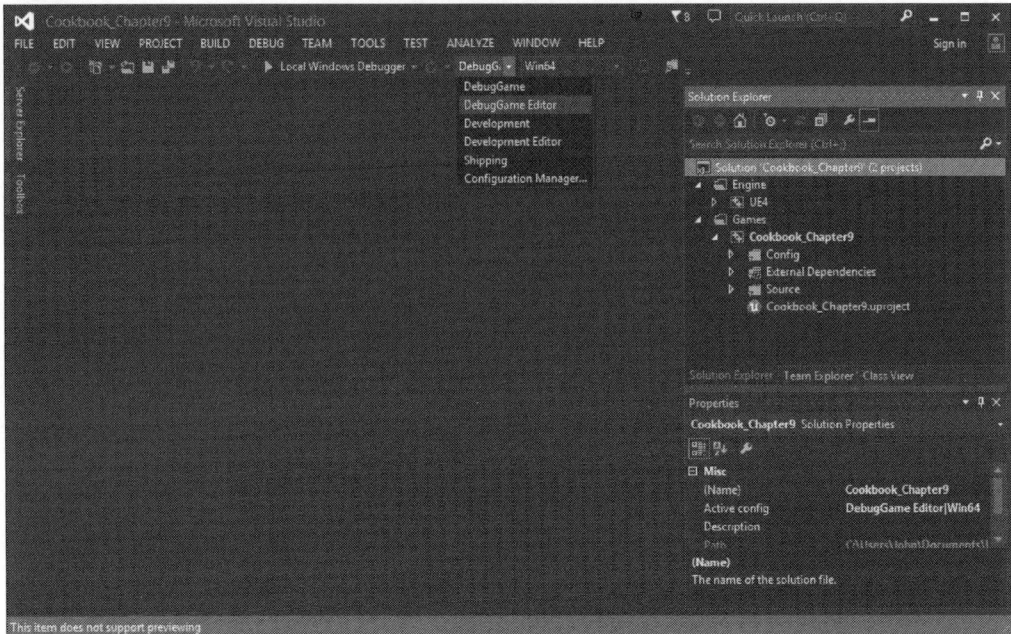

The **Debug Game Editor** mode builds the project with debug symbols enabled for
the Game code but not the Editor. This means that when the game is running, we'll
be able to debug it; you can learn more about this at `https://msdn.microsoft.`
`com/en-us/library/k0k771bt.aspx`.

> For more information on all of the different kinds of configurations,
> refer to `https://docs.unrealengine.com/latest/INT/`
> `Programming/Development/CompilingProjects/index.`
> `html#buildconfiguration`.

9. That being said, it's hard for us to tell what that setting is in the default way that Visual Studio is set up, but thankfully, the program is extremely configurable, so let's increase the width of that dropdown menu. To do this, right-click on the toolbar and select **Customize**.

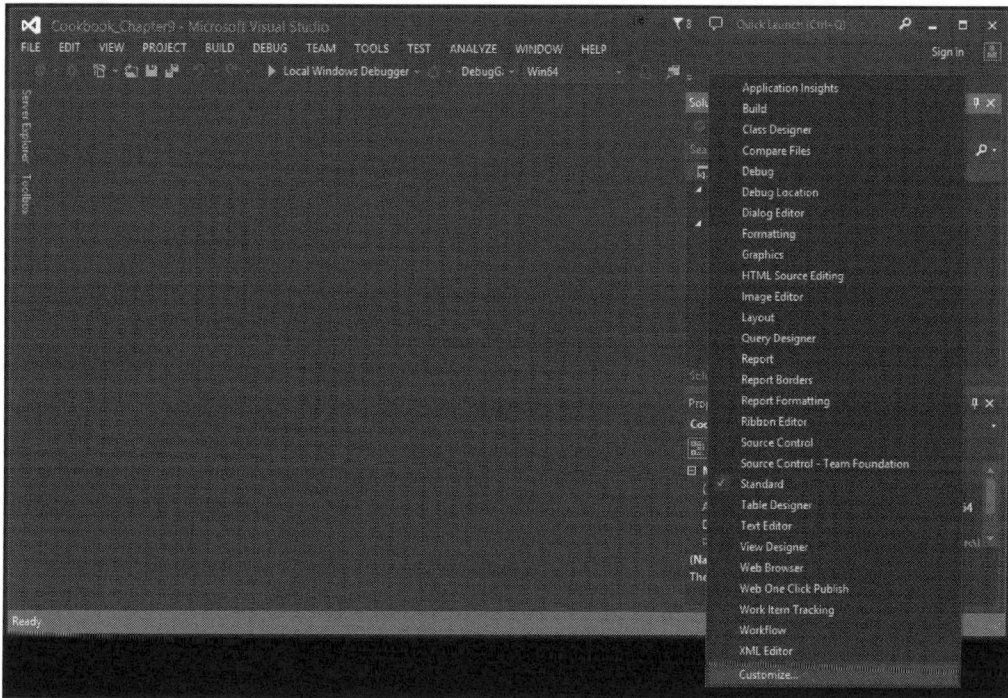

10. From the menu that pops up, select **Commands** and then click on the toggle by **Toolbar**.

11. Select the dropdown next to **Toolbar** and from there, select **Standard**.

12. From the **Controls:** list that pops up from the bottom-right side, scroll down the list until you arrive at the **Solutions Configurations** option and select it.

13. Then, click on the **Modify Selection** dropdown on the right-hand side. From the window that pops up, under **Width:**, type in the value as `150`. You should notice that the area where **DebugGame Editor** is selected is much easier to read now. Afterward, click on the **Close** button.

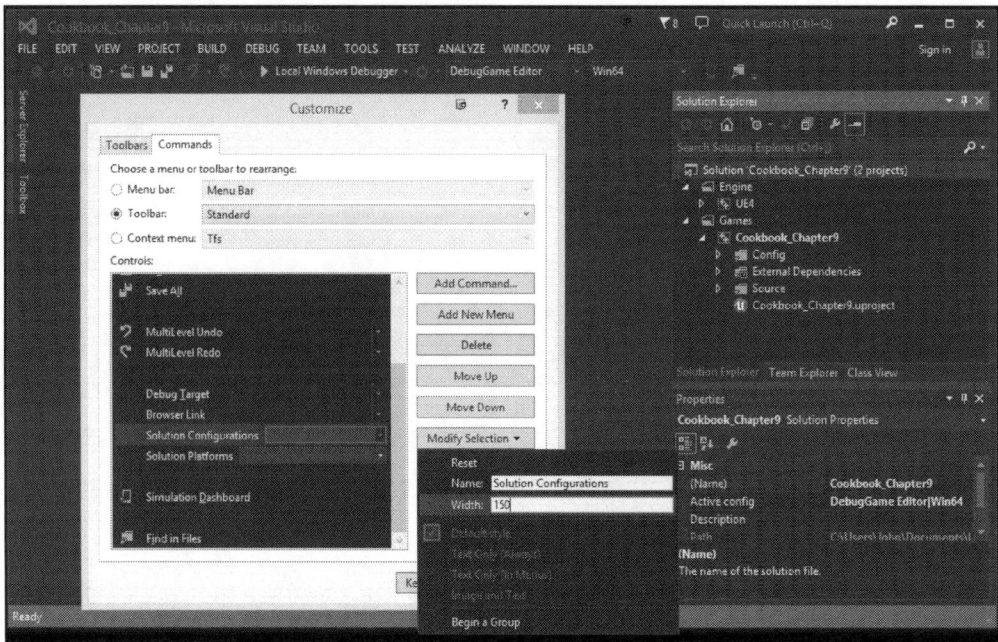

14. Now, let's run the editor to make sure everything's working correctly. In the **Solution Explorer** tab on the right-hand side, right-click on the project name (`Cookbook_Chapter9`) and navigate to **Debug | Start New Instance**.

15. It's going to ask whether you want to build the project, so select **Yes**, and our project will be built.

    The first thing that's happening here is that the **compiler** is going to compile the code. When compiling the code, it's taking all of the files that are part of the project and translating them from the source code that we've written and converting it into object code (something that computers can understand). This is then taken by a **linker**, which is the tool that will combine all of the modules we've created to produce an executable file.

For more information on compiling and linking, refer to `http://www.cprogramming.com/compilingandlinking.html`.

This will take some time when we build a project for the first time, but in future this will be much quicker because it will only compile the files that have changed since the last time you compiled.

If you are using Xcode on the Mac side, navigating to **Product** | **Run** from the menu will launch the UE4 Editor in the **Debug** mode and all the custom C++ code will be available in the editor.

To configure Xcode properly for UE4, make sure the UE4 Editor is selected as the current scheme—Xcode scheme selector.

With this, we should see our project open up!

16. Close the editor and return to Visual Studio.

Now before we go on, I want to talk a little bit about the folders and content that are created automatically for us. On the right-hand side, you'll see a tab called **Solution Explorer** and under that, you'll see two folders—Engine and Games. Engine contains the UE4 Solution, which is the Unreal Engine 4 itself in its full glory. For our purposes, we can use it as a reference, but we will not be modifying it, we will rather be extending from it. The next folder, Games, contains the games that we are creating using UE4, and in my case, I'll see another solution in bold called Cookbook_ Chapter9. Being bolded means that if we click on the Local Windows Debugger button, that'll be the project that'll be built when we tell Visual Studio to compile or run our project. If you extend the solution folder, you'll find the following folders:

- **Config**: This is where all of the configurations that make our game unique will exist, and where settings, input, and so on will live. These files normally have a .ini extension.

- **External Dependences**: This contains all of the headers files for the Unreal Engine. Also known as include files sometimes, header files hold declarations for other files to use without having to see the source code. These files normally have a .h extension to them.

- **Source**: Inside it will be a folder with the same name as your project. This is where we can modify how different modules will work with our projects and add additional files for us to work with. These contain headers (.h) and source files (.cpp).

With this, we now have our environment created to be able to start working in code!

Displaying text during runtime

While you're creating your project, one of the things that can be valuable to know is how to give yourself information while the game is going on. This way, you can check the order of the things being called and/or what values data have.

Since it was first written 40 years ago, it has been a tradition for beginning programmers to write a function that displays "Hello World!" on the screen. Let's do that now!

Getting ready

Before we start working on this we need to have a project created and set up. So, follow the previous recipe all the way to completion.

How to do it...

In this recipe, we will extend and customize the built-in `GameMode` class to do just that:

1. With Visual Studio opened, go over to the **Solution Explorer** tab and open up the `Games/Cookbook_Chapter9/Source/Cookbook_Chapter9` folder, and you should see a number of files. Double-click on the `Cookbook_Chapter9GameMode.h` file to open it.

    This file contains the information for a class called `ACookbook_Chapter9GameMode`. A class is a container that holds variables (data) and functions (series of instructions). Think of this class as a blueprint full of information about what this object is.

    This is a child class of `AGameMode` which means that it contains everything that `AGameMode` has, and we can add additional information to it as well as extend functions that were created previously, which is what we are going to do.

2. Underneath the line `ACookbook_Chapter9GameMode();`, add the following line:

    ```
    void StartMatch();
    ```

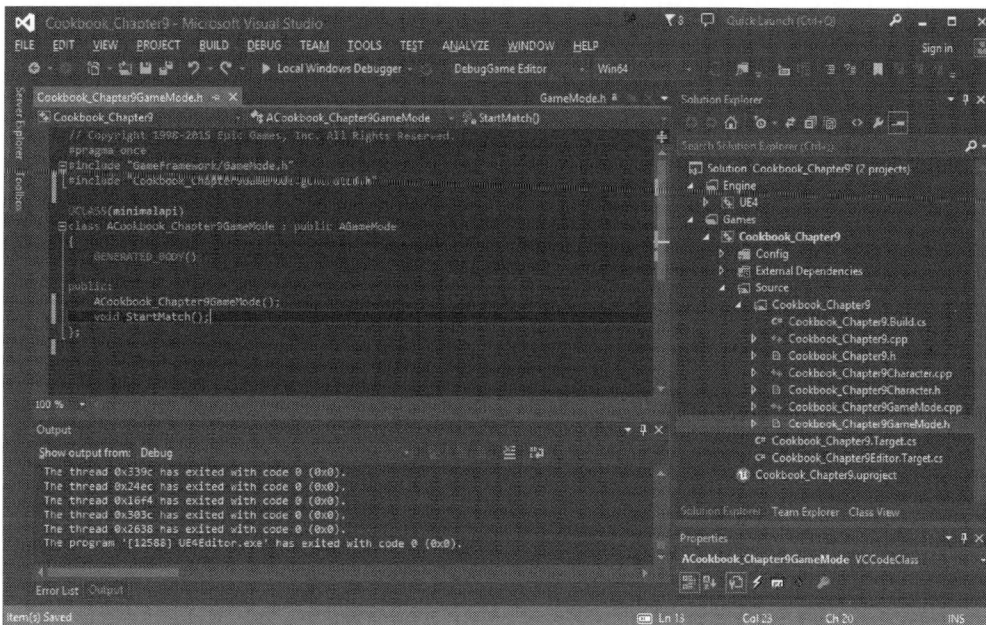

This is what's known as a function declaration and it is saying that somewhere else, there is the implementation of this `StartMatch` function, which takes in no parameters and returns nothing (`void`).

3. Next, we need to write the function definition. To do this, from the **Solution Explorer** tab, double-click on the `Cookbook_Chapter9GameMode.cpp` file to open it.

4. Then we need to write the `StartMatch` function, which will look similar to the following:

```cpp
void ACookbook_Chapter9GameMode::StartMatch()
{
  Super::StartMatch();

  if (GEngine)
  {
    GEngine->AddOnScreenDebugMessage(-1, 10.0f,
                                     FColor::Yellow,
                                     "Hello World!");
  }
}
```

This code is first doing what the parent's version did (by using `Super`). Afterward, it is checking whether the game engine exists (`if (GEngine)`), and if it does, it is adding a debug message on the screen that lasts for 10 seconds on the screen and says **Hello World!**. The `f` at the end of the `10.0` stands for float, as in floating point number which means that it can use a decimal value. The `FColor::Yellow` states that the color of the text will be yellow and the `-1` value lets the function know that we don't want to replace a message if one is already there, we just want to create a new one.

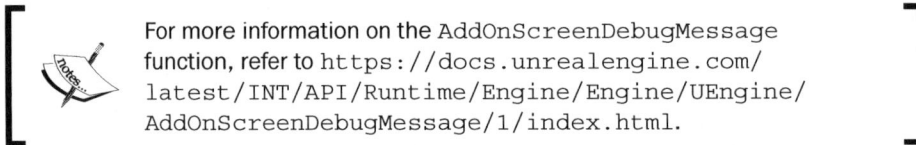

> For more information on the `AddOnScreenDebugMessage` function, refer to https://docs.unrealengine.com/latest/INT/API/Runtime/Engine/Engine/UEngine/AddOnScreenDebugMessage/1/index.html.

After this, you may notice a red squiggly line underneath the `GEngine` part of our code. This is because `GEngine` doesn't exist at this point, or rather it does, but we don't know where it is. To find that variable, we will need to include the `Engine.h` file in our script.

5. At the very top below the other `#include` directives, add the following line:

```cpp
#include "Engine.h" //GEngine
```

The entire file should look similar to the following:

```cpp
// Copyright 1998-2015 Epic Games, Inc. All Rights
    Reserved.

#include "Cookbook_Chapter9.h"
#include "Cookbook_Chapter9GameMode.h"
#include "Cookbook_Chapter9Character.h"
```

```cpp
#include "Engine.h" //GEngine

ACookbook_Chapter9GameMode::ACookbook_Chapter9GameMode()
{
  // set default pawn class to our Blueprinted character
  static ConstructorHelpers::FClassFinder<APawn>
    PlayerPawnBPClass(TEXT("/Game/ThirdPerson/Blueprints/
    ThirdPersonCharacter"));
  if (PlayerPawnBPClass.Class != NULL)
  {
    DefaultPawnClass = PlayerPawnBPClass.Class;
  }
}

void ACookbook_Chapter9GameMode::StartMatch()
{
  Super::StartMatch();

  if (GEngine)
  {
    GEngine->AddOnScreenDebugMessage(-1, 10.0f,
      FColor::Yellow, "Hello World!");
  }
}
```

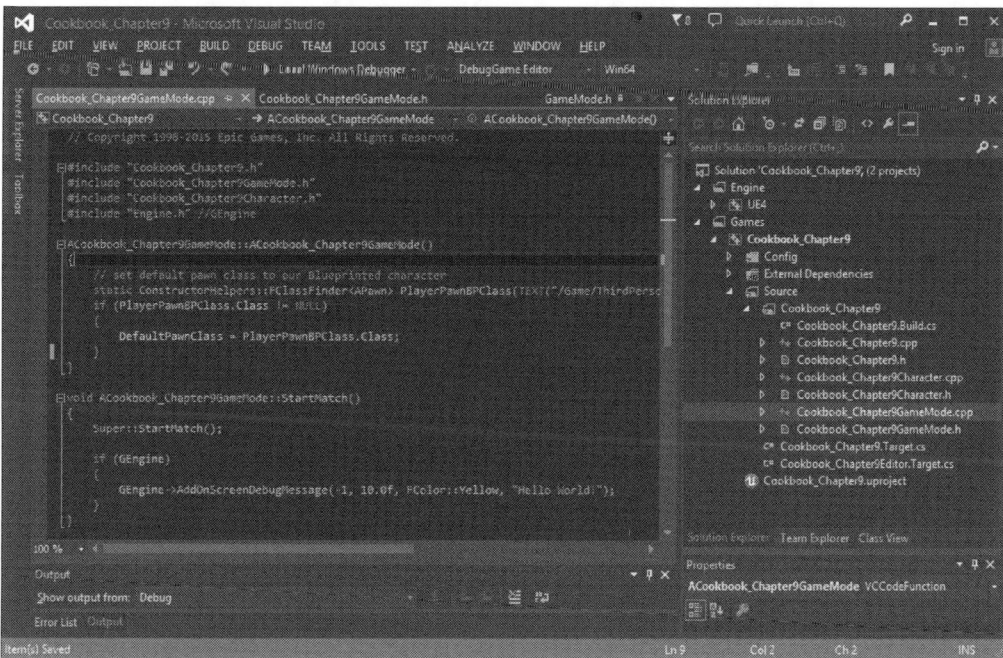

> The lines with // at the beginning are referred to as **comments**. These
> are the texts that don't do anything to the code, but are used to help
> people reading the code understand exactly what something below it is
> doing. Comments can also be created by placing a /*, and until you see
> a */, whatever is in between is commented.

6. After this, we need to compile our code to see any changes. Follow the method
   we used previously or click on the **Local Windows Debugger** button to start it,
   saying **Yes** when it asks you to build.

7. Once the program opens up, again click on the **Play** button.

Just as we thought, when the game starts, it displays the text "Hello World!". Congratulations on entering the world of programming!

> In addition to printing on the screen, it's often useful to write things to a log file so that you have access to the information wherever you are. For information on that, there is an excellent guide at `https://wiki.unrealengine.com/Logs,_Printing_Messages_To_Yourself_During_Runtime`.

Networking 101 – creating collectables with networking

Networking is one of the more complex things you can do as a programmer. Unreal uses a client-server model for communication between multiple computers. In this case, the server is the person who started the game and the clients are those who are playing the game with the first person. In order for things happening on everyone's game to work correctly, we need to call certain code at certain times to certain people.

For example, when a client wants to shoot his/her gun, they send a message to the server, which will then determine whether you hit anything and then tell all the clients what happened using replication. This can be important because some things, such as the Game Mode, only exist on the server.

> For more information on the client-server model, refer to `https://en.wikipedia.org/wiki/Client%E2%80%93server_model`.

Getting ready

Before we start working on this, we need to have a project created and set up. Follow the *Setting up your development environment* recipe all the way to completion.

How to do it...

To give you an idea of how it works, let's do a simple example of a coin collectable:

1. Navigate to **File | New C++ Class**, and you should see the **Choose Parent Class** window pop up. Select **Actor** and then click on **Next**.

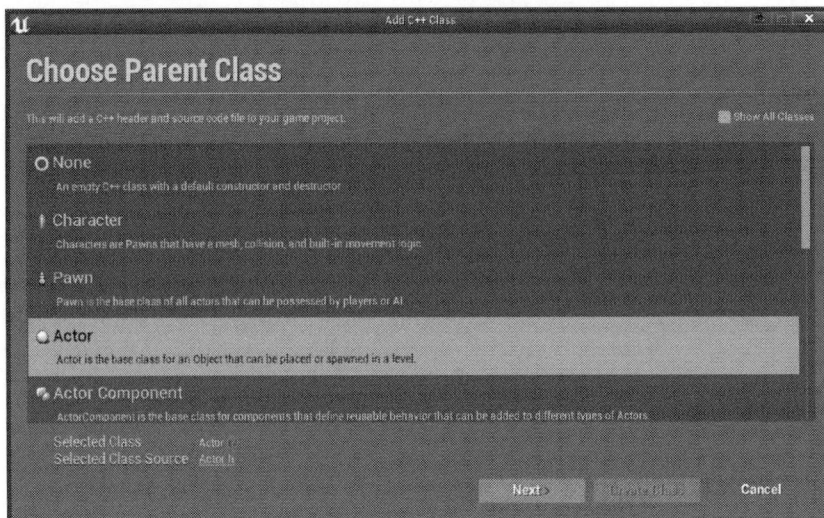

2. From there, we then want to set **Name** of our object to something that makes sense; in this case, I named it `CollectableObject`. Once done, click on the **Create Class** button to add it to the project and compile the code.

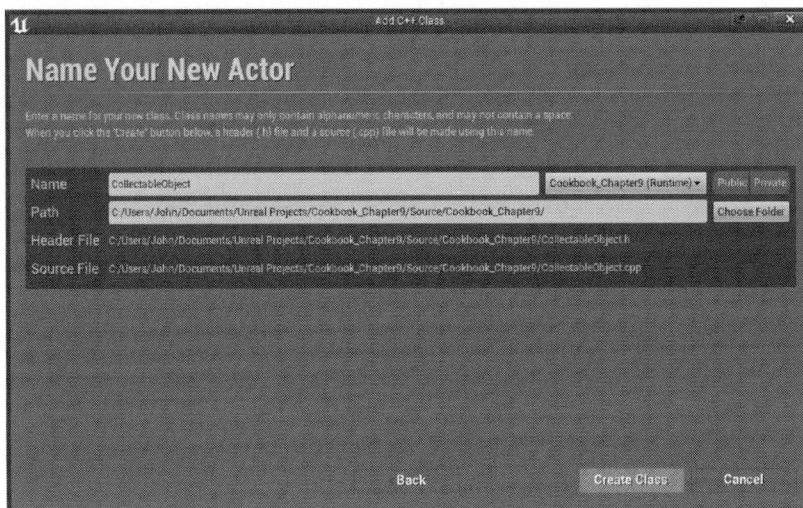

3. Now, we should see two new files being created inside our Visual Studio project: CollectibleObject.cpp and CollectibleObject.h. Open up CollectableObject.h and put in the following code:

```
#pragma once

#include "GameFramework/Actor.h"
#include "CollectableObject.generated.h"

UCLASS()
class COOKBOOK_CHAPTER9_API ACollectableObject : public
  AActor
{
  GENERATED_BODY()

public:
  // Sets default values for this actor's properties
  ACollectableObject(const FObjectInitializer&
    ObjectInitializer);

  // Event called when something starts to overlaps the
  // sphere collider
  UFUNCTION()
  void OnBeginOverlap(class AActor* OtherActor,
                      class UPrimitiveComponent*
                        OtherComp,
                      int32 OtherBodyIndex, bool
                        bFromSweep,
                      const FHitResult& SweepResult);

  // Our server function to update the score.
  UFUNCTION(Reliable, Server, WithValidation)
  void UpdateScore(int32 Amount);
  void UpdateScore_Implementation(int32 Amount);
  bool UpdateScore_Validate(int32 Amount);

};
```

> Note that there is the COOKBOOK_CHAPTER9_API text before ACollectableObject. This automatically-generated part of the code uses the same name as our project. If you did not name your project Cookbook_Chapter9, the name will be different.

We've done a number of things in this new snippet of code. We've replaced the original constructor with a new one that takes in a `FObjectInitializer` object as a parameter. We've done this so that we can add a new component to the object. The next thing we've done is that we have got rid of the `Tick` and `BeginPlay` functions as we won't be using them.

After that, we've added a new function called **OnBeginOverlap**. We will be talking more about what it does later, but for now, it will be a function that'll be called whenever the object will be overlapped with another object (such as the player). Lastly, we have three functions—`UpdateScore`, `UpdateScore_Implementation`, and `UpdateScore_Validate`—which are used to call, implement, and validate the replication properties as we specified in the `UFUNCTION` above its declaration.

> For more information on replication and how the functions are named in their certain way, refer to `https://wiki.unrealengine.com/Replication`.

4. Next, open up the `CollectibleObject.cpp` file and put in the following code:

```cpp
#include "Cookbook_Chapter9.h"
#include "CollectableObject.h"
#include "Engine.h" //GEngine


// Sets default values for this actor's properties
ACollectableObject::ACollectableObject(const
  FObjectInitializer& ObjectInitializer) :
  Super(ObjectInitializer)
{
  // Must be true for an Actor to replicate anything
  bReplicates = true;

  // Create a sphere collider for players to hit
  USphereComponent * SphereCollider =
    ObjectInitializer.CreateDefaultSubobject
    <USphereComponent>(this, TEXT("SphereComponent"));

  // Sets the size of our collider to have a radius of
  // 64 units
  SphereCollider->InitSphereRadius(64.0f);

  // Sets the root of our object to be the sphere collider
  RootComponent = SphereCollider;
```

```
    // Makes it so that OnBeginOverlap will be called
    // whenever something hits this.
    SphereCollider->OnComponentBeginOverlap.AddDynamic(this,
                        &ACollectableObject::OnBeginOverlap);
}


// Event called when something starts to overlaps the
// sphere collider
void ACollectableObject::OnBeginOverlap(
                            class AActor* OtherActor,
                class UPrimitiveComponent* OtherComp,
                                int32 OtherBodyIndex,
                                    bool bFromSweep,
                    const FHitResult& SweepResult)
{
  // If I am the server
  if (Role == ROLE_Authority)
  {
    // Then a coin will be gained!
    UpdateScore(1);
    Destroy();
  }
}


// Do something here that modifies game state.
void ACollectableObject::UpdateScore_Implementation(int32
    Amount)
{
  if (GEngine)
  {
    GEngine->AddOnScreenDebugMessage(-1, 5.0f,
                                FColor::Green,
                                "Collected!");
  }
}


// Optionally validate the request and return false if the
// function should not be run.
bool ACollectableObject::UpdateScore_Validate(int32 Amount)
{
  return true;
}
```

Again, as before, if you have a different name for your project, the `#include "Cookbook_Chapter9.h"` line will also be different.

This code does a number of different things. The first function has the same name as our object's class and has no return type. This special type of function is known as a **constructor**. This function is special because it's the first thing that gets called when an object is created. In this case, we make sure that our object is going to be replicated, and then after that, we create a sphere collider that we tell (via a listener) to call the `OnBeginOverlap` function when it collides with another object it using the `OnComponentBeginOverlap` function.

For more information on the `OnComponentBeginOverlap` function and the function needed to be given to it, refer to `https://docs.unrealengine.com/latest/INT/API/ Runtime/Engine/Components/UPrimitiveComponent/ OnComponentBeginOverlap/index.html`.

After this, inside our `OnBeginOverlap` function, we first check if we are currently on the server. We don't want things to get called multiple times, and we want the server to be the one that tells the other clients that we've increased our score. We also call the `UpdateScore` function, which will, in turn, call the `UpdateScore_ Implementation` function that we created and it will display a message, saying that we've collected the object via printing out some text like we used earlier.

Finally, the `UpdateScore_Validate` function is required for us to have and just tells the game that we should always run the implementation for the `UpdateScore` function.

5. Save both files and go back into the Unreal Editor. From there, click on the **Compile** button in order to update the game with the changes we've made without having to close the game.

6. Once you see a message at the bottom-right of the screen that says the compilation is complete with no errors, we can then actually add our collectable objects to the scene. From the **Content Browser** tab, select the `ThirdPerson` folder and then click on the green **Add New** button and select **Blueprint Class**.

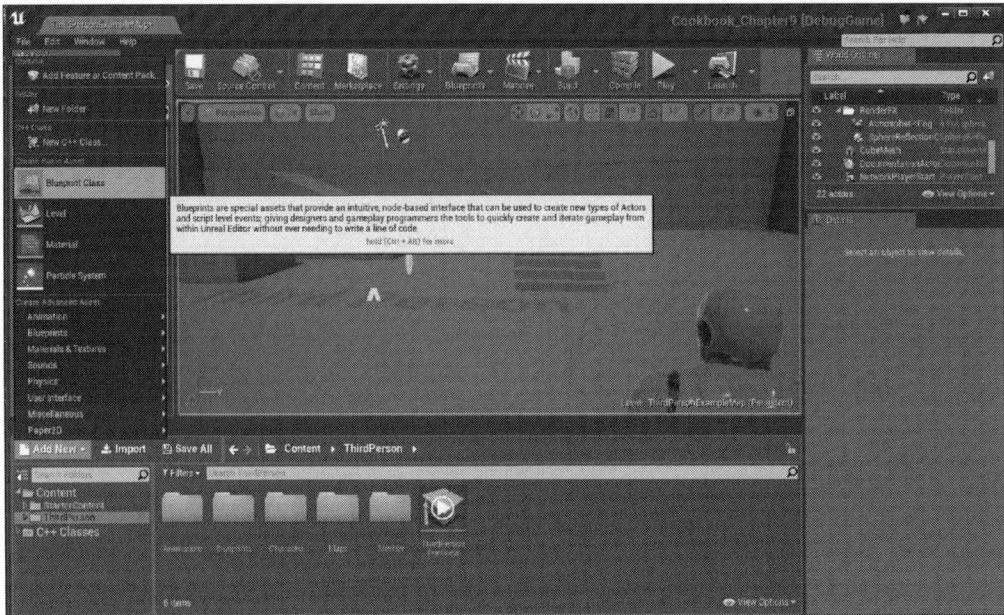

7. From the popup asking you to select the parent class, go to the **All Classes** section at the bottom and start typing in `CollectableObject`, then select it from the list. Once selected, click on the **Select** button.

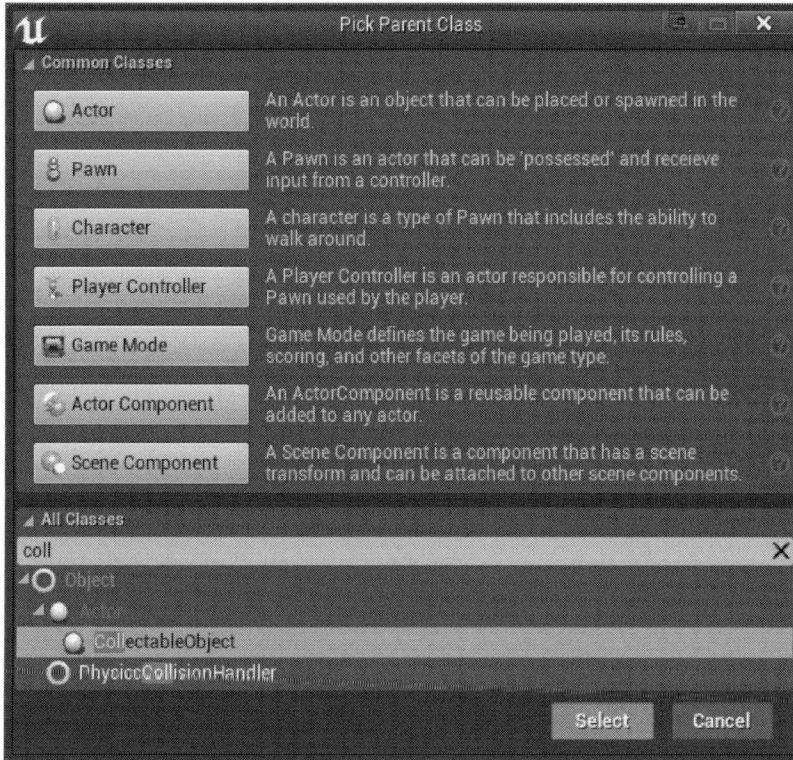

8. After this, it will have the newly-created object selected, which will need a name. Type in `Collectible` and then press *Enter*.

9. Double-click on our newly-created `Collectible` object to open up the Blueprints Editor.

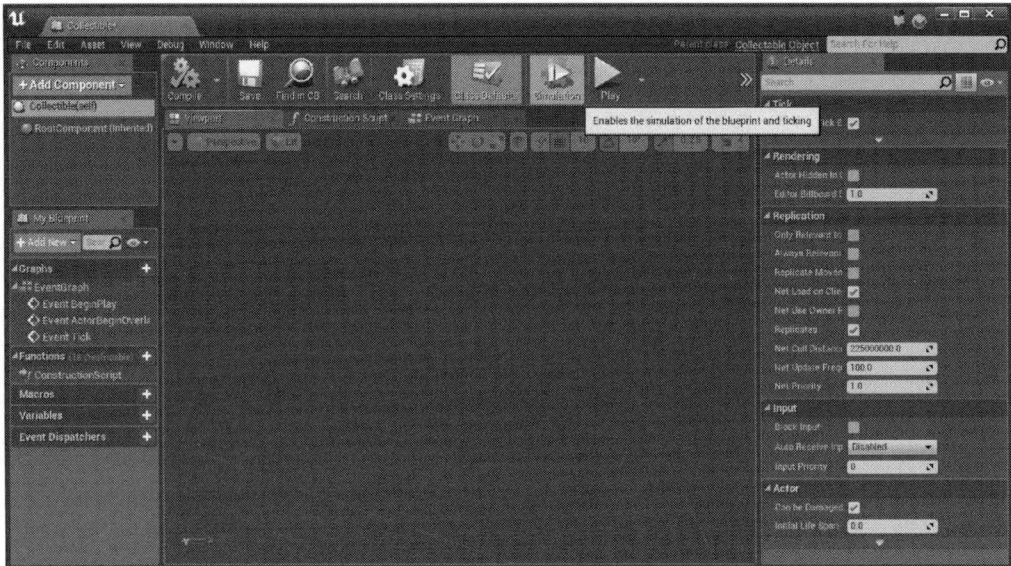

Blueprint editor for the Collectible object

You'll notice that there is a red sphere in the level, just like we wanted to be created in our class file! Right now though, it'll almost be impossible for us to hit it because we can't see anything. Let's add a particle system to make it easy to see.

10. From the **Components** tab, select **Add Component** and then **Particle System**. From the **Details** tab under the **Particles** section, select the dropdown to the right of the **Template** property and then select P_Fire, and you should see the particle system start playing.

Adding a fire particle system to the collectible

11. Hit the **Compile** and **Save** buttons and then close the Blueprint Editor. After this, drag and drop two of the objects in the world and set their **Z Location** to 200 so that you can see the whole thing.

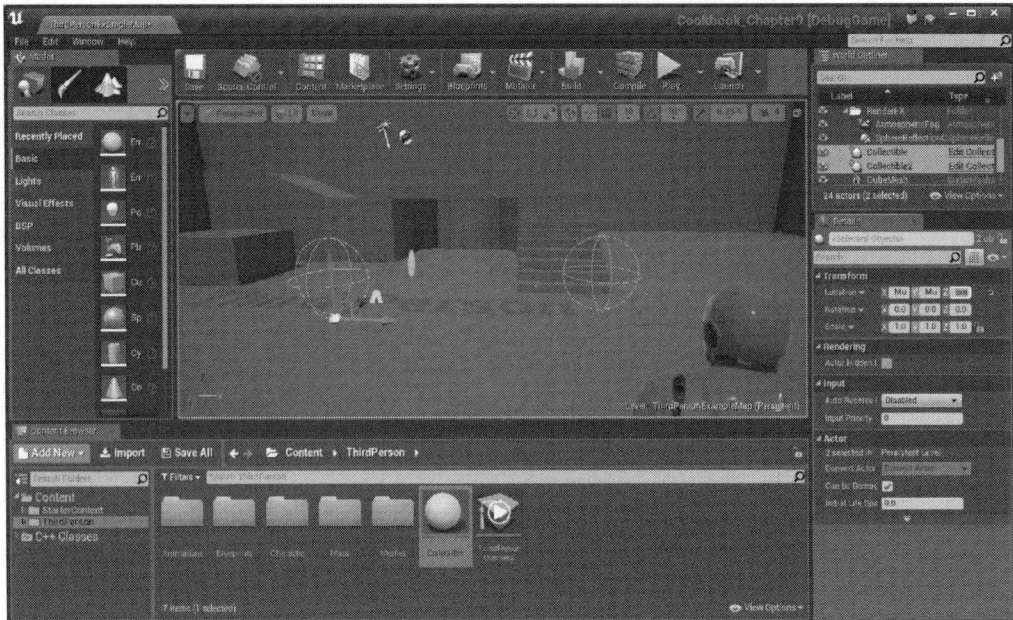

The level view after compilation

12. Lastly, we'll need to have a way to play two versions of the project at once to see what happens. Click on the dropdown to the right of the **Play** button and change **Number of Players** to 2 and then click on the **New Editor Window** option, which will open two windows with players.

Opening two simultaneous windows

And with this, you can see the message is replicated from the server to the client!

> If you're interested in seeing another example of using networking and replication, refer to `https://wiki.unrealengine.com/Networking/Replication`.
>
> In addition, you can also check out the Shooter Game example project included with Unreal Engine 4 and read the files to get a feeling for how it's used in a complete example.

Saving or loading games and keyboard input with C++

As games get more and more complex and longer and longer, players will often need to play a game within multiple sessions. However, by default, players will need to start over from scratch. In this recipe, we will be going over how to save a variable and load it at runtime.

Getting ready

Before we start working on this, we need to have a project created and set up. Follow the *Setting up your development environment* recipe all the way to completion.

How to do it...

To give you an idea of how it works, let's do a simple example of saving a player's position and rotation, which we can return to using keyboard input:

1. Navigate to **File | New C++ Class**, and you should see the **Choose Parent Class** window pop up. Check the **Show All Classes** option, select **SaveGame**, and click on **Next**.

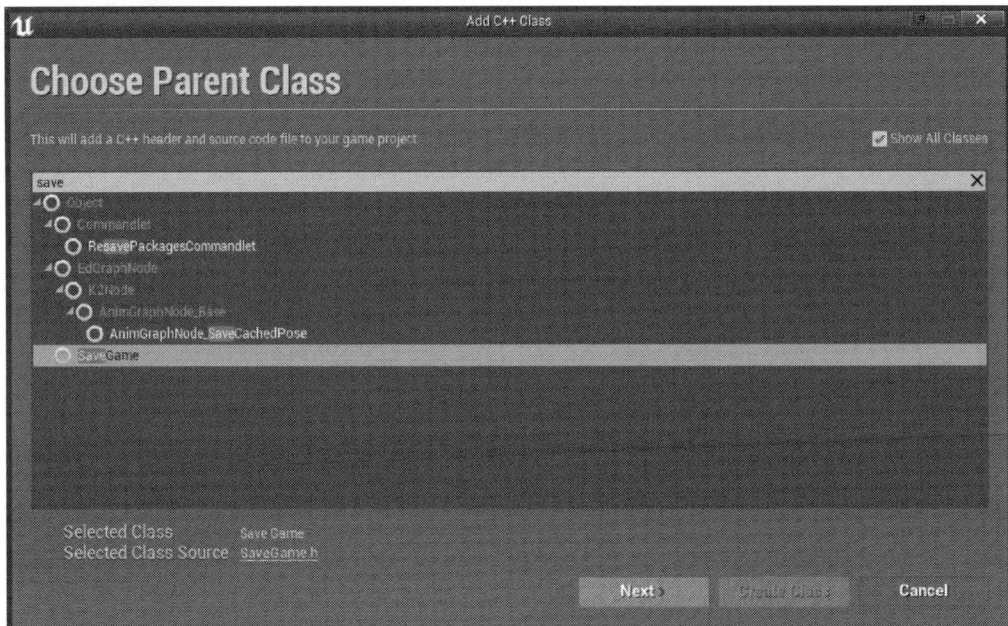

2. Next, it'll ask you for the name of your save class. In this instance, I'm going to leave it as `MySaveGame` and click on **Create Class** and wait for it to finish compiling.

3. In the header file for the object, we'll need to add any variables that we want to save. In this case, I want to save my player's position and rotation, so I'm going to do the following:

```
#pragma once

#include "GameFramework/SaveGame.h"
#include "MySaveGame.generated.h"

/**
 *
 */
UCLASS()
class COOKBOOK_CHAPTER9_API UMySaveGame : public USaveGame
{
    GENERATED_BODY()

    public:

        UPROPERTY(VisibleAnywhere, Category = Basic)
        FVector PlayerPosition;

        UPROPERTY(VisibleAnywhere, Category = Basic)
        FRotator PlayerRotation;

};
```

The `PlayerPosition` variable is of type `FVector`, more commonly referred to as a vector. A **vector** is a series of three values, X, Y, and Z, which we've been using already for every object's position, and scaled in the appropriate axis. The rotation of an object is stored in a special type called `FRotator`.

4. We aren't doing anything special inside the `.cpp` file, but that would be where we would have set any default values. Instead, open up the `Cookbook_Chapter9Character.h` file. Under the `public` section of the class, add in the following bolded code:

```
// Copyright 1998-2015 Epic Games, Inc. All Rights Reserved.
#pragma once
#include "GameFramework/Character.h"
#include "Cookbook_Chapter9Character.generated.h"
```

```cpp
UCLASS(config=Game)
class ACookbook_Chapter9Character : public ACharacter
{
  GENERATED_BODY()

  /** Camera boom positioning the camera behind the
    character */
  UPROPERTY(VisibleAnywhere, BlueprintReadOnly, Category =
    Camera, meta = (AllowPrivateAccess = "true"))
    class USpringArmComponent* CameraBoom;

/** Follow camera */
  UPROPERTY(VisibleAnywhere, BlueprintReadOnly, Category =
    Camera, meta = (AllowPrivateAccess = "true"))
  class UCameraComponent* FollowCamera;

public:
  ACookbook_Chapter9Character();

  /** Base turn rate, in deg/sec. Other scaling may affect
    final turn rate. */
  UPROPERTY(VisibleAnywhere, BlueprintReadOnly,
    Category=Camera)
  float BaseTurnRate;

  /** Base look up/down rate, in deg/sec. Other scaling may
    affect final rate. */
  UPROPERTY(VisibleAnywhere, BlueprintReadOnly,
    Category=Camera)
  float BaseLookUpRate;

  // Saves the game
  void SaveMyGameFile();

  // Loads the game
  void LoadMyGameFile();

  // Called every frame
  void Tick(float DeltaTime);

protected:

  /** Called for forwards/backward input */
  void MoveForward(float Value);

    // Other declarations below
```

5. Next, we need to implement the functionality in the `MySaveGame.cpp` file. At the top, we need to add in some includes, so below the others, add the following:

```
#include "MySaveGame.h"
#include "Kismet/GameplayStatics.h"
#include "Engine.h" //GEngine
```

This will allow us to use the `MySaveGame` class and `GEngine` inside of the file.

6. After that we need to enable the ability for the `Tick` function to be called. To do this, go to the constructor of the `Character` class (`ACookbook_Chapter9Character`) and add the following bold line:

```
ACookbook_Chapter9Character::ACookbook_Chapter9Character()
{
    PrimaryActorTick.bCanEverTick = true;

    // Set size for collision capsule
    GetCapsuleComponent()->InitCapsuleSize(42.f, 96.0f);

    // Other code below
```

7. Now we can implement the `Tick` function:

```
void ACookbook_Chapter9Character::Tick(float DeltaTime)
{
    APlayerController * PController =
      Cast<APlayerController>(Controller);

    // Any time we cast, we need to check if the variable is
      valid
    if (PController != NULL)
    {
        //  If Q is pressed, save the game
        if (PController->WasInputKeyJustPressed(EKeys::Q))
        {
            SaveMyGameFile();
        }
        // Otherwise, if E is pressed we will load
        else if (PController->WasInputKeyJustPressed(EKeys::E))
        {
            LoadMyGameFile();
        }
    }
}
```

The `Tick` function is called in every frame in the game (at 60 FPS, the game is running 60 frames per second), so it'll happen quite often, which is important when it comes to checking input. If the player presses the *Q* or *E* key, we will call the `Save` and/or `Load` functions, respectively.

8. After that, let's implement the function that will save the game:

```cpp
void ACookbook_Chapter9Character::SaveMyGameFile()
{
  // Create a save object for us to store values
  UMySaveGame* SaveGameInstance =
    Cast<UMySaveGame>(UGameplayStatics::
    CreateSaveGameObject(UMySaveGame::StaticClass()));

  // Set the player's current location and rotation
  SaveGameInstance->PlayerPosition = GetActorLocation();
  SaveGameInstance->PlayerRotation = GetActorRotation();

  //Saves the new save file into the first save slot (0)
    with
  // a name of "SaveSlot"
  UGameplayStatics::SaveGameToSlot(SaveGameInstance,
                                   "SaveSlot", 0);

  if (GEngine)
  {
    // Notify the player that we saved
    GEngine->AddOnScreenDebugMessage(-1, 10.0f,
              FColor::Yellow, "Game Saved!");
  }
}
```

9. Finally, we need to implement the way to load the game:

```cpp
void ACookbook_Chapter9Character::LoadMyGameFile()
{
  // Create a save object for us to store values to load
  UMySaveGame* LoadGameInstance =
    Cast<UMySaveGame>(UGameplayStatics::
    CreateSaveGameObject(UMySaveGame::StaticClass()));

  // Loads the save slot we created previously
  LoadGameInstance = Cast<UMySaveGame>
    (UGameplayStatics::LoadGameFromSlot("SaveSlot", 0));
```

```
//Set the player's location and rotation to what we saved
SetActorLocationAndRotation(
            LoadGameInstance->PlayerPosition,
            LoadGameInstance->PlayerRotation);

if (GEngine)
{
  // Notify the player that we loaded
  GEngine->AddOnScreenDebugMessage(-1, 10.0f,
                  FColor::Yellow, "Loaded!");
}
}
```

10. With all that done, save all of the files, go back into the Unreal Editor and then hit the **Compile** button.

11. Once the compilation finishes, start up the game by using the **Play** button.

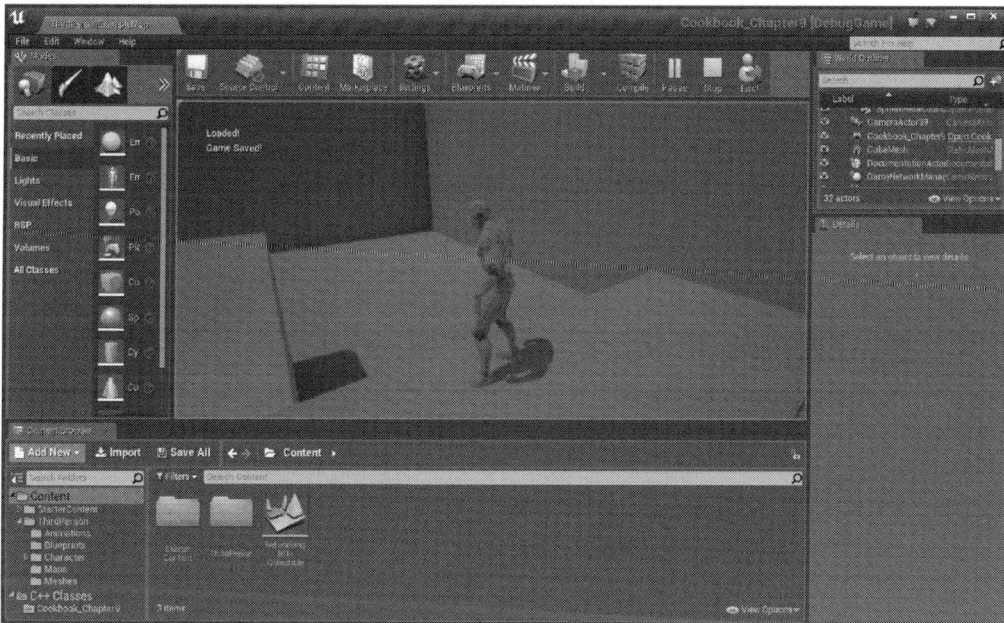

Starting the game with Play button

Now, whenever you press the *Q* button, your position and rotation will be saved and if you walk around and then hit the *E* key, you'll be brought exactly to where you last left it!

> If you're interested in taking this to the next level, there is a tutorial on how to do file management, being able to create and modify files on the player's hard drive at `https://wiki.unrealengine.com/File_Management,_Create_Folders,_Delete_Files,_and_More`.

Creating custom blueprint nodes

Blueprint is very powerful and has access to most of the functions that are created for a particular class, but there may be certain pieces of code that you want to be always available for use inside Blueprints. Thankfully, we can make use of a custom class extending from Blueprint Function Library to do so.

Getting ready

Before we start working on this, we need to have a project created and set up. Follow the *Setting up your development environment* recipe all the way to completion.

How to do it...

Often games will display a copyright notice on the main menu. We also do this at the beginning of every class that we create at the header with it, by default, displaying this:

```
//Fill out your copyright notice in the Description page of
  //Project Settings.
```

Rather than typing it in every time we want to show it, let's create a note that will get it for us and in the process, teach us how we can create custom blueprint nodes that can do whatever actions we'd like in the future:

1. Navigate to **File | New C++ Class**, and you should see the **Choose Parent Class** window pop up. Scroll down and select **Blueprint Function Library** and then click on **Next**.

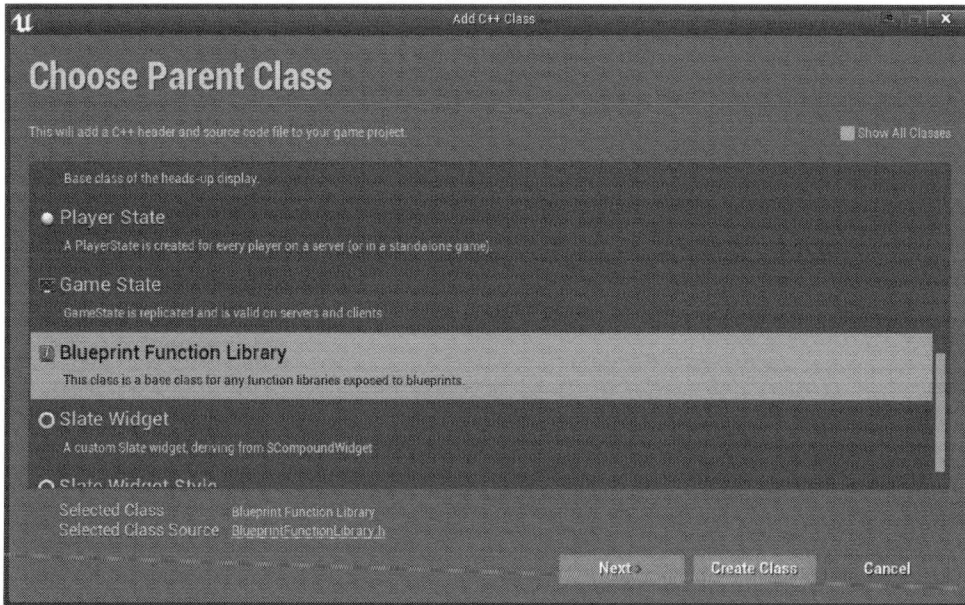

2. Select the name you'd like for this class and then click on the **Create Class** button and wait for it to compile.

3. Once compiled, go into the .h file and set it to the following code:

```
#pragma once

#include "Kismet/BlueprintFunctionLibrary.h"
#include "MyBlueprintFunctionLibrary.generated.h"

UCLASS()
class COOKBOOK_CHAPTER9_API UMyBlueprintFunctionLibrary :
    public UBlueprintFunctionLibrary
```

```
  {
    GENERATED_BODY()

public:
    // Create the Blueprint node and give it a name and category.
    // The next line is the function that is associated with this
    UFUNCTION(BlueprintPure, meta = (DisplayName =
      "Copyright Notice", CompactNodeTitle =
      "Copyright Notice"), Category = "Project Settings")
    static FString GetCopyrightNotice();

  };
```

4. Now we need to implement the function in the .cpp file:

```
#include "Cookbook_Chapter9.h"
#include "MyBlueprintFunctionLibrary.h"

FString UMyBlueprintFunctionLibrary::GetCopyrightNotice()
{
  FString CopyrightNotice;

  // Get a string from a configuration file.
  GConfig->GetString(
    // Location of the string you want.
    TEXT("/Script/EngineSettings.GeneralProjectSettings"),

    // Name of the string you want.
    TEXT("CopyrightNotice"),

    // Variable you want to put the string in.
    CopyrightNotice,

    // Which ini file do you want to grab from
    GGameIni
    );

  // Return the value of the variable ProjectVersion you've
  // just set.
  return CopyrightNotice;

}
```

5. Go to **Edit | Project Settings**, and you should have a window pop up that has a number of different properties you can assign. For our purposes, scroll down to **Legal** and under **Copyright Notice**, put in what you'd like your copyright to say. In my case, I'll change it to `Copyright 2015 John P. Doran. All Rights Reserved`.

Once you leave the window, these properties are actually saved to the `DefaultGame.ini` file, which is located in the `Config` folder in the **Solution Explorer** tab.

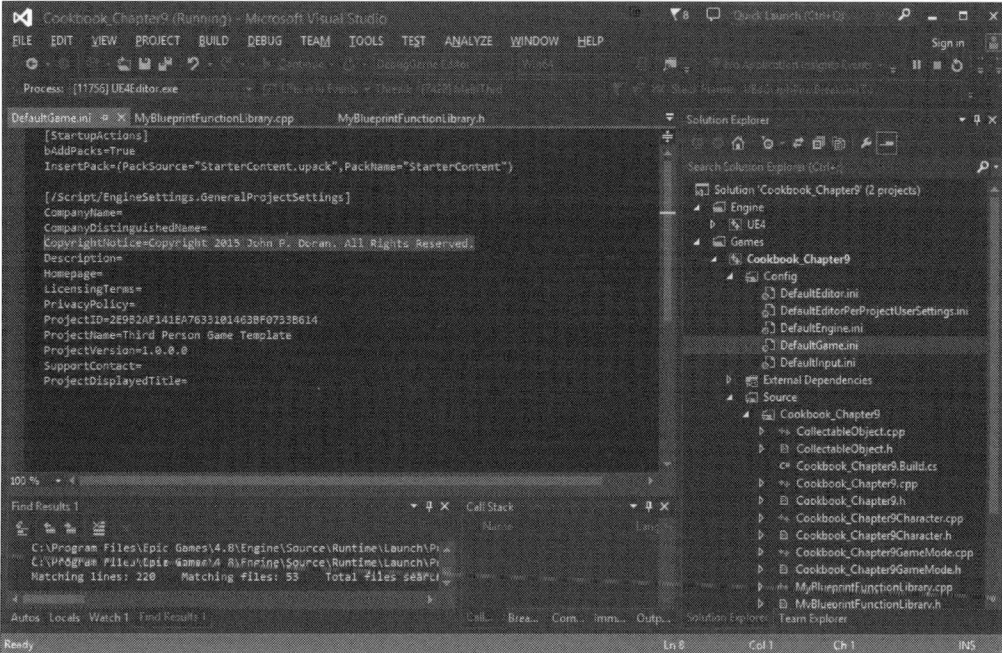

As you can see, the property name is `CopyrightNotice` and it's located in the `/Script/EngineSettings.GeneralProjectSettings` section, just as we did in the code we created earlier.

> For more information on reading and writing values from config files, refer to `https://wiki.unrealengine.com/Config_Files,_Read_%26_Write_to_Config_Files`.

6. Now that our code is complete, save all of the files and compile the project.

7. After it compiles correctly, let's use our newly-created blueprint node. Click on the **Blueprints** dropdown and select **Open Level Blueprint**.

8. Right-click and search for `Copyright Notice`, and you'll see that there is a node located in our custom-made **Project Settings** category called **Copyright Notice**. Select it, and you'll see it added to the screen with some large text displayed.

> This text displayed is the content of the `CompactNodeTitle` property. If left blank, it will show up like a normal node. Also notice that the text displayed when you highlight the node is the comment above the `UFUNCTION` line. Keep that in mind in the future when you want to provide details to users about what your action does.

9. Let's display this string. So, to do this, right-click on the right-hand side of the **Copyright Notice** node and select a **Print String** action. Connect the output of the **Copyright Notice** to the **In String** variable of the **Print String** node.

10. Finally, create **Event BeginPlay** to connect to the **Print String** input. The final level blueprint should look similar to this:

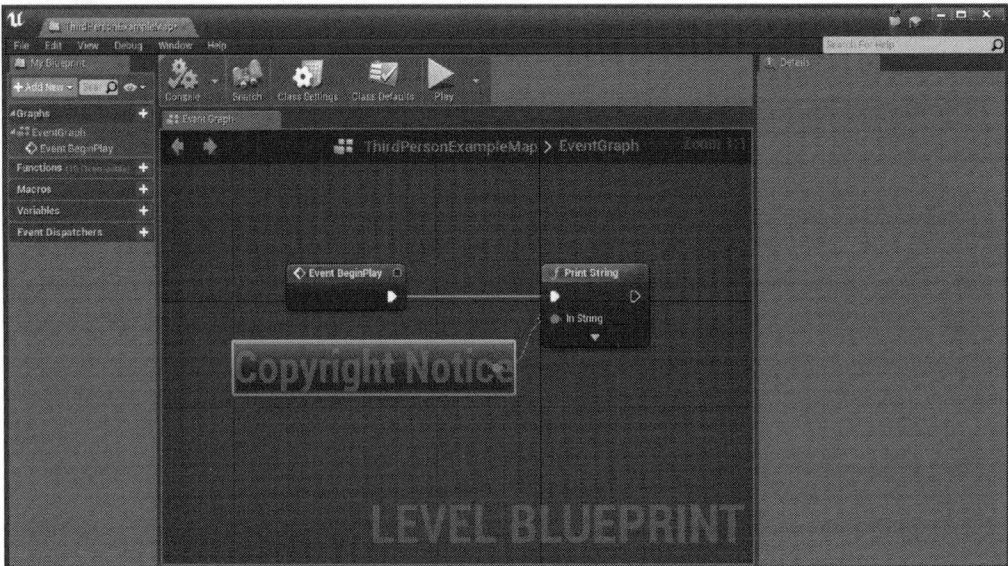

11. Compile and close the level blueprint and from there, start the game!

Game view after compilation of level blueprint

With this, our copyright is displayed!

> For more examples of how to create custom blueprint notes, refer to `https://wiki.unrealengine.com/Custom_Blueprint_Node_Creation`.

See also

Programming is a way of life, and you can spend years becoming better and better at it. Once you feel comfortable with the content in this chapter, take a look at some additional tutorials and/or resources, which will hopefully be useful for you in the future:

- Epic's official programming guide goes though a number of simple examples, introducing content about the API as well as the way the architecture of the engine is built. Check it out at `https://docs.unrealengine.com/latest/INT/Programming/index.html`.

- It may be outdated in terms of images, but the content of this tutorial goes through the steps of creating an FPS game from scratch. It can be found at `https://wiki.unrealengine.com/First_Person_Shooter_C%2B%2B_Tutorial`.

- A number of official C++ Programming tutorials can be found at `https://docs.unrealengine.com/latest/INT/Programming/Tutorials/index.html`.

- For those wanting to take their networking game further, there is another tutorial by Tom Looman about creating a survival game in the same vein as *Day Z*. You can find this at `http://www.tomlooman.com/survival-sample-game-for-ue4/`.

10

User Interface

In this chapter, we'll cover the following recipes:

- Create a Health/Damage system, part 2 – creating a healthbar
- Dynamic enemy healthbars
- Creating a main menu
- Animating a menu

Introduction

In order to create a good game project, you need to be able to communicate information to the player. To do this, we need to create a **user interface** (**UI**), which will allow us to display information such as the player's health, inventory, and others.

Inside Unreal 4, we use the Slate UI framework to create user interfaces, however, it's a very complex system. To make things easier for end users, Unreal also released the **Unreal Motion Graphics** (**UMG**) UI Designer, which is a visual UI authoring tool with a much easier workflow. This is what we will be using in this chapter.

> For more information on Slate, refer to `https://docs.unrealengine.com/latest/INT/Programming/Slate/index.html`.

Creating a Health/Damage system, part 2 – creating a healthbar

Something that you'll be using often as a game developer is some kind of healthbar. In this recipe, we will learn how to display a healthbar on the screen that will update based off of the values of variables inside of blueprints.

Getting ready

Before we start working on this, we need to have a project created and set up for our character. To do this, complete the *Creating a Health/Damage system, part 1 – taking damage* recipe in *Chapter 8, Blueprint Scripting – Level Effects*.

How to do it...

Let's see how we can use the UMG editor to display a healthbar:

1. From the **Content Browser** tab, select the `Content` folder and then click on the **Add New** button and select **New Folder**. Name this new folder `UI`.

2. Click on the **Add New** button once again and then go to **User Interface | Widget Blueprint**. When it comes up, name it `HUD` (short for Heads Up Display).

   The **Widget Blueprint** is a tool that can be used to place all of our UI elements into a scene.

   > For more information on **Widget Blueprints**, refer to `https://docs.unrealengine.com/latest/INT/Engine/UMG/UserGuide/WidgetBlueprints/index.html`.

3. Double-click on the HUD to open it up inside the UMG Editor.

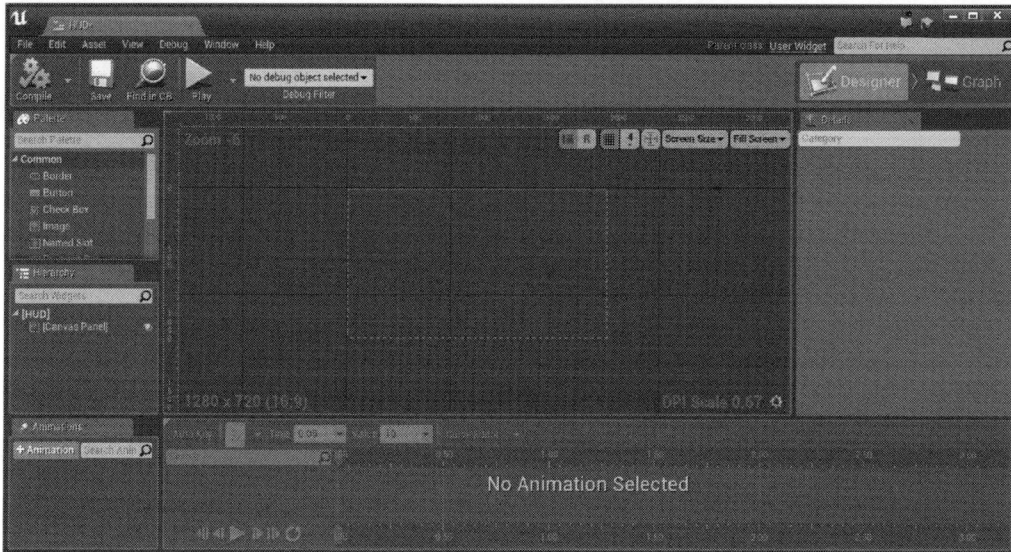

4. First things first! We are going to display a bar for our health, so from the **Palette** tab on the left-hand side, open **Common** and then drag and drop **Progress Bar** onto the middle screen.

5. With the newly-created **Progress Bar** selected, in the **Details** tab on the right-hand side, rename **Progress Bar** to HealthBar and under **Slot**, click on the **Anchors** dropdown and then click on the top-left side to have the bar move according to our liking; I selected it and changed **Size X** to 600. Under **Progress**, you can move the **Percent** property to see how the bar changes or how the value moves (note that it is a value from 0 to 1).

6. Under the **Details** tab from **Appearance**, change **Fill Color** to any color you like (I chose red) and hit **Okay**.

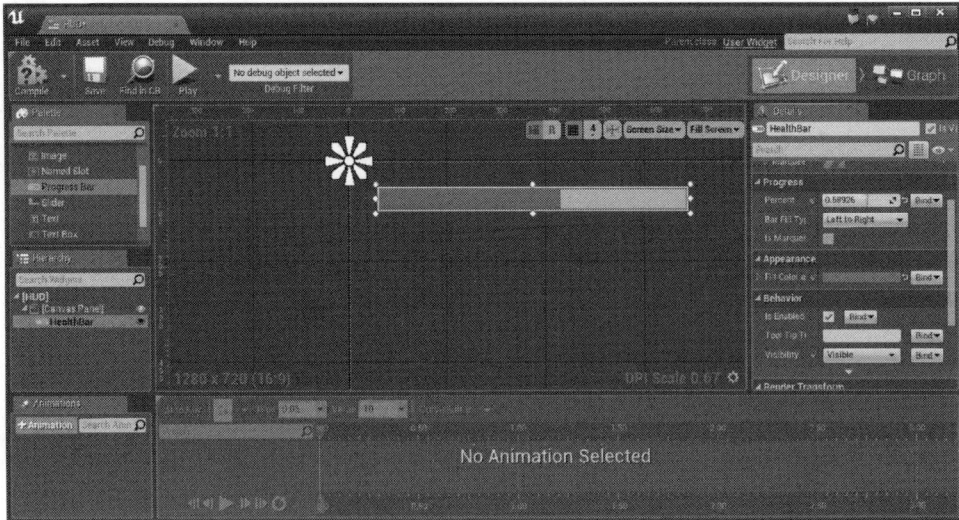

Now that we have the visuals down, let's get to the implementation of our elements:

1. From the **Details** tab under the **Progress** component's **Percent** property, click on the **Bind** button and then select **Create Binding**.

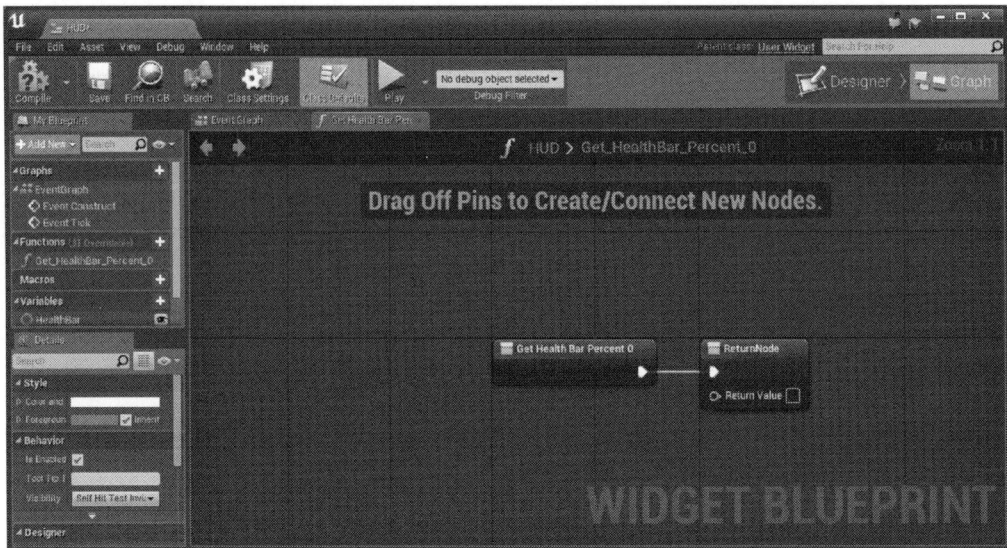

This will take us to the object's **Graph** mode with the appropriate node being created.

2. Let's first rename this function to `GetHealthPercentage` by double-clicking on its name from the **Function** dropdown.

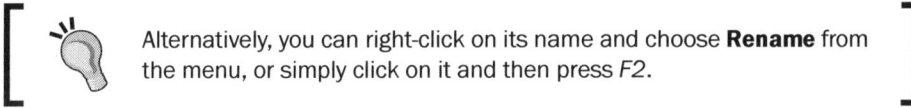

> 💡 Alternatively, you can right-click on its name and choose **Rename** from the menu, or simply click on it and then press *F2*.

3. After this, let's set the correct value of our character. From the graph, right-click and select **Get Player Character**.

   This will give us `Character Reference`, but this is the default version of the character, not the one we created in our blueprint, so we are going to need to cast the object to our class (`ThirdPersonCharacter`).

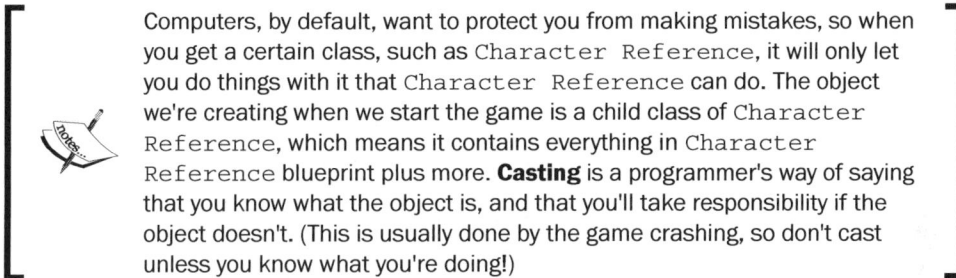

> 📝 Computers, by default, want to protect you from making mistakes, so when you get a certain class, such as `Character Reference`, it will only let you do things with it that `Character Reference` can do. The object we're creating when we start the game is a child class of `Character Reference`, which means it contains everything in `Character Reference` blueprint plus more. **Casting** is a programmer's way of saying that you know what the object is, and that you'll take responsibility if the object doesn't. (This is usually done by the game crashing, so don't cast unless you know what you're doing!)

4. Click and drag from the **Return Value** variable and from the action, select **Cast to ThirdPersonCharacter**.

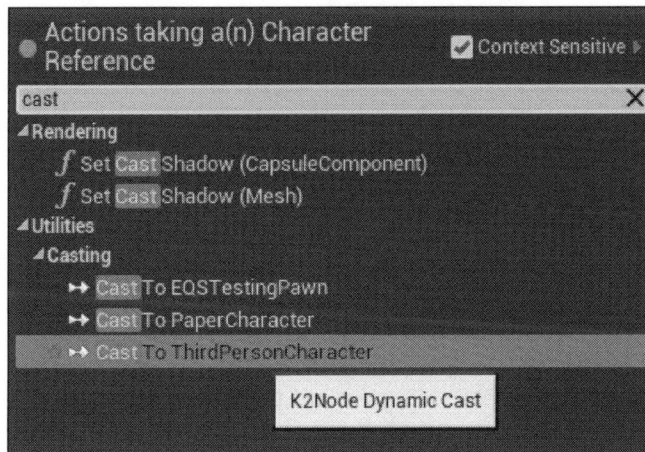

5. Now that we have the cast, delete the connection from **Get Health Percentage** and **Return Node** and then connect the output from **Get Health Percentage** to the input of **Cast to Third Person Character**. Then, connect the output of the **Cast to Third Person Character** action to the input of **ReturnNode**.

6. We still need to set the correct value, so from the **As Third Person Character** output, this time create two **Get** actions—one for **Current Health** and the other for **Max Health**.

7. After this, create a **float/float** action (divide a float by another float) and connect **CurrentHealth** to the top and **Max Health** to the bottom.

8. Finally, connect the output of the division to **Return Value** of **Return Node**.

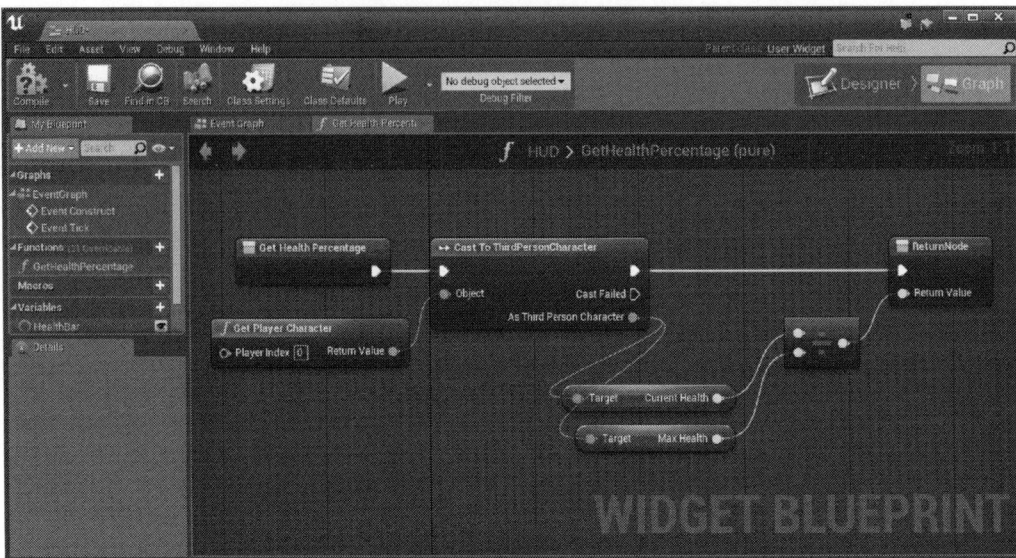

9. Compile, save, and then exit the editor.

10. Next, we need to tell the widget to display on the screen. Go to **Blueprints | Open Level Blueprint** and this time, create an **EventBeginPlay** event.

> Note that it is also possible to put the following blueprint actions into the character's blueprint. For more information on converting from a level to a class blueprint, refer to *Chapter 8, Blueprint Scripting – Level Effects*.

11. Then, to the right of this, right-click and create a **Create Widget** action. Under **Class** from the dropdown, select HUD and connect the arrow from **Event Begin Play** to the input of **Create HUD_C Widget** action.

12. After this, click and drag from the output arrow and create an **Add to Viewport** event. Then, connect the **Return Value** variable of our **Create Widget** action to the **Target** variable of the **Add to Viewport** action.

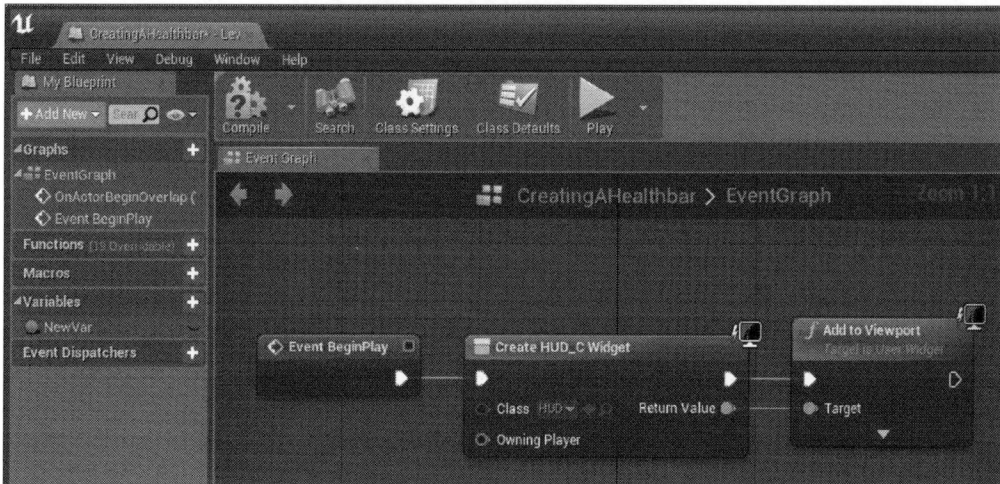

13. Now let's compile, save our game, and play the level!

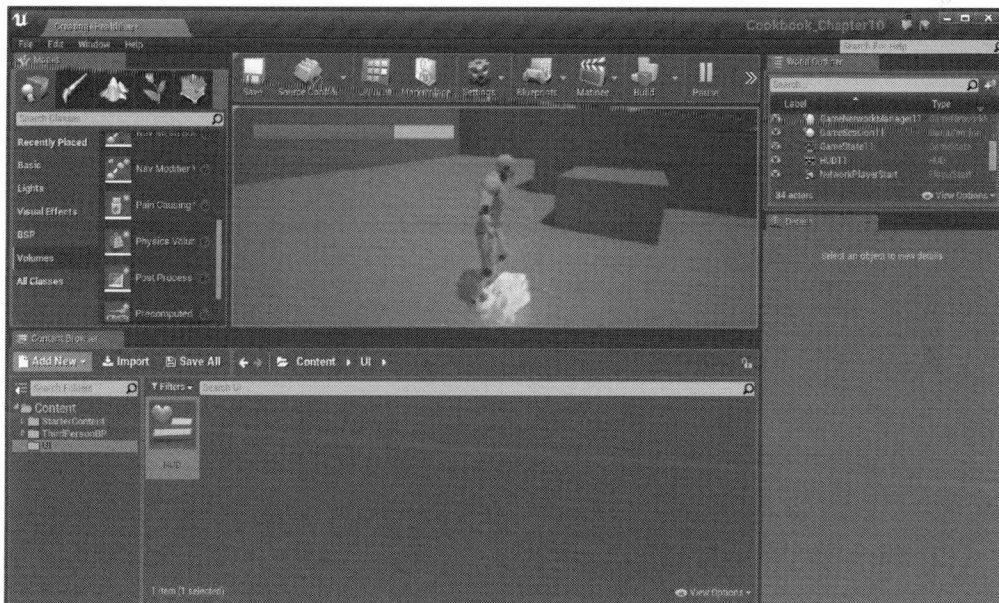

With this, we now have a simple healthbar system working for us! With this example in place, you can make much more complex actions dealing with any kind of variable being displayed!

Dynamic enemy healthbars

Another thing that you'll often see in games are healthbars for enemies that will appear over their heads, changing as the game is being played. In this recipe, we will learn how we can do what we've learned from the previous recipe and apply it here.

Getting ready

Before we start working on this, we need to have a project created and set up. Do the previous recipe all the way to completion.

How to do it...

Of course, to actually have enemy healthbars, we will need to actually have an enemy, so let's get that implemented first:

1. Go to the **Content Browser** tab and then to the `ThirdPersonBP/Blueprints` folder. Right-click on the `ThirdPersonCharacter` object and then select **Duplicate** and name the duplicated object `AI`.

2. Double-click on the blueprint to open up its **EventGraph**. We actually don't need any of the previously-created stuff in **Event Graph**, so select all of the Unreal-created content and then delete it. Do note that we do have the `CurrentHealth` and `MaxHealth` properties and `Event AnyDamage` that we created earlier.

   We won't be using the **Event AnyDamage** action in this recipe, but it will be good for you to use it in your own internal testing.

Blueprint of the new AI object

3. Close out of the blueprint for right now. We're going to create our enemy healthbar.

4. From the **Content Browser** tab, open the UI folder and navigate to **Add New | User Interface | Widget Blueprint**. Give it a name (EnemyHealthbar). Double-click on it to open up its editor.

> It's important to note the lack of spaces between words when naming anything in Unreal Engine 4. Either use _ or just capitalize the next word's first letter.

5. Now the first thing we're going to do is create a custom resolution. We can do this by clicking on the top-right button, **Fill Screen**, and then selecting **Custom**.

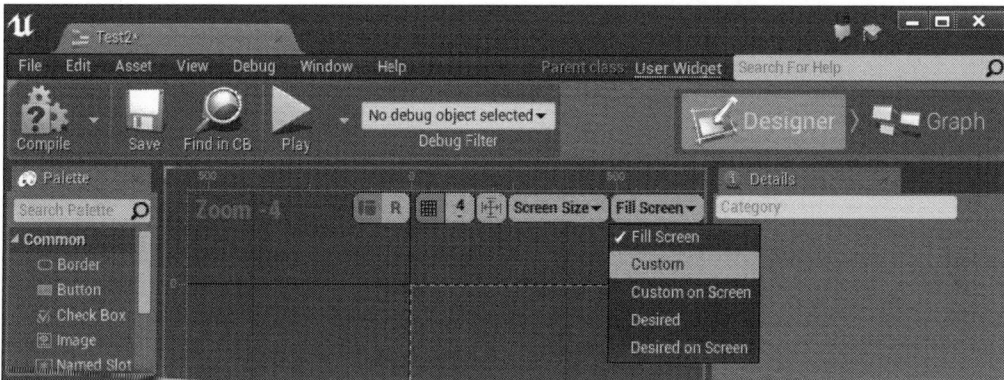

6. From here, let's keep the **Width** value at 100 and change the **Height** value to 25.

7. Next, drag and drop a **Progress Bar** into the level and scale it to fit into the box. Change the color again if you want to.

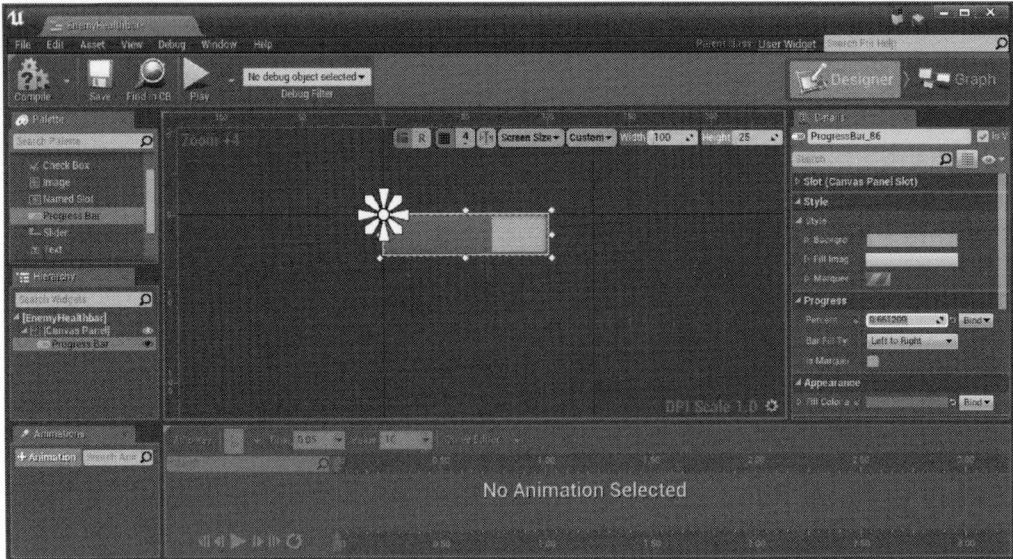

8. Next, rename the progress bar to something a little easier to read, such as `HealthProgressBar`.

9. Compile and save the widget and exit out of the editor. Next, open our `AI` blueprint again and this time, go into the **Viewport** tab.

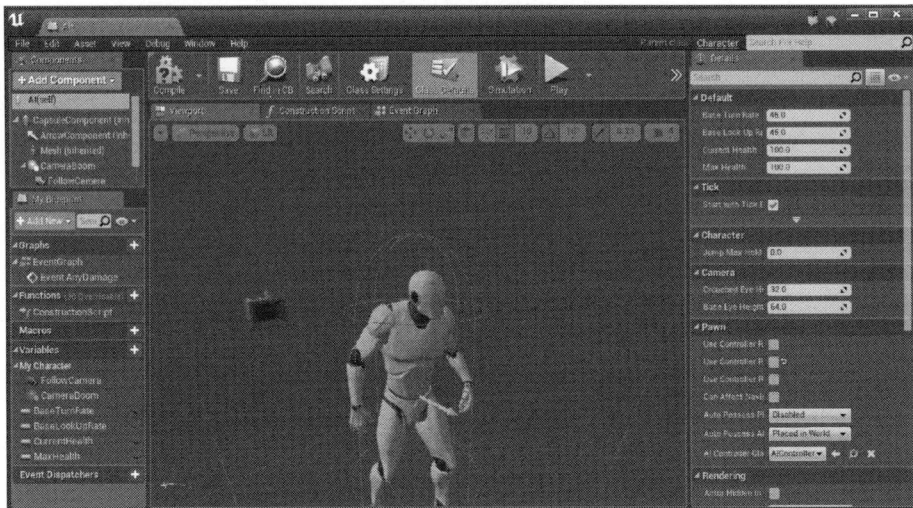

Viewport tab of the AI blueprint

10. Go into **Add Component** and select **Widget**. Once created, rename it to `Healthbar`. Under the **UI** component, set the **Widget Class** property to `EnemyHealthbar`. Then, under **Draw Size**, set **X** to `100` and **Y** to `25` (what we made the resolution earlier). Then, rotate the healthbar until it is positioned above the enemy's head and rotates appropriately.

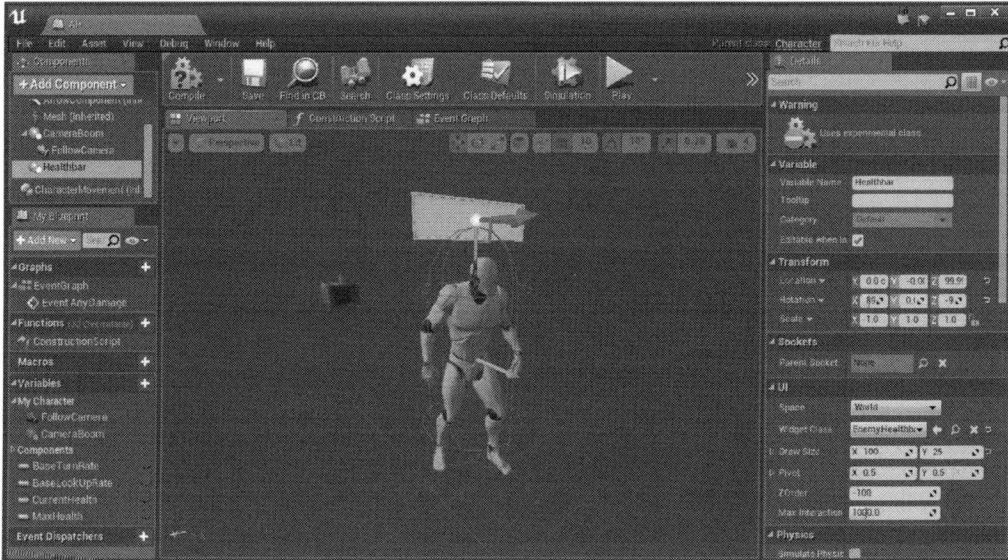

Now, unlike our previous version of the healthbar where we only had to worry about having one player, we can have multiple enemies on the screen. So, instead of having the widget assign its appropriate value, we will use the enemy's blueprint:

1. Select the **Event Graph** tab and then drag and drop the `Healthbar` object from the **Components** tab into **Event Graph**.

2. From the output of the **Healthbar** object, drag out and then create a **Get User Widget Object** action.

3. From the **Return Value** output of the **Get User Widget Object** action, drag out and then create a **CastToEnemyHealthbar** action.

4. Next, from the **As Enemy Healthbar** output, create a **Get Health Progress Bar** action.

5. Finally, drag out **Health Progress Bar** to select the **Set Percent** action.

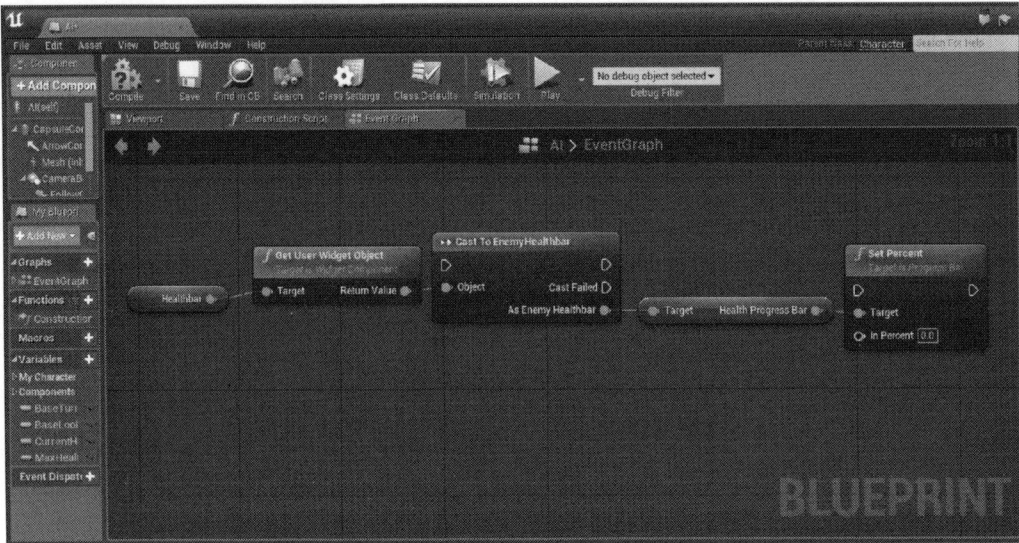

6. Next, we need to divide **Current Health** by **Max Health** once again. Drag and drop the **Current Health** and **Max Health** objects from the **Variables** section and select **Get** both times.

7. To the right of these, create a **float/float** action and connect **Current Health** to the top and **Max Health** on the bottom.

8. Finally, create an **Event Tick** event and connect its output to the input of the **Cast to EnemyHealthbar** action and then connect the output of the **Cast to EnemyHealthbar** action to the input of the **Set Percent** action.

9. Compile and save the **Blueprint** and then exit the editor.

10. After this, drag and drop an `AI` blueprint into our scene and then play the game.

When we are facing the enemy, we can now see the widget clearly, and we can see that it's updated using its health values!

However, we will want to fix an issue, that is, if we aren't facing the enemy, we can't see the UI for it, as you can see in the following screenshot with two enemies, each facing in the opposite direction:

To fix this, we will have the healthbar rotate toward the player.

11. Open up the AI blueprint once again. We need to get a couple of variables, namely the player's position and the healthbars. Drag and drop a **Healthbar** variable from the **Components** tab and to the right of it, create a **Get World Location** action.

12. Below this, create a **Get Player Character** action and to the right of that, create another **GetWorldLocation (Mesh)** to get the information for the **Mesh** component.

13. To the right of that, create a **Find Look at Rotation** action and connect the **Start** variable to the **Healthbar** object's location and the **Target** variable to the player's.

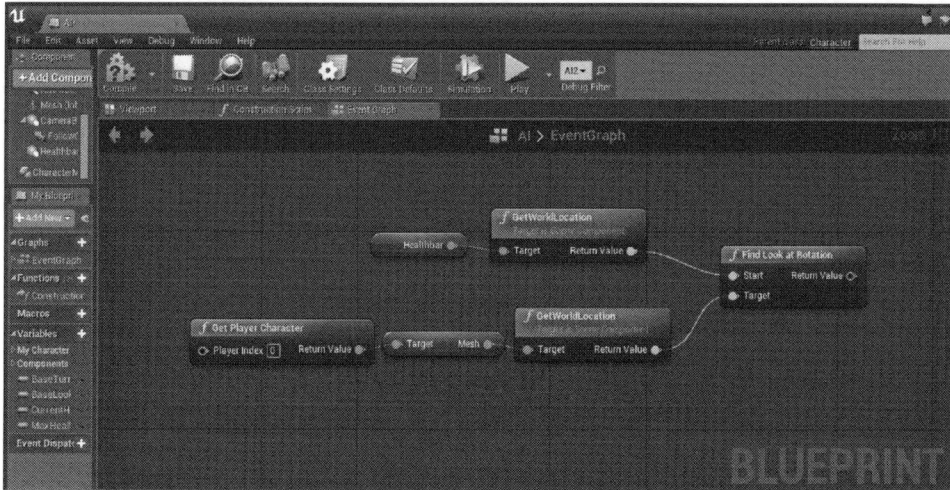

Finding the Look at Rotation of the healthbar to the player

The rotational value that this will contain will make the object rotate toward us, but it will look strange if we just set it because the bar will move up and down as we move around it.

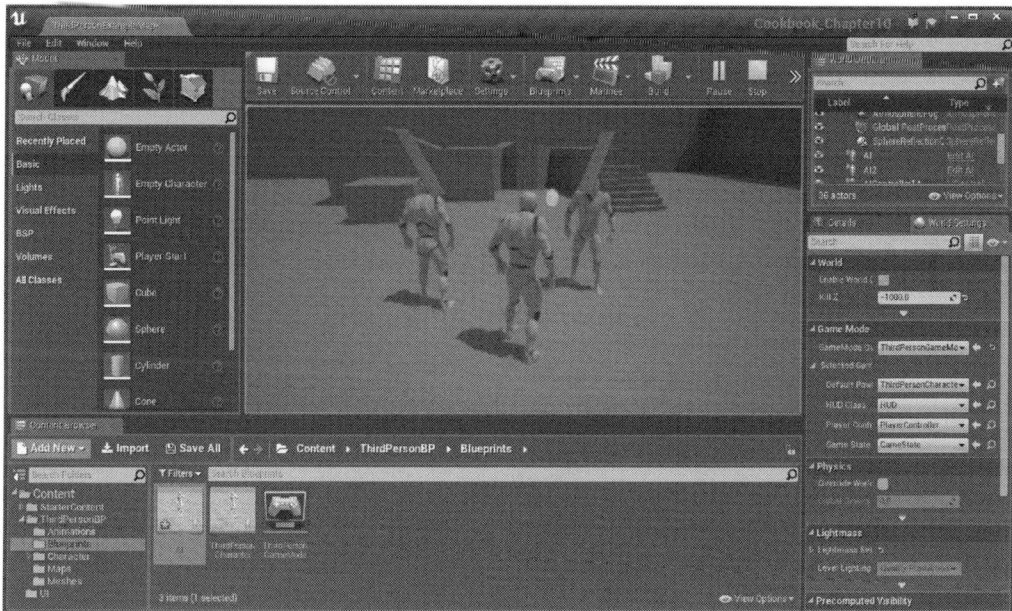

This is due to the pivot point of the object that it's being rotated to being in the top-left corner rather than in the center. To fix this, we can create a new object as a parent that will work correctly.

14. Open up the `AI` Blueprint and with the **Viewport** tab being selected, go to the **Components** tab and navigate to **Add Component | Scene**.

   A scene component is a kind of an empty slate, but it has a **Transfrom** component so that we can use it as holder or custom pivot, as in this case.

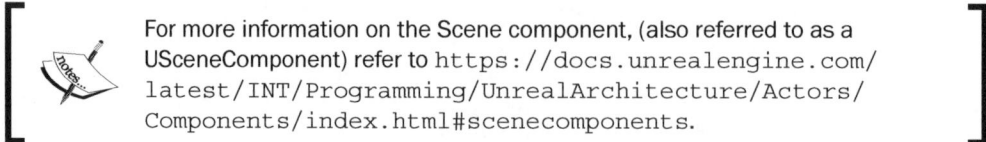

> For more information on the Scene component, (also referred to as a USceneComponent) refer to `https://docs.unrealengine.com/latest/INT/Programming/UnrealArchitecture/Actors/Components/index.html#scenecomponents`.

15. Move the **Scene** object until its centered around the **Healthbar** object and then from the **Components** tab, drag and drop the **Healthbar** object on top of the **Scene object** to make the **Scene object** the parent of the **Healthbar** object.

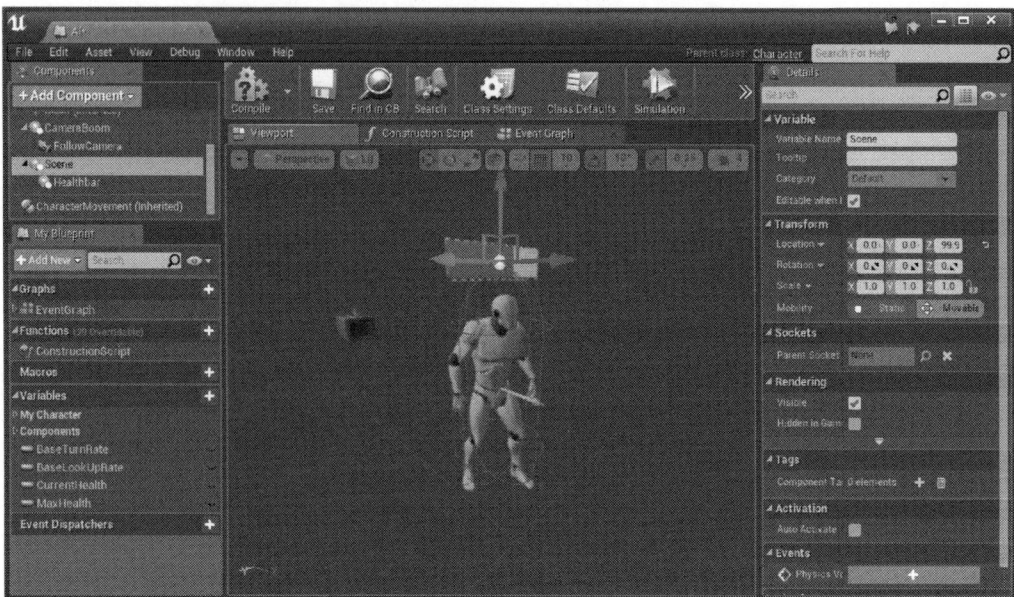

16. Next, we will need to replace the **Healthbar** variable with the **Scene** variable for the **GetWorldLocation** action (select the **Healthbar** variable, press *Delete* and then move **Scene** in and connect it).

    Now, this is much better, but there's still some issues when jumping or getting too near. This is because in reality, we only want **Yaw** to move.

17. From **Return Value** of the **Find Look at Rotation** action, drag out and select **Break Rot** , which will give us each part of the rotation by itself.

18. To the right of this newly-created rotation, right-click and select **Make Rot** and connect **Yaw** of the **Break Rot** action to **Yaw** of the **Make Rot** action.

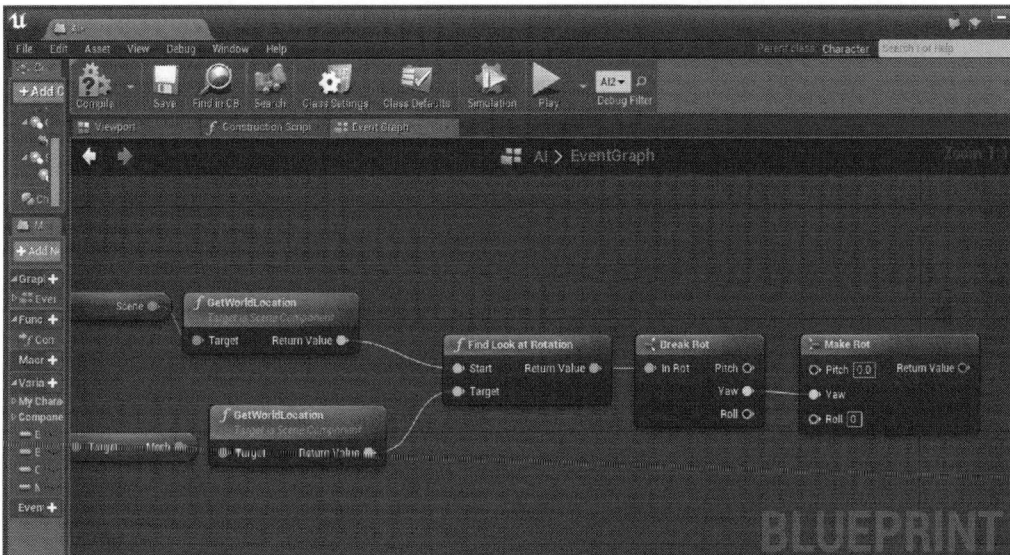

19. Now, we need to right-click and select a **Set World Rotation (Scene)** action and connect **Return Value** to **New Rotation**.

20. Finally, connect the output of the **Set Percent** action to the input of the **SetWorldRotation** action.

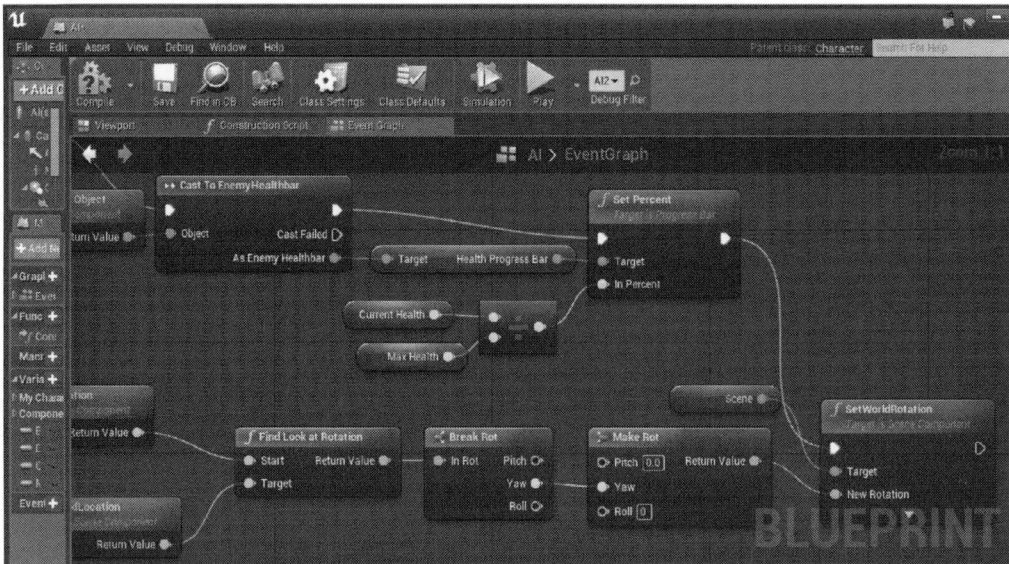

21. Compile the **Blueprint**, save it, and start the game!

Now our enemy's healthbars will rotate toward our player at all times!

Creating a main menu

A main menu can serve as an introduction to your game and is a great place for us to discuss some additional things that UMG has, such as texts and buttons. We'll also learn how we can make buttons do things. Let's spend some time to see just how easy it is to create one!

> For more information on the client-server model, refer to `https://en.wikipedia.org/wiki/Client%E2%80%93server_model`.

How to do it...

To give you an idea of how it works, let's create an empty level to hold our menu:

1. Create a new level by going to **File | New Level** and select **Empty Level**.

2. Next, inside the **Content Browser** tab, go to our `UI` folder and navigate to **Add New | User Interface | Widget Blueprint** and give it a name (`MainMenu`). Double-click on it to open up the editor.

   In this menu, we are going to have the title of the game, and then a series of buttons the player can press.

3. From the **Palette** tab, open up the **Common** section and drag and drop a **Button** onto the middle of the screen.

4. Select the button and change its **Size X** to `400` and **Size Y** to `80`. We will also rename the button to `Play Game`.

5. Drag and drop a **Text** object onto the **Play Game** button, and you should see it snap onto the button as a child. Under **Content**, change **Text** to **Play Game**. Under **Appearance**, change the color of the button to black and change the **Font** size to `32`.

6. From the **Hierarchy** tab, select the **Play Game** button and copy and paste it to create a duplicate. Move the button down, rename it to `Quit Game`, and change the text `Content` as well.

7. Move both of the objects so that they're on the bottom part of the HUD, slightly above and side by side, as shown in the following image:

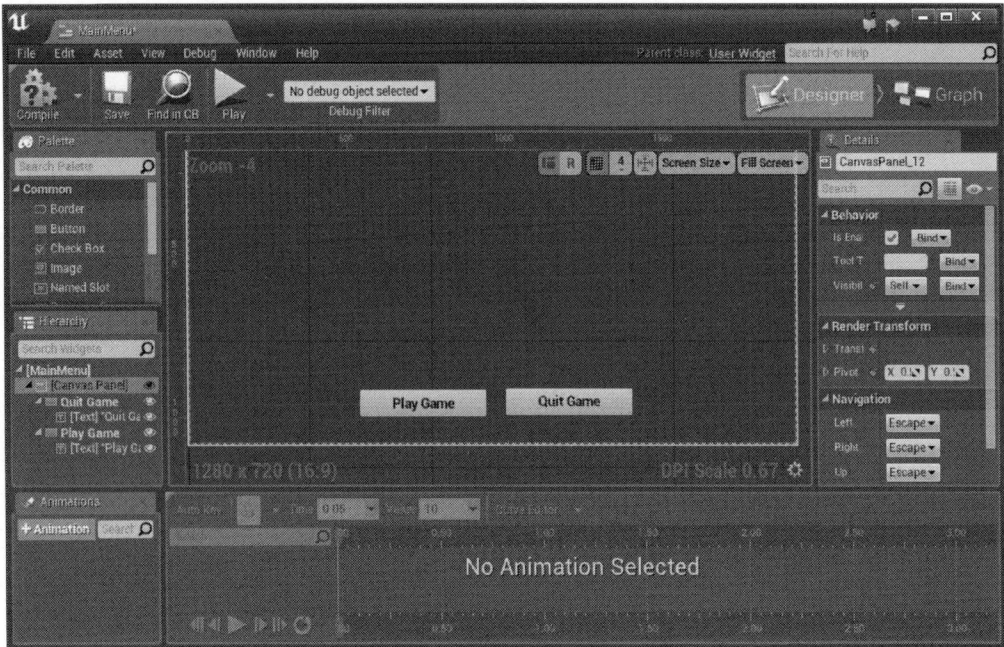

8. Lastly, we'll want to set our pivots and anchors accordingly. When you select either the **Quit Game** or **Play Game** buttons, you may notice a sun-like widget that displays the **Anchors** of the object (known as the Anchor Medallion). In our case, open **Anchors** from the **Details** panel and click on the bottom center option.

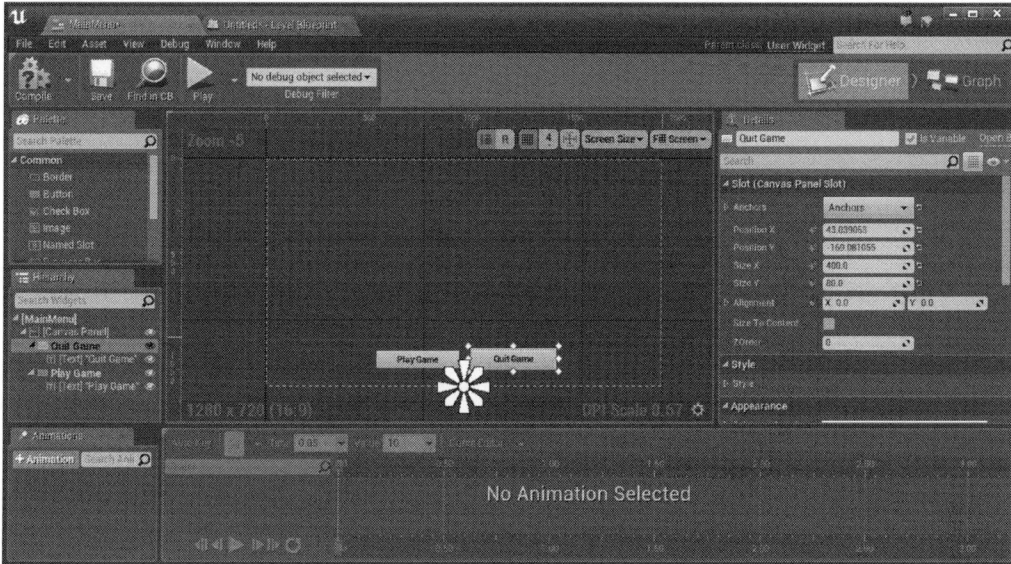

9. Now that we have the buttons created, we want them to actually do something when we click on them. Select the **Play Game** button and from the **Details** tab, scroll down until you see the **Events** component. There should be a series of big green **+** buttons. Click on the green button beside **OnClicked**.

10. Next, it will take us to **Event Graph** with the appropriate event created for us. To the right of the event, right-click and create an **Open Level** action. Under **Level Name**, put in whatever level you like (for example, StarterMap) and then connect the output of the **OnClicked** action to the input of the **Open Level** action.

11. To the right of that, create a **Remove from Parent** action to make sure that when we leave it, the menu doesn't stay.

12. Finally, create a **Get Player Controller** action and to the right of it, a **Set Show Mouse Cursor** action disabled so that the mouse will no longer be visible as we want to see the mouse in the menu (drag from **Return Value** of the Player Controller to create a new node and search for the mouse cursor action).

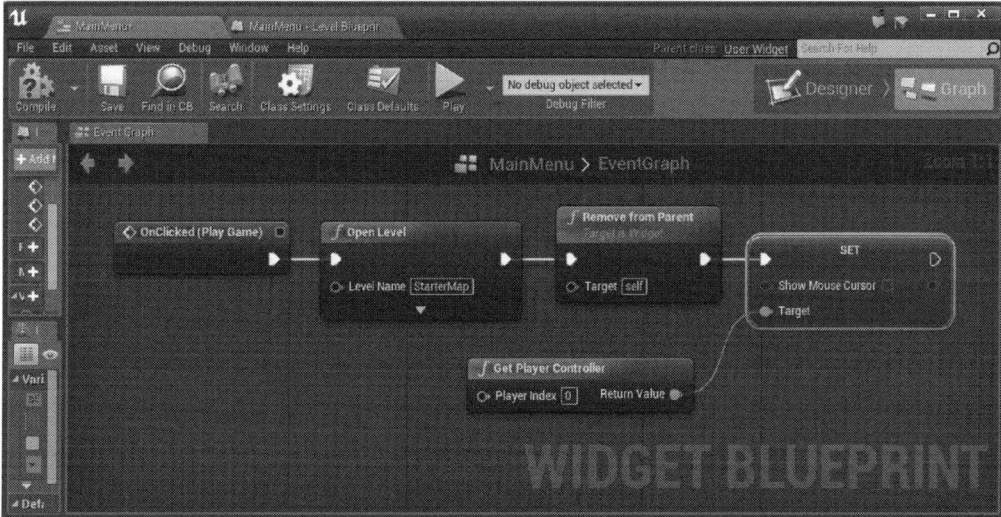

13. Now, go back to the **Designer** button and then select the **Quit Game** button. Click on the **OnClicked** button as well and to the right of this one, create a **Quit Game** action and connect the output of the **OnClicked** action to the input of the **Quit Game** action.

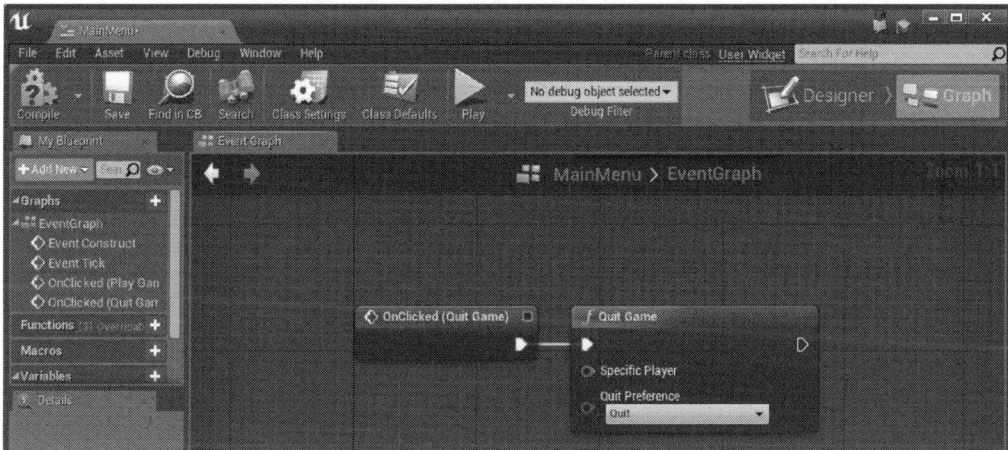

14. Lastly, as a bit of polish, let's add our game title to the screen. Drag and drop another **Text** object onto the scene, this time with **Anchor** at the top of center. From here, change **Position X** to 0 and **Position Y** to 176.

15. Change the **Alignment** value of the **X** axis to .5 and check the **Size to Content** option for it to automatically resize.

16. Set the **Content** component's **Text** property to the game's name (in my case, Game Name).

17. Under the **Appearance** component, set the **Font** size to 93 and set the **Justification** property to **Center**.

> There are a number of other styling options that you may wish to use when developing your HUDs. For more information on that, refer to https://docs.unrealengine.com/latest/INT/Engine/ UMG/UserGuide/Styling/index.html.

18. Compile the menu, and save it, and now we need to actually have the widget show up. To do so, we need to take the same steps as we did previously.

19. Open up **Level Blueprint** by going to to **Blueprints | Open Level Blueprint** and create an **EventBeginPlay** event.

20. Then, to the right of that, right-click and create a **Create Widget** action. Under **Class**, from the dropdown, select `MainMenu` and connect the arrow from **Event Begin Play** to the input of **Create MainMenu_C Widget**.

21. After this, click and drag from the output arrow and create an **Add to Viewport** event. Then, connect **Return Value** of our **Create Widget** action to **Target** of the **Add to Viewport** action.

22. Lastly, we also want to display the player's cursor on the screen to show buttons. To do that, right-click and select **Get Player Controller**. Then, from **Return Value** of that, create a **Set Show Mouse Cursor** object. Connect the output of the **Add to Viewport** action to the input of the **Show Mouse Cursor** action.

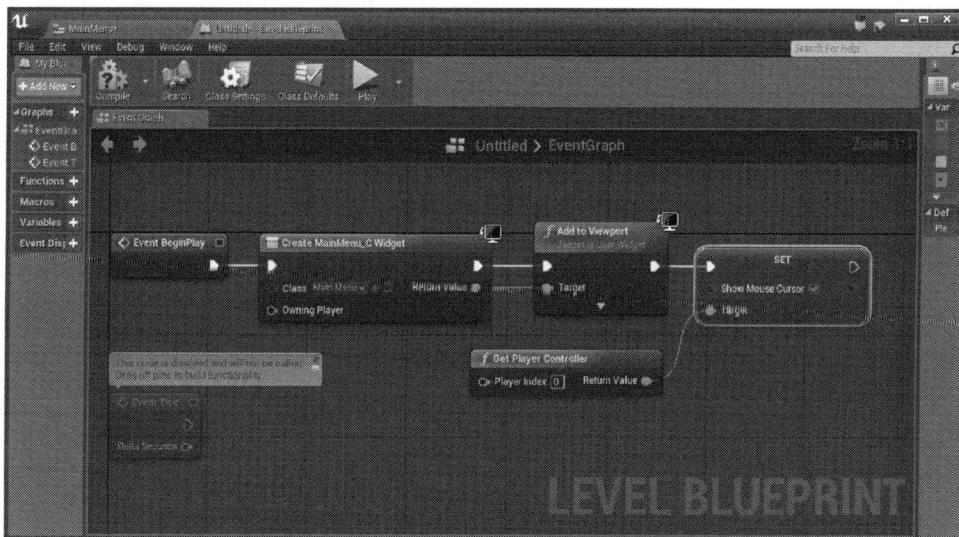

Blueprint to show player's cursor on the screen

23. Compile, save, and run the project!

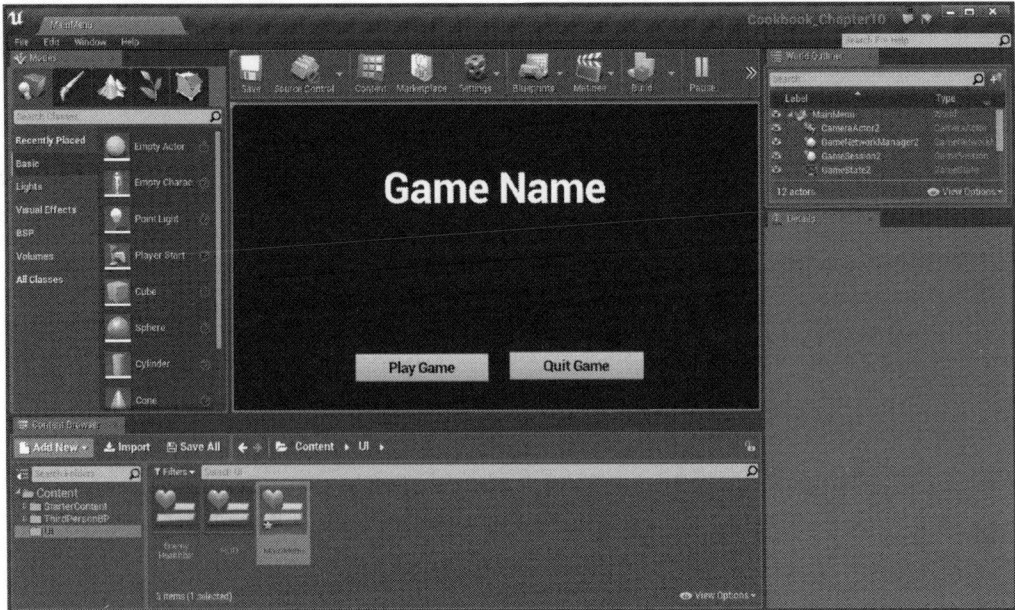

With this our menu is completed! We can quit the game with no problems, and pressing the **Play Game** button will start our level!

Animating a menu

You may have created a menu or UI element at some point, but rather than having it static and non-moving, let's spend some time looking at how we can animate the menus by having them fly in and out or animate in some way. This will help add polish to the title as well as enable players to notice things easier as they move in.

Getting ready

Before we start working on this, we need to have a project created and set up. Follow the previous recipe all the way to completion.

How to do it...

1. Open up the `MainMenu` blueprint once more and from the bottom-left in the **Animations** tab, click on the **+Animation** button and give the new animation a name (`MenuFlyIn`).

2. Select the newly-created animation, and you should see the window on the right-hand side brighten up.

Creating a new animation

3. Next, click on the **Auto Key** toggle to have the animation editor automatically set keys that are appropriate for our implementation.

4. If it's not there already, move the **timeline** bar (the white line with two orange ends on the top and bottom) to the `0.00` mark on the animation timeline.

5. Next, select the **Game Name** object and under the **Color and Opacity** option, open it up and change the **A** (alpha) value to `0`.

6. Now, move the timeline bar to the 1.00 mark and then open the color again and set the **A** value to 1.

You'll notice that now there is a transition going from a completely transparent text to a fully shown one. This is a good start. Let's have the buttons fly in after the text appears.

7. Next, move the timeline bar to the 2.00 mark and select the **Play Game** button. Now from the **Details** tab, you'll notice that under the variables there are new **+** icons to the left of variables. This will save the value for use in the animations. Click on the **+** icon by the **Position Y** value.

> If you use your scroll wheel while inside the dark gray portion of the timeline, (where the keyframe numbers are displayed) it zooms in and out. This can be quite useful as you create more complex animations.

8. Now move the timeline bar to the `1.00` mark and move the **Play Game** button off the screen. By doing the animation in this way, we are saving where we want it to be at the end, and then we will go back and do the animations.

9. Do the same animation for the **Quit Game** button.

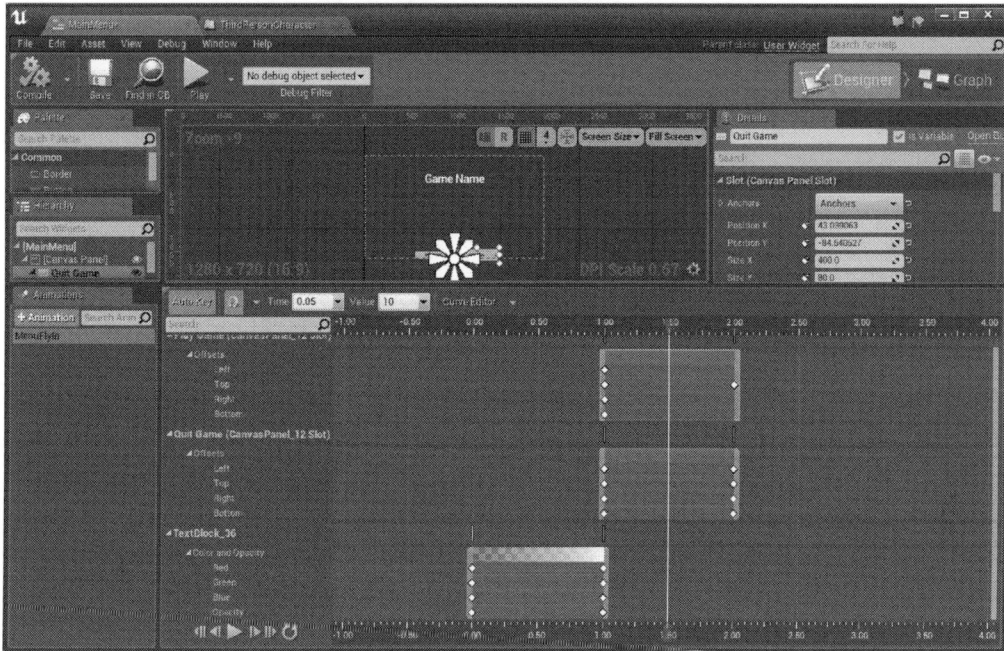

Animation for the Quit Game button

Now that our animation is created, let's make it so that when the object starts, it plays this animation:

1. Click on the **Graph** button and from the **MyBlueprint** tab under the **Graphs** section, double-click on the **Event Construct** event, which is called as soon as we add the menu to the scene. Grab the pin on the end of it and create a **Play Animation** action.

2. Drag and drop a **MenuFlyIn** animation into the scene and select **Get**. Connect its output pin to the **In Animation** property of the **Play Animation** action.

Now that we have the animation working for the menu, let's have it play when we leave the menu:

1. Select the **Play Animation** and **Menu Fly In** variables and copy them. Then, move to the **OnClicked (Play Game)** action, drag the **OnClicked** event over to the left, and remove its original connection to the **Open Level** action by holding down *Alt* and clicking.

2. Paste (*Ctrl + V*) the new objects and connect the output of **OnClicked (Play Game)** to the input of **Play Animation**. Now change the **Play Mode** to **Reverse**.

3. To the right of that, create a **Delay** action. For the **Duration** variable, we want to wait as long as the animation is, so from the **Menu Fly In** variable, create another pin and a **Get End Time** action. Connect **Return Value** of the **Get End Time** variable to the input of the **Delay** action.

4. Connect the output of the **Play Animation** variable to the input of the **Delay** variable and the **Completed** output of the **Delay** variable to the input of the **Open Level** action.

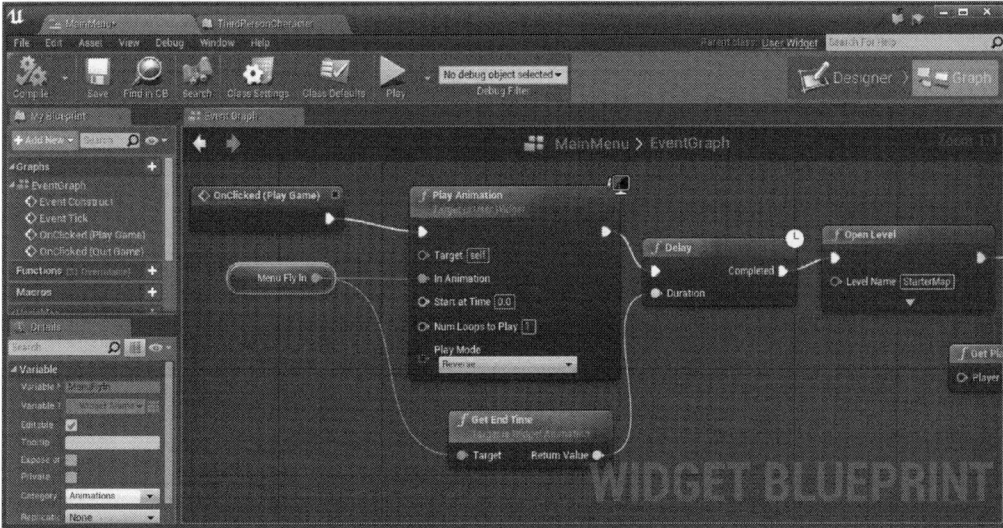

5. Now, we need to do the same for the **OnClicked (Quit Game)** event.

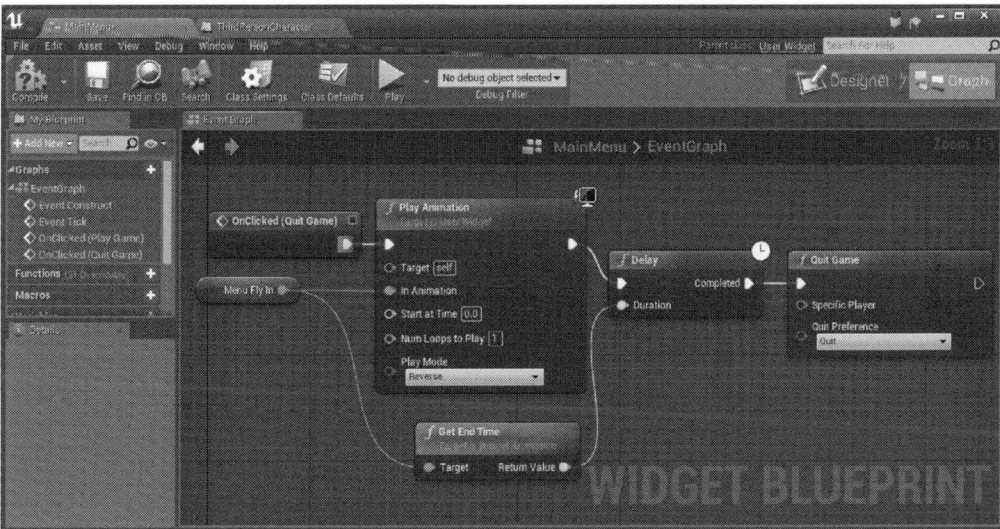

6. Now compile, save, and run the game!

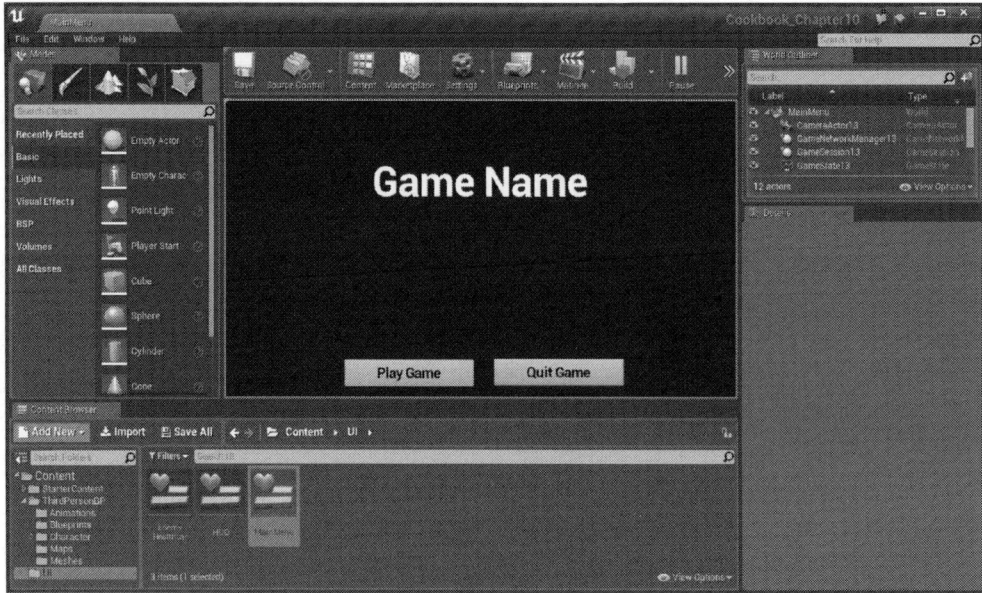

Our menu is now completed! You learned about how animation works inside UMG.

> For more examples of using UMG for animation, refer to `https://docs.unrealengine.com/latest/INT/Engine/UMG/UserGuide/Animation/index.html`.

See also

I would love to write an entire book about creating UIs for games, but there just isn't enough space in this book to dive deeply into it. However, for those interested in doing more complex UI, here are some additional tutorials, which may prove to be beneficial:

▶ **Basic Inventory System in Blueprint**: `http://www.tomlooman.com/tutorial-basic-inventory-system-in-blueprint/`

▶ **Creating / Scripting an In-Game Pause Menu**: `https://docs.unrealengine.com/latest/INT/Engine/UMG/QuickStart/5/index.html`

▶ **Level Menus (UMG)**: `https://www.youtube.com/watch?v=wPzIvBP8-PA`

▶ **UMG Using a Gamepad**: `https://www.youtube.com/watch?v=tCXuNu4RETs`

▶ **UMG, Create Scrollable List of Clickable Buttons From Dynamic Array**: `https://wiki.unrealengine.com/UMG,_Create_Scrollable_List_of_Clickable_Buttons_From_Dynamic_Array`

11
Publishing and Deployment

In this chapter, we'll cover the following recipes:

- ▸ Packaging your project
- ▸ Creating an installer for Windows

Introduction

At this point, you should have created an entire project, but taking the time to get the projects out into the world is just as important. Playing the game inside the editor is nice and all, but playing the game as a standalone title has a special feel to it that you can't duplicate.

After exporting it to the computer, it is possible for you to just zip it up and send someone that file, but you spent quality time on your project, and so, give it the respect it deserves. With that in mind, people notice the polish that is put into games and the little things, such as an installer, can help get people into the mood of your project early on and see your game as a professional title.

Packaging your project

Before we can export our project and share it with others, we first need to package it. Packaging is the name for a series of different steps, including compiling your project, then cooking content into a format that the platform understands before finally putting the project in a certain format. This will allow you to test/play your full game (instead of a single map) in the same way that it would be when published.

Getting ready

Before we start working on this, we need to have a completed project. In my example, I created a new blank project, but any of the things we worked on in the book should work fine.

How to do it...

Let's see just how the packaging works! Follow these steps:

1. From the **File** menu, navigate to **Package Project | Windows | Windows (64 Bit)**.

2. From there, you should see a **Browse For Folder** dialog window pop up. Here, we will want to place the files for the game. In my case, I selected Desktop and then selected **Make New Folder**. From here, I renamed this new folder to UE4 EXPORT:

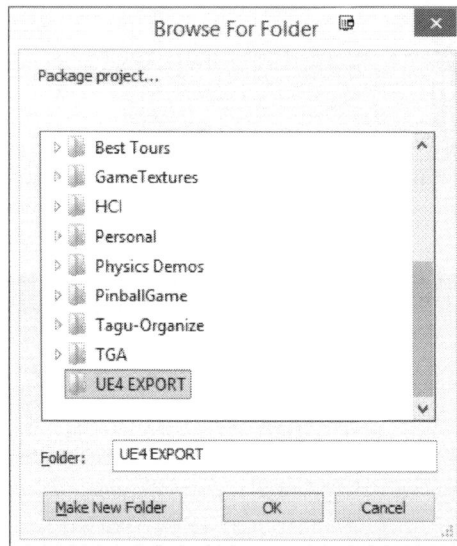

3. After you've selected your folder, click on the **OK** button and you'll notice a new message on the bottom-right of your screen, saying that the project is currently being packaged.

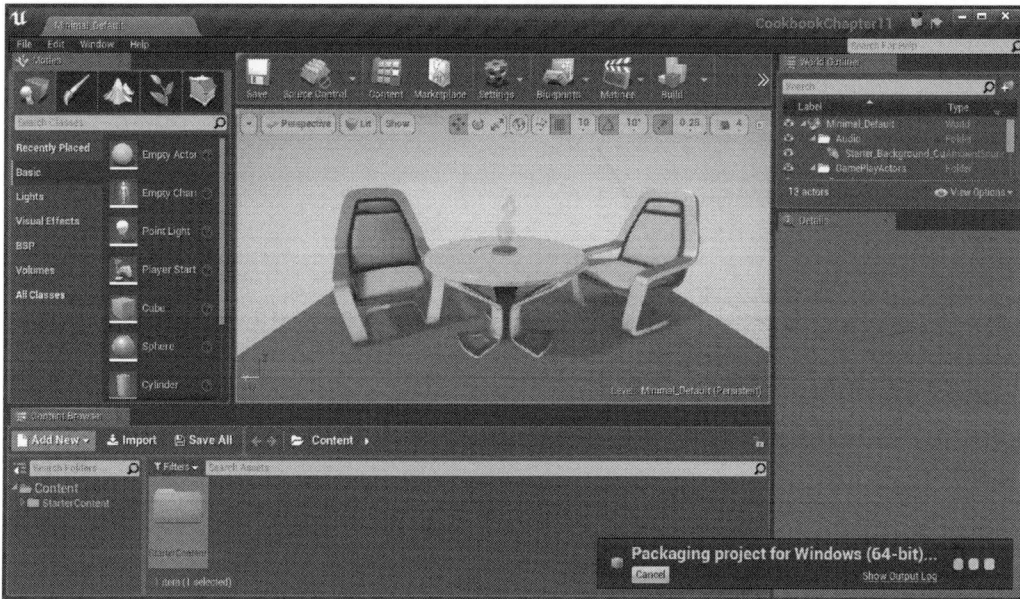

This is done as a background process as it will often take some time, so you can still make changes and work with the editor; note that the changes made during this period will not be reflected in your packaged project.

It is also possible to display additional information about what's going on by clicking the **Show Log** button. The output log can be useful in case something went wrong:

1. Once you see the message disappear, you should go back to the exported folder, and once there, you should see a folder called `WindowsNoEditor`. Double-click on that folder and you should see a number of files.

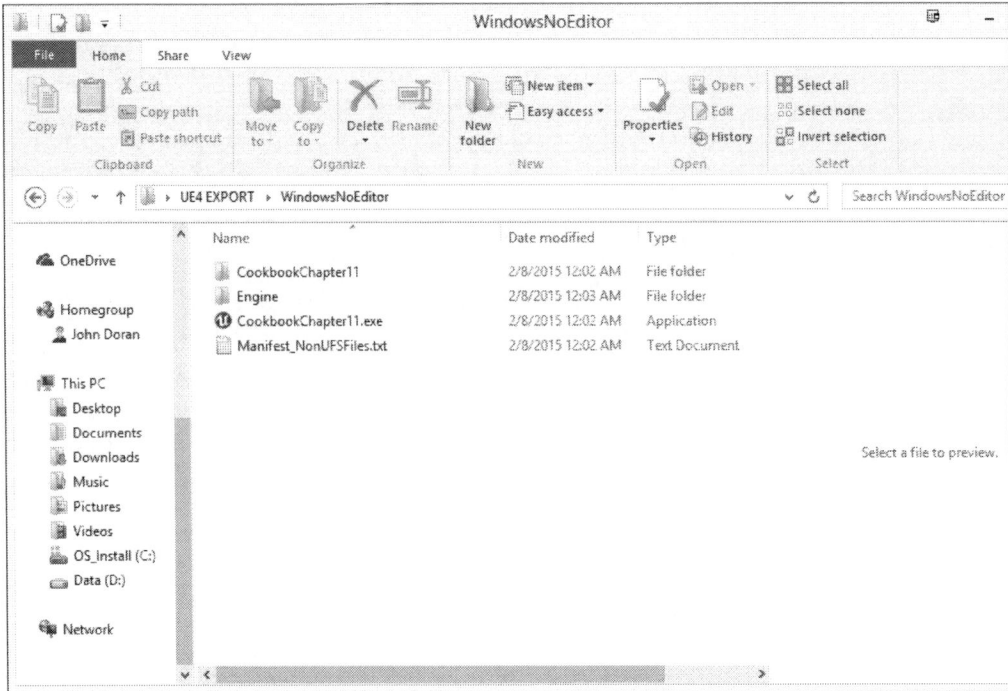

2. Double-click on the `.exe` file and you should see your game started!

With this, we've now exported our project for others to play!

> If, like this generic example, you do not have functionality for exiting the game, feel free to press *Alt + Tab* to exit the game and then just simply click on the **X** in the top-right.

> For more information on exporting projects to different platforms, such as iOS and Android, visit `https://docs.unrealengine.com/latest/INT/Engine/Basics/Projects/Packaging/index.html#distribution`.
>
> If you're specifically interested in exporting to iOS, refer to `https://docs.unrealengine.com/latest/INT/Platforms/iOS/QuickStart/index.html`.
>
> In addition, if you're specifically interested in exporting to Android, visit `https://docs.unrealengine.com/latest/INT/Platforms/Android/GettingStarted/index.html`.
>
> For specifics on working with mobile projects, read *Learning Unreal Engine Android Game Development* and *Learning Unreal® Engine iOS Game Development*, both by Packt Publishing.

Creating an installer for Windows

As I mentioned previously, having multiple folders that need to be included with our `.exe` is somewhat of a pain. Rather than giving people a `.zip` file and hoping that they will extract it all and then keep everything in the same folder, I'd rather have the process be automatic and give the person an opportunity to have it installed, just like a professional game. With that in mind, I'm going to go over a free way to create a Windows installer.

Getting ready

Before we start working on this, we need to have an exported project. If you do not have that already, follow the previous recipe all the way to completion.

How to do it...

The first thing we need to do is get our setup program. For our demonstration, I will be using Jordan Russell's Inno setup. Let's get started by first downloading it:

1. Go to `http://jrsoftware.org/isinfo.php` and from there, click on the **Download Inno Setup** link.

2. From here, click on the **Stable Release** button and select the **isetup-5.5.6.exe** file. Once it's finished, double-click on the executable to open it, clicking on the **Run** button if it shows a Security Warning and **Yes** to allow changes.

3. Under the **Select Setup Language** window, leave it as `English` and then click on **Ok**.

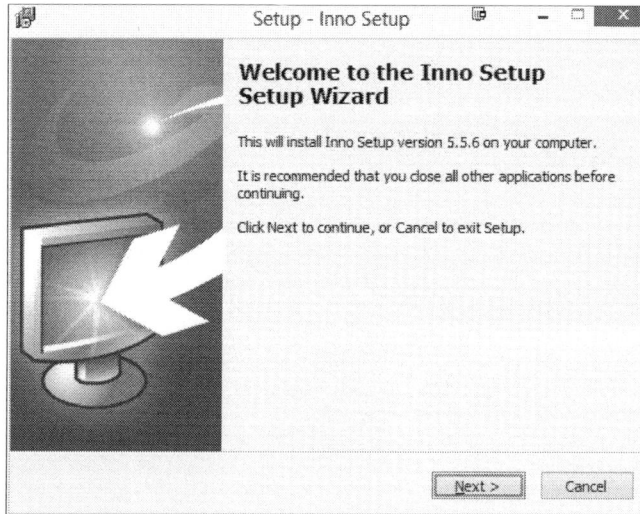

4. From here, run through the installation, making sure to uncheck the **Install Inno Setup Preprocessor** option since we won't be using it. Upon finishing, make sure that **Launch Inno Setup** is checked and then press the **Finish** button.

When you open the program, it will look something similar to this:

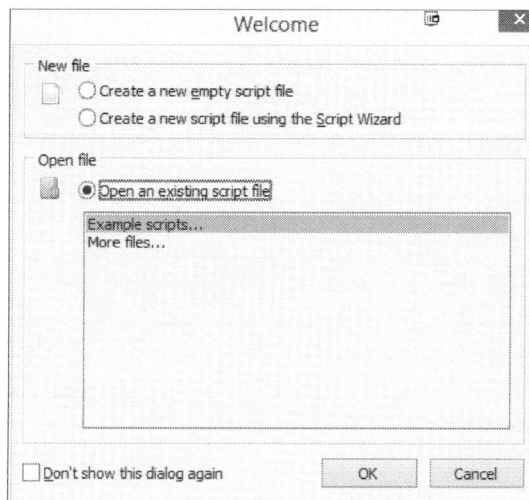

5. From here, choose **Create a new script file using the Script Wizard** and then select **OK**.

6. Now click on the **Next** button, and you'll come to the **Application Information** section. Fill in your information and then click on **Next**.

7. Next, you'll come up to some information about the Application folder. In general, you will not want to change this information, so I'd click **Next**.

8. From here, we'll be brought to the **Application Files** section, where we need to specify the files we want to install. Under **Application main executable file:**, select **Browse** to go to the location of your `Export` folder, select the `.exe` file, and then click on **Open**.

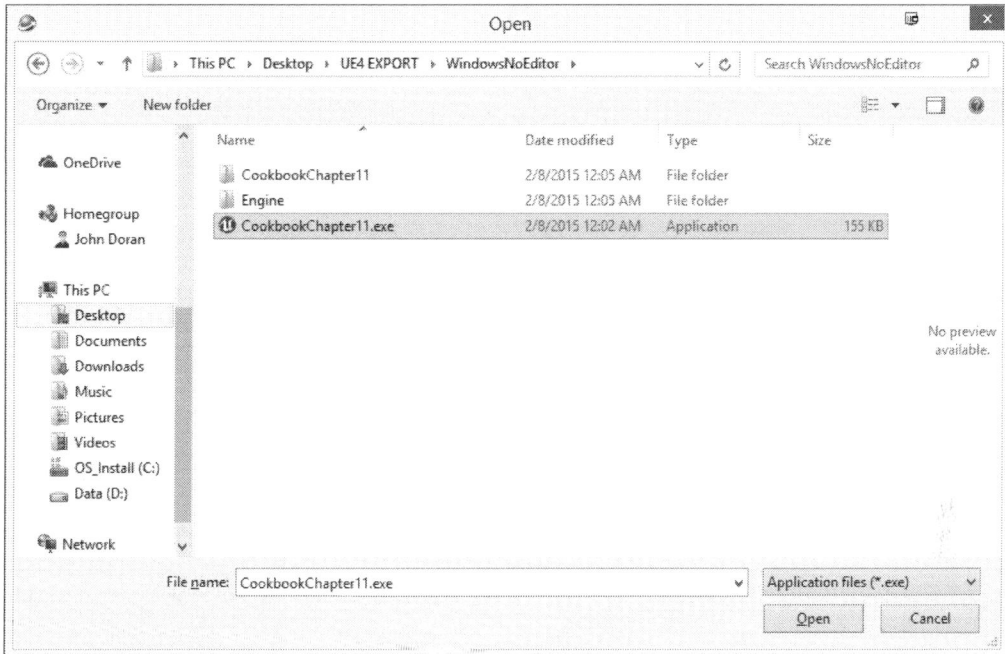

9. Now, we need to add in the project's folder (the same name as the `.exe` file). Click on the **Add Folder...** button, select the project's name folder, and then click on **OK**. In the popup that appears and asks whether you should include files in the subfolders, click on **Yes**.

10. After that, we need to also add in the `Engine` folder. Click on the **Add Folder...** button, select the `Engine` folder, and then click on **OK**. In the popup that appears and asks whether you should include files in the subfolders, click on the **Yes** button.

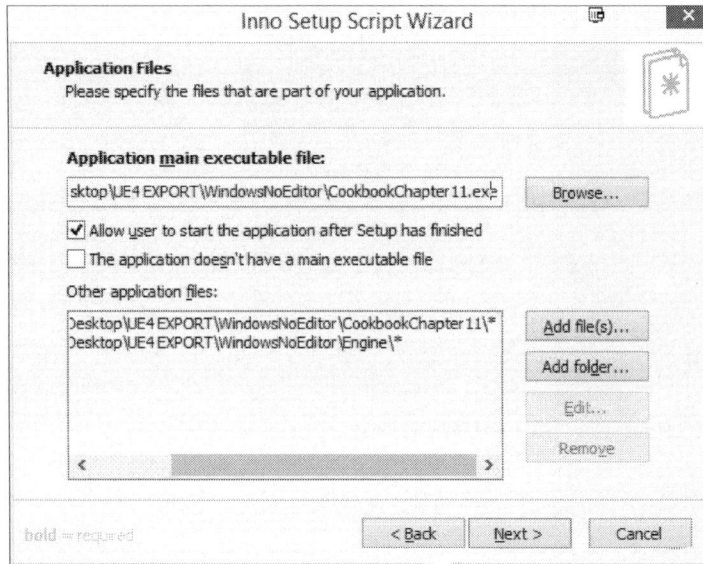

11. Then, select each folder in the **Other Applications files:** section and click on the **Edit** button. From here, set the **Destination subfolder** property to the same name as the folder and then click on **OK**.

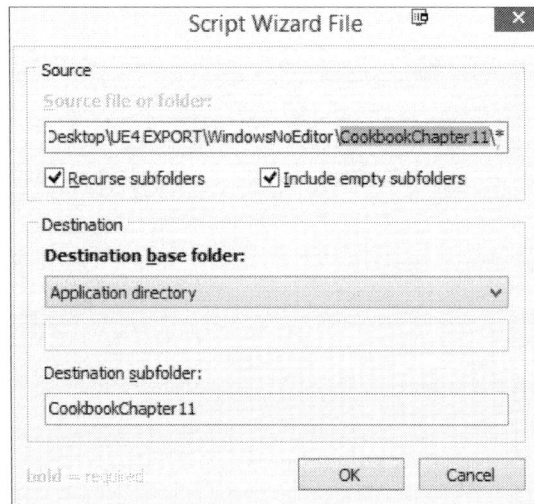

12. Make sure that you do the same with the `Engine` folder as well and then click on the **Next** button.

13. In the next menu, check whichever options you'd like, and then click on **Next**.

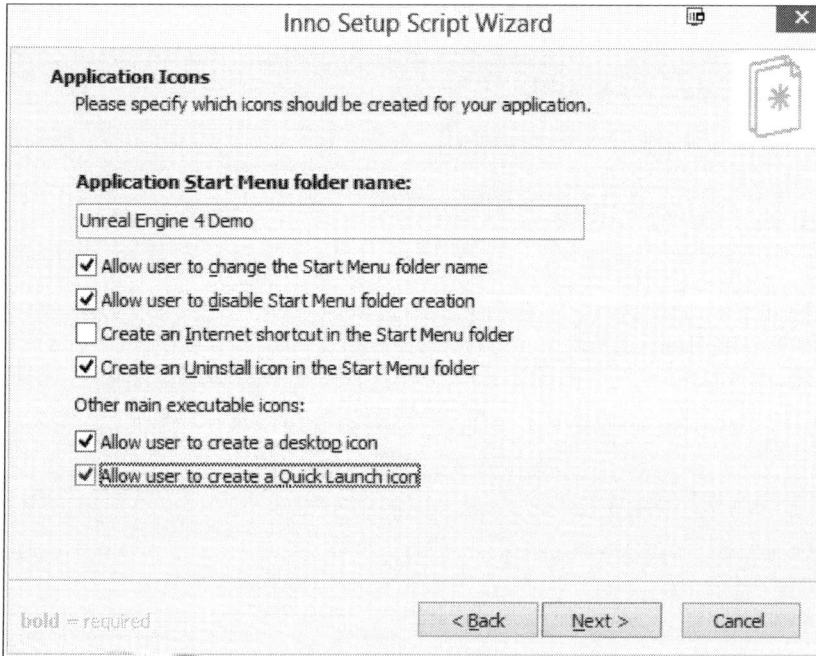

14. Now, you'll have an option to include a license file, such as a EULA or whatever your publisher may require, and any personal stuff you want to tell your users before or after installation. The program accepts `.txt` and `.rtf` files. Once you're ready, click on the **Next** button.

15. Next, they'll allow you to specify what languages you want the installation to work for. I'll just go for English, but you can add more. Afterward, click on **Next**.

16. We need to set where we want the setup to be placed as well as the icon for it or a password. I created a new folder on my desktop called `UE4DemoSetup` and used it. Then click on **Next**!

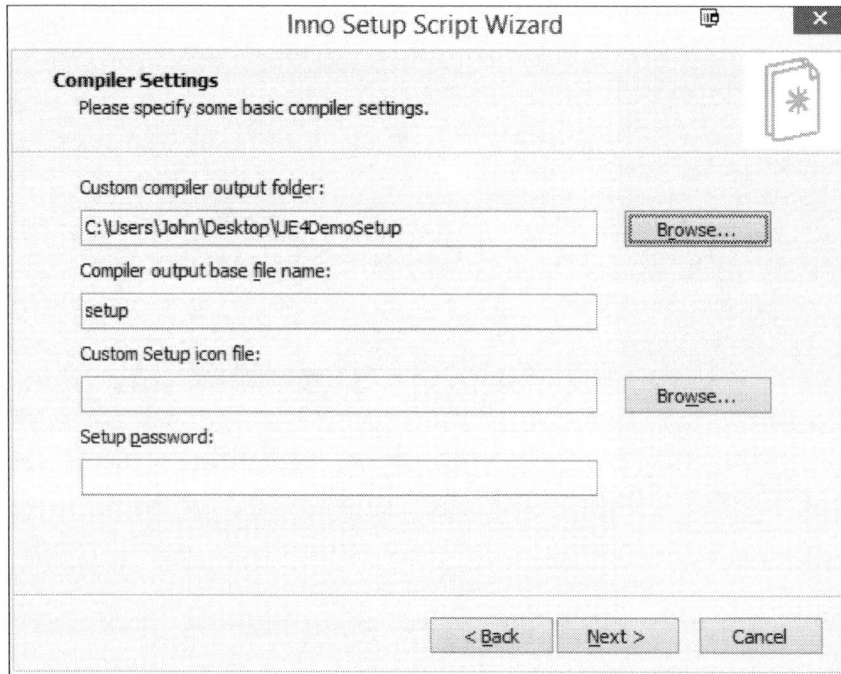

If you want to include a custom icon but don't have a `.ico` file, you can visit `http://www.icoconverter.com/` to create one from an image file.

17. Next, you'll be brought to the **Successfully Completed Script Wizard** screen. After this, click on **Finish**!

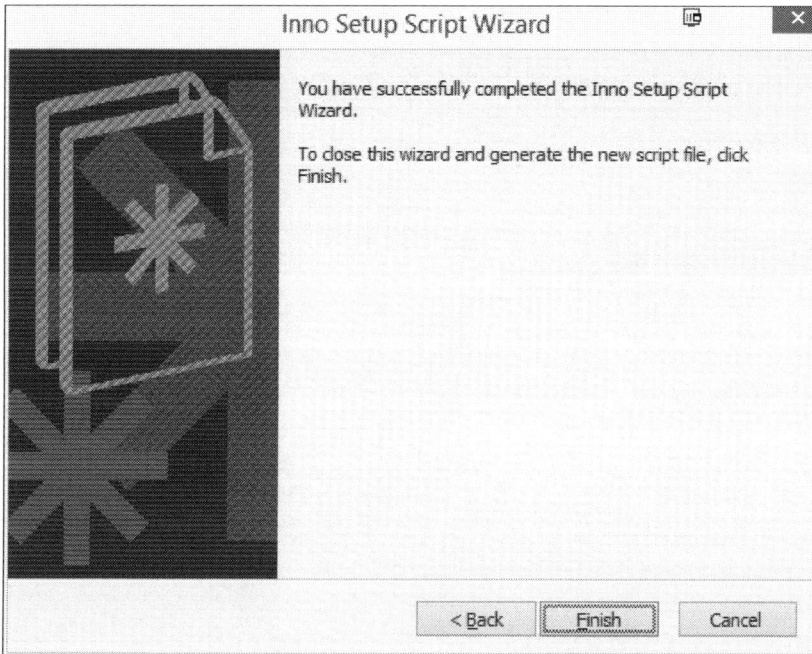

18. Now it will ask you whether you'd like to compile the script immediately. Select **Yes**. It'll also ask you whether you want to save your script. Again, click on **Yes**. I saved it to the same folder as my exporting directory. It'll take a while, but as soon as you see `Finished` in the console window, it should be ready!

19. If you go to the same place as your export folder, you should see your installer!

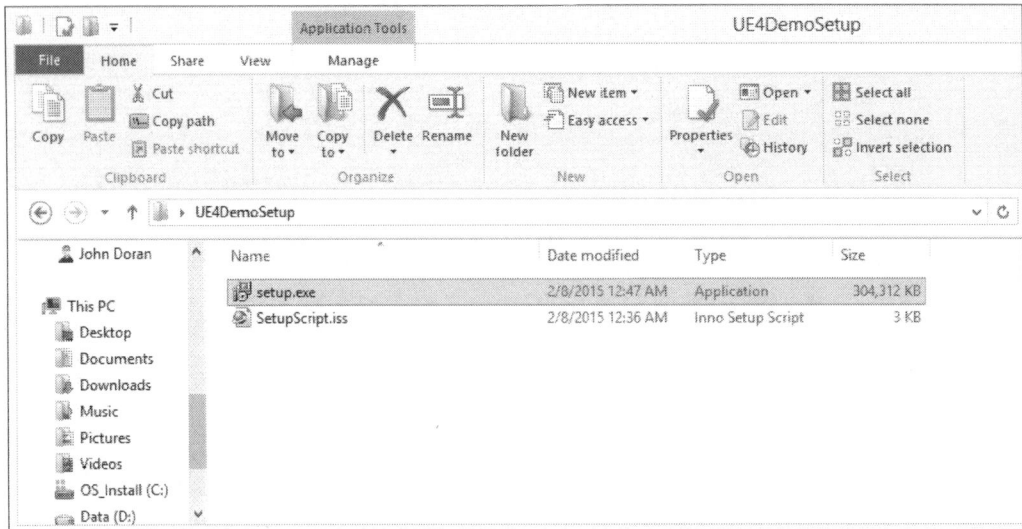

20. If you run the project, you should see something similar to this:

With this, we now have a working installer for our game and a single file that we can share with anyone. This will install everything correctly!

Index

Thank you for buying
iOS 9 Game Development Essentials

About Packt Publishing

Packt, pronounced 'packed', published its first book, *Mastering phpMyAdmin for Effective MySQL Management*, in April 2004, and subsequently continued to specialize in publishing highly focused books on specific technologies and solutions.

Our books and publications share the experiences of your fellow IT professionals in adapting and customizing today's systems, applications, and frameworks. Our solution-based books give you the knowledge and power to customize the software and technologies you're using to get the job done. Packt books are more specific and less general than the IT books you have seen in the past. Our unique business model allows us to bring you more focused information, giving you more of what you need to know, and less of what you don't.

Packt is a modern yet unique publishing company that focuses on producing quality, cutting-edge books for communities of developers, administrators, and newbies alike. For more information, please visit our website at www.packtpub.com.

About Packt Open Source

In 2010, Packt launched two new brands, Packt Open Source and Packt Enterprise, in order to continue its focus on specialization. This book is part of the Packt Open Source brand, home to books published on software built around open source licenses, and offering information to anybody from advanced developers to budding web designers. The Open Source brand also runs Packt's Open Source Royalty Scheme, by which Packt gives a royalty to each open source project about whose software a book is sold.

Writing for Packt

We welcome all inquiries from people who are interested in authoring. Book proposals should be sent to author@packtpub.com. If your book idea is still at an early stage and you would like to discuss it first before writing a formal book proposal, then please contact us; one of our commissioning editors will get in touch with you.

We're not just looking for published authors; if you have strong technical skills but no writing experience, our experienced editors can help you develop a writing career, or simply get some additional reward for your expertise.

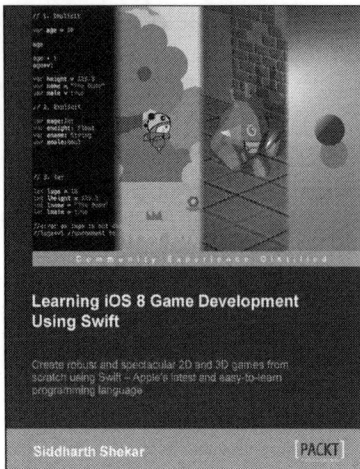

Learning iOS 8 Game Development Using Swift

ISBN: 978-1-78439-355-7   Paperback: 366 pages

Create robust and spectacular 2D and 3D games from scratch using Swift – Apple's latest and easy-to-learn programming language

1. Create engaging games from the ground up using SpriteKit and SceneKit.

2. Boost your game's visual performance using Metal - Apple's new graphics library.

3. A step-by-step approach to exploring the world of game development using Swift.

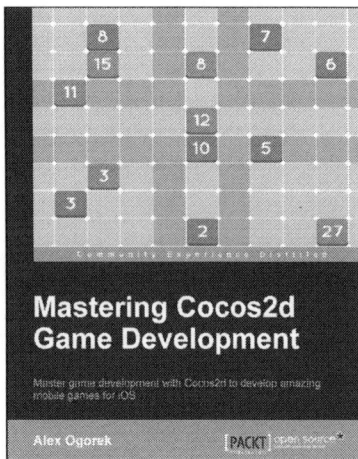

Mastering Cocos2d Game Development

ISBN: 978-1-78439-671-8   Paperback: 290 pages

Master game development with Cocos2d to develop amazing mobile games for iOS

1. Learn how to create beautiful and engaging mobile games using Cocos2D-Swift.

2. Explore the cross-platform capabilities of Cocos2d.

3. Get to grips with Cocos2d game development tools and learn Swift, a powerful modern approach to game development.

Please check **www.PacktPub.com** for information on our titles

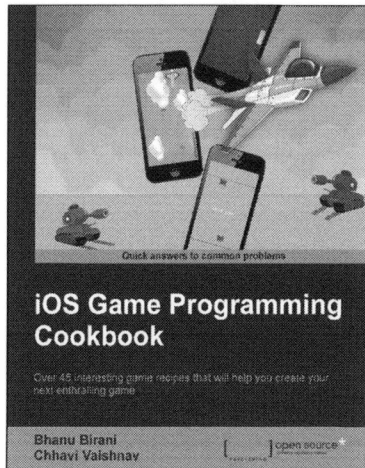

iOS Game Programming Cookbook

ISBN: 978-1-78439-825-5   Paperback: 300 pages

Over 45 interesting game recipes that will help you create your next enthralling game

1. Learn to create 2D graphics with Sprite Kit, game physics, AI behaviours, 3D game programming, and multiplayer gaming.

2. Use native iOS frameworks for OpenGL to create 3D textures, allowing you to explore 3D animations and game programming.

3. Explore powerful iOS game features through detailed step-by-step recipes.

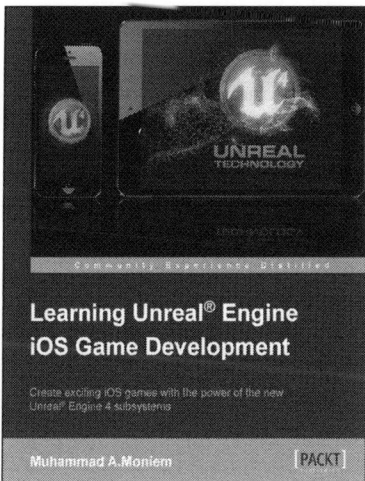

Learning Unreal® Engine iOS Game Development

ISBN: 978-1-78439-771-5   Paperback: 212 pages

Create exciting iOS games with the power of the new Unreal® Engine 4 subsystems

1. Learn each step in the iOS game development process, from start to finish.

2. Develop exciting iOS games with the Unreal Engine 4.x toolset.

3. Step-by-step tutorials to build optimized iOS games.

Please check **www.PacktPub.com** for information on our titles

Printed in Great Britain
by Amazon.co.uk, Ltd.,
Marston Gate.